ARNE JACOBSEN
ヤコブセンの建築とデザイン

TOTO出版

Arne Jacobsen

First published in Japan on June 20, 2014
Third published on January 20, 2021

TOTO Publishing (TOTO LTD.)
TOTO Nogizaka Bldg., 2F,
1-24-3 Minami-aoyama, Minato-ku, Tokyo 107-0062, Japan
[Sales] Telephone: +81-3-3402-7138 Facsimile: +81-3-3402-7187
[Editorial] Telephone: +81-3-3497-1010
URL: https://jp.toto.com/publishing

Photographs	Yukio Yoshimura
Text	Toshihiko Suzuki
Publisher	Takeshi Ito
Art Direction & Design	Hiroko Ogata
Printer	Tosho Printing Co., Ltd.

Except as permitted under copyright law, this book may not be reproduced, in whole or in part, in any form or by any means, including photocopying, scanning, digitizing, or otherwise, without prior permission. Scanning or digitizing this book through a third party, even for personal or home use, is also strictly prohibited.
The list price is indicated on the cover.

ISBN978-4-88706-343-3

CONTENTS

- 4 — はじめに　PREFACE
  鈴木敏彦　TOSHIHIKO SUZUKI
- 6 — ヤコブセンの予見　未来の家　ARNE JACOBSEN'S FORESIGHT, HOUSE OF THE FUTURE
- 9 — 略歴　PROFILE
- 10 — アルネ・ヤコブセンのトータルデザイン　THE TOTAL DESIGN OF ARNE JACOBSEN
  鈴木敏彦　TOSHIHIKO SUZUKI

- 32 — ベルビュー地区　THE BELLEVUE AREA 1930〜
- 34 — ベルビュー海水浴場　THE BELLEVUE BEACH 1930
- 38 — ベラヴィスタ集合住宅　BELLAVISTA HOUSING COMPLEX 1934
- 46 — ベルビューシアター　BELLEVUE THEATER 1937
- 60 — テキサコ・ガソリンスタンド　TEXACO SERVICE STATION 1937
- 64 — ノヴォ治療ラボラトリウム　NOVO TERAPEUTISK LABORATORIUM 1935〜
- 72 — ステリング・ビル　THE STELLING BUILDING 1937
- 78 — オーフス市庁舎　AARHUS CITY HALL 1942
- 102 — スレロド市庁舎　SOLLEROD CITY HALL 1942
- 116 — スモーク・ハウス　FISH SMOKEHOUSE 1943
- 120 — スーホルム I　SOHOLM I 1950
- 128 — ホービュー・セントラルスクール　HARBY CENTRAL SCHOOL 1950
- 140 — シモニュー邸　THE SIMONY HOUSE 1954
- 152 — ムンケゴー小学校　MUNKEGARD ELEMENTARY SCHOOL 1957
- 168 — ニュエア小学校　NYAGER ELEMENTARY SCHOOL 1964
- 180 — ラウンド・ハウス　ROUND HOUSE 1956
- 188 — ロドオア市庁舎　RODOVRE CITY HALL 1956
- 200 — ロドオア中央図書館　RODOVRE LIBRARY 1969
- 212 — SASロイヤルホテル　SAS ROYAL HOTEL 1960
- 230 — セント・キャサリンズ・カレッジ　ST CATHERINE'S COLLEGE 1964
- 278 — デンマーク国立銀行　DANMARKS NATIONALBANK 1971

- 300 — アルネ・ヤコブセンのプロダクトデザイン　THE PRODUCT DESIGN BY ARNE JACOBSEN
  鈴木敏彦　TOSHIHIKO SUZUKI
- 320 — 掲載作品MAP　A MAP OF THE WORKS LISTED IN THIS BOOK
- 322 — 主要参考文献　A COMPLETE LIST OF REFERENCES
- 323 — クレジット　CREDITS
- 324 — あとがき　POSTSCRIPT
  吉村行雄　YUKIO YOSHIMURA
- 327 — 謝辞　ACKNOWLEDGEMENT

はじめに
鈴木敏彦

　本書は、アルネ・ヤコブセンの建築、インテリア、プロダクトを網羅した、日本初の本格的な作品集である。建築写真家・吉村行雄氏がこれまでに撮りためた膨大な建築写真に加え、2013年夏に吉村氏と筆者、編集者らで共にデンマークを訪ね、新たに撮影と調査を行った。日本では、ヤコブセンは建築家というよりデザイナーとして名声を博しているが、本書を通じて、ヤコブセンの建築家としての総合的な取り組みを認識することができるだろう。

　まず、「アルネ・ヤコブセンのトータルデザイン」と題し、建築作品について時系列に論じた。家具、プロダクト、インテリア、建築の領域を横断し、ヤコブセンが人びとの生活を隅々までデザインしたことがうかがえる。建築家として独立した直後に、地元のベルビュー地区のリゾート開発で実現した一連の白い建築群から、晩年に一期工事を見届けた生涯最後の作品である「デンマーク国立銀行」まで、21の主要な建築作品を掲載した。中でも、デンマーク国外におけるヤコブセンのトータルデザインの傑作のひとつとして、「セント・キャサリンズ・カレッジ」には十分な紙面を割いた。家具から建築まで何ひとつ変わることなく大事に使われている事実を、撮り下ろしの写真で伝えることに本書を今日刊行する意義がある。21世紀となった今でも、ヤコブセンの魅力は古びるどころか、むしろ今日的なデザインのアイコンとして人びとに認識されている。この事実により「今、なぜヤコブセンなのか」という問い掛けからの論考は、「今もなお、ヤコブセンである」という結論に達した。

　次に、「アルネ・ヤコブセンのプロダクトデザイン」と題し、プロダクトデザインの視点から作品を時系列に記述した。ヤコブセンのプロダクトはインテリアを構成し、空間を機能させるために、常に建築と同時に開発された。1925年、23歳のヤコブセンが「パリ万国博覧会デンマーク館」のためにデザインした椅子が銀メダルを受賞したことから彼のプロダクトデザインが始まる。「ノヴォ治療ラボラトリウム」のために開発した「アントチェア」の成功は、その後のプロダクトデザイン開発に拍車をかけ、さらには「SASロイヤルホテル」のすべてをデザインするトータルデザインの実現につながっていく。メーカーから製品化され、商業的に成功し、生産されるプロダクトが、常にヤコブセンの建築の中で使い続けられていく。この新陳代謝がヤコブセンの建築を色あせないものにしている。ここでは、家具や照明に始まり、テーブルウェア、テキスタイル、ドアノブ、そして遺作の「デンマーク国立銀行」において開発した「ボーラ」の水栓金具まで76作品を掲載している。

　ヤコブセンは建築をシェルターとして考えるのではなく、人びとが生き生きと生活する場として捉えた。そのために、建築の内外の環境を構成するあらゆる要素を総合的にデザインした。ヤコブセンの仕事ぶりを追っていくと、すべてを自らデザインしようという意気込みがうかがえる。現在、私たちは生活用品をプロダクトデザイナーの仕事、椅子を家具デザイナーの仕事、建築を建築家の仕事と考えがちだが、理想的な生活を実現するには、そんな区分は必要ないのだとヤコブセンは教えてくれる。本書こそ、建築の全体から細部に至るまでのデザインの在り方を学べる一冊だと確信している。

Preface
Toshihiko Suzuki

This is the first genuine book in Japanese that contains the works of Arne Jacobsen: architecture, interior design, product design. Architectural photographer, Mr. Yukio Yoshimura, has taken a great number of photographs. In addition, during the summer of 2013, the editors and I accompanied him to Denmark to take further pictures and to conduct research together. Although Jacobsen is renowned more as a designer than as an architect in Japan, this book will confirm his wide-ranging achievements as an architect.

First, I wrote "The total design of Arne Jacobsen" in which I introduced his architectural works in chronological order. It is obvious that Jacobsen designed the complete lives of people in every detail and took a cross-sectional approach to furniture, products and architecture. We listed 21 main architectural works that he begin with a series of white buildings that he created at the resort development of his local Bellevue Beach area, and ended with his final work, "Danmarks Nationalbank." We devoted many pages to "St Catherine's College," in particular, as it is one of the masterpieces of his total design that is located outside of Denmark. There is a reason to publish this book today with new photographs, because it is important to convey the fact that everything, including furniture and architecture, is used carefully and there is nothing to change. Jacobsen's charm never faded during the 21st century and he is still regarded as an icon today. Because of this, my article, which begins with the question, "Why should we consider Jacobsen now?" concludes with "Jacobsen is still worth considering."

Next, I wrote "The product design by Arne Jacobsen" in chronological order from a product point of view. His products were developed at the same time as his architecture to create the interior and to add functionality to the space. His career as a product designer began when he was awarded a silver medal in 1925 at 23 years of age with a chair for the "Danish Pavilion" in the Paris Exhibition. Then, the creation of "The Ant," which he developed for "Novo Terapeutisk Laboratorium," expedited further development of his product design. It finally led him to the establishment of the total design that he implemented by designing everything for the "SAS Royal Hotel." The products that they continued to use in his buildings are those that, having been commercialized by manufacturers and having met with success, continued to be produced. This causes his architecture to appear fresh. In this book, we introduced 76 products that he designed. They include furniture, lighting fixtures, tableware, textiles, door knobs and "Vola" water facets that he developed for his posthumous work, "Danmarks Nationalbank."

Jacobsen grasped architecture not as shelter, but as a stage on which people live dynamically. Therefore he designed comprehensively all elements of the environment, inside and outside of the architecture. As we follow his achievements, we can understand his enthusiasm to design everything by himself. Nevertheless, we tend to think that household goods are made by product designers, chairs are made by furniture designers, and buildings are constructed by architects. However, Jacobsen has told us that, to achieve ideal lives, such thinking is nonsense. I am convinced that this is the book to study to learn how design and architecture should proceed from outline to details.

ヤコブセンの予見　未来の家
Arne Jacobsen's foresight, House of the Future

1927年、北欧の小国デンマークからひとりの建築家が「未来の家」のコンペに勝利して鮮烈なデビューを飾った。後に北欧を代表する偉大な建築家として一世を風靡する、当時27歳のアルネ・ヤコブセンである。特筆すべきことは、彼は「未来の家」を設計しただけではなく、未来の生活を構想したことだ。1920年代後半、過去のすべてを否定し機械時代を宣言するヨーロッパ中央のモダニズムの潮流が北欧に到達しようとしていた。ヤコブセンは、モダニズムに影響を受けながらも、さらにその先にある未来の暮らしをこの住宅で提示した。陸・海・空からのアプローチ。1階には車のガレージ、地下にスピードボートを係留するための水上ガレージ、屋上にはオートジャイロ(回転翼をもつ飛行機)用の発着台がある。送電機能を備えた無線のアンテナ。車が近付くと自動的に開閉するガレージのドア。来客の靴の埃を吸い取る排気ファン付きの玄関マット。電気床暖房。タイプライターがビルトインされたオフィスのスチールデスク。温風ドライヤーのある浴室。手紙は郵便局まで圧縮空気のチューブで送られる。自動車の窓のようにハンドルで上下に開閉する窓ガラス。食事の配達を前提としたシンプルで最小限のキッチン。ダイニングルームの壁と天井は黄色、床は赤という斬新な配色。建築のスタイリングのみならず暮らしのイメージまでを提示した姿勢がミッドセンチュリーの北欧デザインを予見している。「未来の家」はコペンハーゲンのフォーラム住宅展示会にて実物展示されて高い評判を呼んだ。ヤコブセンの下には次々と仕事が舞い込み順風満帆の船出となった。しかし「未来の家」のアイデアはヤコブセンの心の中にずっと温められていて、29年後の1956年、「ラウンド・ハウス」で実現させることになる。

In 1927, one architect won the competition of "House of the Future" and debuted brilliantly in Denmark, a small country in Scandinavia. It was Arne Jacobsen at 27 years of age, who later took the world by storm as a representative of Scandinavia. It is noteworthy that he designed not only "House of the Future," but also envisaged life in the future. In the late 1920's, the tide of modernism in Central Europe, which ignored the past and embraced the machine age, was about to reach to Scandinavia. While Jacobsen was influenced by the modernism, he proposed life in this house that was far into the future: It involved approaches from ground, sea and sky. There was a garage for a car on the ground floor, an underground aqua garage for a speed boat and an airport on the rooftop for an autogiro, which was an aircraft that had rotating wings. Moreover, there were an antenna with a transmission function on the roof, an automatic garage door that would open and close when a car approached, a doormat that was equipped with a fan to draw the dust from the shoes of visitors, electric floor heating, a steel desk in an office that had a built-in typewriter, a bathroom with a hot dryer, a tube that used compressed air to send a letter to the post office, a glass window with handles like a window in a car to open or close, and simple and compact kitchen in which to prepare meals. The color coordination was novel the dining room's walls and ceiling were yellow, and the floor was red. His approach was to propose not only architectural styling, but also a new Scandinavian design of mid-century lifestyle. A full size model of "House of the Future" was displayed at the Housing Exhibition at the Forum and gained favorable reviews. Jacobsen received many offers and he had an exceedingly smooth start as an architect. Nevertheless, he took 29 years to form his ideas of "House of the Future." He finally achieved it at "Round House" in 1956.

Arne Jacobsen's foresight, House of the Future

略歴
PROFILE

アルネ・ヤコブセン（1902-1971）

1902年、デンマーク、コペンハーゲンに生まれる。画家を目指したが父の反対にあい、1924年に22歳でデンマーク王立芸術アカデミーに入学し建築の道に進む。卒業設計はアカデミーのゴールドメダルに輝いた。1927年に卒業。

以後、本書に取り上げた作品を中心に年代を追っていくと、卒業2年後の1929年にフレミング・ラッセンと共同で応募した「未来の家」で優勝。一躍有名になり、独立し事務所を開設。1931年、コペンハーゲン郊外のクランペンボー地区のリゾート開発のコンペに優勝し、ベルビュービーチ沿いに一連の白い建築群（1938）を完成させる。1937年、デンマーク第2の都市である「オーフス市庁舎」（1942）のコンペに勝利。1943年、ユダヤ人のヤコブセンは、ナチスの迫害を恐れスウェーデンに亡命。1946年、帰国後、クランペンボー地区に「スーホルムⅠ」（1950）を設計し、そこに自宅兼オフィスを構える。1952年に、世界初の成形合板一体型の「アントチェア」を世に送り出し、1955年には「セブンチェア」を発表する。1956年、母校の王立芸術アカデミーの教授に就任。1960年、デンマーク発の高層建築となった「SASロイヤルホテル」を竣工。「エッグチェア」（1958）、「スワンチェア」（1958）、「AJランプ」（1957）、「AJカトラリー」（1957）等は、すべてこの建築のためにデザインしたものである。1959年、「ムンケゴー小学校」（1957）の成功が評価され、イギリスのオックスフォード大学の「セント・キャサリンズ・カレッジ」（1964）の正式な設計者となる。1971年、コペンハーゲン中心部の「デンマーク国立銀行」（1978）の完成を見ぬままに自宅にて心臓発作で急逝。享年69歳。

ARNE JACOBSEN (1902-1971)

Arne Jacobsen was born in Copenhagen. Although he wanted to become an artist, his father was against the idea. In 1924, Jacobsen, at 22 years of age, enrolled in The Royal Danish Academy of Fine Arts, where he studied architecture. Jacobsen won the gold medal in 1927 for his graduation work at the Academy. I now summarize his works that were introduced in this book:

In 1929, two years after his graduation, Jacobsen won the "House of the Future" design competition with Fleming Lassen. As a result, he suddenly became famous, and opened his office as an independent architect. In 1931, he won a competition for a resort development at Klampenborg, a suburb of Copenhagen. The resort development, which consisted of a series of white buildings along Bellevue Beach, was completed a few years later. In 1937, Jacobsen won the "Aarhus City Hall" competition. At that time, Aarhus was the second largest city in Denmark. In 1943, as a Danish Jew, he sought refuge in Sweden from Nazi persecution. He returned to Denmark in 1946 and designed "Soholm I" at Klampenborg and established his studio and residence there. In 1952, he succeeded in becoming first in the world to develop a molded plywood chair, "The Ant," and in 1955 he released "The Seven." Jacobsen became a professor at his old school in 1956, The Royal Danish Academy of Fine Arts. In 1960, he completed the first high-rise building in Denmark, "SAS Royal Hotel" using of curtain walls. "The Egg," "The Swan," "AJ Lamp" and "AJ Cutlery" were developed for this building. In 1959, the succession of "Munkegard Elementary School" was evaluated well and he became an official designer of "St Catherine's College." In 1971, Arne Jacobsen died of a heart attack in his house at the age of 69, without making sure of the completion of "Danmarks Nationalbank."

アルネ・ヤコブセンのトータルデザイン
鈴木敏彦

1 はじめに

アルネ・ヤコブセンは、20世紀のデンマークモダニズムを代表する建築家である。1929年の「未来の家」コンペの華々しい勝利と共にデビューし、その後43年間にわたって、あらゆるジャンルの建築とさまざまなプロダクトデザインに携わってきた。建築ではデンマークの国立銀行と4つの市庁舎をはじめとして、住宅、集合住宅、学校、図書館、ホテル、銀行、大使館、ガソリンスタンド、スポーツ施設、工場等を設計し、そのプロジェクト数は優に100を超える。プロダクトデザインにおいては、家具、照明器具はもちろんのこと、カトラリーやコーヒーポット等のテーブルウェア、時計、ドアハンドル、さらには浴室の水栓金具に至るまでデザインし、シリーズ展開を含めるとその数は300を超える。これらは自ら設計した建築のインテリアとして置くためにデザインし、その後製品化されたものである。そして現在においても、そのほとんどが北欧デザインを代表するプロダクトとして、確固たる商品価値を維持している。ヤコブセンにとって建築とはインテリアエレメントを含む総体であり、「暮らしの場を創出すること」を意味した。暮らしに必要なすべてのものをデザインすることは、彼にとって当然の帰結であった。

本稿では、彼の誕生から時系列で代表的な作品とその背景について考察し、ヤコブセンのトータルデザインの今日的意味を明らかにする。

2 アルネ・ヤコブセンの生い立ち 1902-1923

アルネ・ヤコブセンは、1902年2月11日にデンマークの首都コペンハーゲンに生まれた。ユダヤ系デンマーク人の家系で、父ヨハンは安全ピンや小物をデパートや大型店舗に卸す貿易商。母パウリーンはデンマークで初めて銀行に勤務した女性で、植物を愛し、花の絵を好んで描く芸術的な感性の持ち主であった。ヤコブセンは父親から商才を、母親から絵心を、そしてユダヤという血筋からコスモポリタンとしての世界的な視野と行動力を受け継いだ。

小学校に入学する頃、コペンハーゲン中心部から郊外のクランペンボーの住宅地に引っ越したが、落ち着きのなさや授業を妨害する振る舞いが原因で、11歳の時に全寮制の学校へ転校することになった。そこで、後にデンマークを代表する建築家となるフレミング(1902-1984)とモーエンス(1901-1987)のラッセン兄弟と運命的に出会う。ヤコブセンには、美術講師が絵の具箱を彼に買い与えるほど水彩画の才能があり、絵描きを志していた。しかしフレミング・ラッセンと父親の勧めで、絵の才能を生かすもうひとつの道として建築家になることを決意する。

技術学校に進学して製図法や建設技術を学び、1920年の夏休みにはドイツに行き煉瓦職人の下で修行した。ヤ

11歳から入学したネラム寄宿学校での写真。右端にアルネ・ヤコブセン、左端にフレミングとモーエンスのラッセン兄弟。

Photo at Nærum boarding school where Jacobsen entered at 11 years of age. At the far right is Arne Jacobsen, Mogence and Fleming Lassen are on the left.

The total design of Arne Jacobsen
Toshihiko Suzuki

1 | Introduction

Arne Jacobsen is an architect who was the principal figure in Denmark's modernism during the 20th century. He won the competition of "House of the Future" and debuted brilliantly in 1929. He then designed every type of architecture and created various product designs over the next 43 years. Jacobsen designed a total of more than 100 works of architecture: These included the central bank of Denmark and four city halls, private residences, apartments, schools, hotels, banks, an embassy, a gas station, sport halls and factories. He designed more than 300 products. The list of these includes families of products: furniture, lighting fixtures, tableware such as cutlery, coffee pots, clocks, door handles and water faucets for their bathroom. These are the items with which he intended to equip his architectural works. Later, many companies sold them as products designed by him. Most of them still maintain high commercial value and are representative of Scandinavian design. For Jacobsen, architecture meant everything, including interior elements and a field where "he created life." To create everything that others need in their lives was a natural concern for him. In this article, I will discuss his representative works from his birth to his death, and conclude with his total design which still has meaning today.

2 | The childfood of Arne Jacobsen | 1902–1923

Arne Jacobsen was born in Copenhagen, the capital of Denmark, on February 11th 1902. He was of Danish Jewish descent. His father, Johan, was a trader who sold safety-pins and small articles to department stores. His mother, Pauline, was one of the first women to work in a bank in Denmark. She loved plants and often painted flowers. Jacobsen inherited his father's talent for business and his mother's artistic taste, and a breadth of view and cosmopolitan action orientation from his Jewish bloodline.

After he enrolled on elementary school, his family moved from the center of Copenhagen to Klampenborg. However, he was soon sent away to boarding school because of his restless character and disruptive activities. When he was 11 years old, he met the Lassen brothers, Fleming (1902-1984) and Mogence (1901-1987). Jacobsen was very gifted in painting in water colors. So, his art teacher supplied him with art supplies. Although he initially wanted to become an artist, he decided to take advantage of his talent by becoming an architect on the advice of Fleming Lassen and Johan Jacobsen.

Accordingly, he entered architecture school where he learned drafting and building techniques. In 1920, he went to Germany where he trained as a bricklayer during his summer vacation. It was at that time that Jacobsen visited an exhibition of Mies van der Rohe (1886-1969)

1921年のニューヨークの街並み。フレデリックⅧ号の客室係としてニューヨークに渡った時にヤコブセン自身が撮影した。

A street in New York. Jacobsen took this photograph when he traveled to New York as a cabin boy of the ship Frederic VIII.

コブセンはこの時ベルリンでミース・ファン・デル・ローエ(1886-1969)の展覧会を見ている。ミースを中心とするドイツのモダニズムがヤコブセンに大きな影響を与えたことは想像に難くない。

1921年、デンマークに戻ったヤコブセンは海外に目を向け、19歳でフレデリックⅧ号に客室係として乗り込んだ。船酔いと戦いながら一路ニューヨークに向かうと、摩天楼やブルックリン橋をその眼とフィルムに焼き付けた。1920年代初頭のニューヨークは急激な経済成長に伴い、高層ビルが競うように建てられ、ロンドンを抜いて世界最大の人口を抱える都市になっていた。ヤコブセンは同年代のヨーロッパの建築家の誰よりも早く、アメリカの摩天楼の強烈な洗礼を青年期に受けたのである。デンマークに戻った彼は、1924年に22歳で技術学校を卒業し、同年デンマーク王立芸術アカデミーに入学した。

3 │ 北欧モダニズムの到来 │ 1919–1930

ヤコブセンが建築を本格的に学び始めた1920年代初頭、アメリカだけでなくヨーロッパの建築界も大きな変革期を迎えていた。1919年にドイツのワイマールではバウハウスが開校した。初代学長のワルター・グロピウス (1883-1969) は建築を中心とする総合芸術を提唱し、産業デザインを標榜した。1920年にはフランスでル・コルビュジエ (1887-1965) が『エスプリ・ヌーヴォー』誌を創刊して機械時代の到来を宣言した。そして1925年のパリ万国博覧会では、装飾のない機能的な住空間「エスプリ・ヌーヴォー館」を発表し、新しい時代の暮らしの在り方を提示した。その2年後、ドイツのシュトゥットガルトにて同様のテーマに沿ったモデルハウス群が完成する。ドイツ工作連盟の副会長としてミースが全体計画を取り仕切り、ペーター・ベーレンス(1868-1940)、グロピウス、ル・コルビュジエ、ブルーノ・タウト(1880-1938)らが、白い壁とフラットルーフで出来た機能主義的な集合住宅群を建設した。1927年開催の「シュトゥットガルト住宅展」である。

「ストックホルム国際博覧会」(1930) の航空写真。
Aerial view of "Stockholm International Exhibition" (1930).

このようにドイツやフランスで勃興したモダニズムの潮流は、北欧では異なるかたちで受け入れられていく。当時、北欧では民族主義的な機運が熟し、工芸を尊重する風潮にあった。機能主義を額面通りに受け取るのではなく、北欧の伝統的な工芸技術とのブレンドが求められる中で、スウェーデンのエーリック・グンナール・アスプルンド (1885-1940)、フィンランドのアルヴァ・アールト (1898-1976)、そしてデンマークのアルネ・ヤコブセン (1902-1971) という3国の建築家が北欧モダニズムを牽引していく。

ヨーロッパの機能主義を北欧流にアレンジした成果は1930年開催の「ストックホルム国際博覧会 (住宅工芸デザイン展)」に見られる。この博覧会は、スウェーデン工芸協会理事であったグレゴール・パウルソン(1889-1977)が総監督となり、アスプルンドに主任建築家を任じて組織したものである。パウルソンはこの博覧会を、フランスの「エスプリ・ヌーヴォー館」やドイツの「シュトゥットガルト住宅展」が提示したヨーロッパ中央のモダニズムから遅れを取り戻し、追い付くためだけのイベントとしては考えていなかった。むしろ、1919年の「イェーテボリ博覧会」でスウェーデン工芸協会が掲げた「日用品をより美しく」というスローガンを体現するため、そして、モダニ

in Berlin. It is easy to imagine that German modernism in which Mies plays a leading role had a great influence on him.

In 1921, Jacobsen moved back to Denmark. However, his thoughts were elsewhere. When he was 19 years old, he boarded the ship Frederic VIII as a cabin boy and headed to New York. During the voyage, he became seasick. On arrival in New York, Jacobsen was dazzled by the skyscrapers and the Brooklyn Bridge. New York had overtaken London and become the world's most populated city, as a result of rapid economic growth. High rise buildings mushroomed throughout the city. Jacobsen took many photographs of the city's architecture with his camera. Thus, he became immersed in the American skyscraper-style during his adolescence, earlier than any architect of his age. After his return to Denmark and graduation from technical school in 1924 he entered The Royal Danish Academy of Fine Arts at the age of 22.

3 | The advent of Scandinavian Modernism | 1919–1930

When Jacobsen really began his career in architecture in the early 1920s, the field of architecture was undergoing a revolution, not only in the U.S.A, but also in Europa. In 1919, the Bauhaus opened an academy in Weimar, Germany. Its first president, Walter Gropius (1883-1969) advocated the total work of art emphasizing architecture and producing industrial design. In 1929, Le Corbusier (1887-1965) started a magazine entitled *L'Esprit Nouveau* as a declaration of the machine age. In 1925, he presented a new living style for the new age at the "Pavillon de l'Esprit Nouveau." It expressed functional living space without embellishment in the Paris Exhibition. Two years later, new model buildings that embodied the same theme opened in Stuttgart in Germany in 1927. It was "Weissenhofsiedlung Exhibition", in which Mies van der Rohe took charge of that, and Peter Behrens (1868-1940), Bruno Taut (1880-1938), Gropius and Le Corbusier and others created functional buildings and apartments that featured white walls and flat roofs.

「ストックホルム国際博覧会」(1930)。アスプルンドがデザインした博覧会建築を目の当りにしてヤコブセンは熱狂し、多くの写真を撮影した。

"Stockholm International Exhibition" (1930). Jacobsen was excited to see the architectural pavilion that Asplund designed and took many photographs.

Then the current of modernism that arose in Germany and France spread in different way to the Scandinavian countries, where the time was ripe for nationalism, although there was respect for handicrafts. Functionalism as it was practiced did not succeed. Instead, it was blended with Scandinavian historical and industrial arts. The three architects who played leading roles in this Scandinavian Modernism were Erik Gunnar Asplund (1885-1940) from Sweden, Alvar Aalto (1898-1976) from Finland, and Arne Jacobsen (1902-1971) from Denmark.

"Stockholm International Exhibition" that was held in 1930 showed us the result of transforming European functionalism into Scandinavian style. As chief manager, Gregor Paulsson (1889-1977), a director of the Swedish Society of Industrial Design, ordered Asplund as chief architect to create and organize all design. Paulsson did not rank the Stockholm event as a second "Pavillon de l'Esprit Nouveau" of France or "Weissenhofsiedlung" of Germany to express Eurocentric Modernism. Instead of using the event to catch up with the latter, he intended to express "Better Things for Everyday Life," which the Swedish arts and crafts society had already advocated in "Gothenburg Exhibition" in 1919, and which was based on

ズムをベースにしながらも、使いやすさ、美しさ、そして人びとの暮らしを豊かにするデザインを意図していた。アスプルンドはパウルソンの解釈を理解した上で、博覧会の会場を鉄とガラスのモダンなパビリオンで構成し、近代建築の精神を見事に視覚化した。

　この博覧会を契機に、北欧諸国における建築とデザインの近代化が本格化していく。アールトは「ストックホルム国際博覧会」のオープニング・セレモニーに参加し、友人アスプルンドが成し得た、北欧流の機能主義の社会的メッセージを賞賛した。そして1933年完成の「パイミオのサナトリウム」で、名実共に機能主義をフィンランドの地に開花させた。同様に、「ストックホルム国際博覧会」に足を運んだヤコブセンは、1929年、機能主義の象徴であるフラットルーフで白い箱型の「自邸」を完成させる。1929年に建築家として独立し、モダニズムの旗手として活動を始めた矢先のことである。

　しかしその後、時期は異なるが、アスプルンドもアールトもヤコブセンもモダニズムを卒業して、それぞれが自国の地に根差した表現に移行していった。3人の北欧モダニズムは、機能主義を受け入れながらも、北欧特有の木材や職人の工芸技術を再評価するまでの通過点であった。それはまさにバウハウス初期にグロピウスが目指した「建築を中心とする総合芸術」の具現化への道のりだった。

4 ｜ デンマーク王立芸術アカデミー ｜ 1924–1927

1924年、22歳のヤコブセンはデンマーク王立芸術アカデミーに進学し、建築学部の教授であった建築家のカイ・フィスカ(1893-1965)に師事した。同年、家具科が新設され初代講師にコーレ・クリント(1888-1954)が着任する。クリントは、人間工学の観点から人の動作や日用品のサイズに合わせて家具の寸法を標準化したデザイナーであり、建築家でもあった。また、過去の事例を徹底的に研究した上で現代的な形に作り上げる手法を確立していた。バウハウスが過去を否定してゼロから素材や技術を開発したのに対して、クリントの手法は、18世紀のイギリスの家具に美的な合理性を見出し、機能と形のプロセスを見直して、より洗練した形に仕上げていくものだった。このように再びデザインする手法を「リ・デザイン」という。リ・デザインの手法は、以降のデンマークのデザイナーが共有するデザイン原理となったが、単なる模倣だと思われる危険性もはらんでいた。

ヤコブセンが25歳の時にアカデミーのゴールドメダルを受賞した「国立ミュージアム」設計案の外観透視図。
A perspective of "National Museum" with which Jacobsen won the Golden medal at the academy at 25 years of age.

Modernism. The Stockholm event focused on ease, beauty and enrichment of use. Asplund understood Paulson's intention and visualized the spirit of Modern Architecture thoroughly as the exhibition consisted of modern pavilions constructed from glass and steel.

After this, a trend to Modernism in architecture and design began in earnest in Scandinavian countries. Aalto joined in the opening ceremony of "Stockholm International Exhibition" and praised his friend, Asplund, who had caused Scandinavian functionalism to become socially significant. In 1933, Aalto created "Paimio Sanatorium" and functionalism blossomed in name and reality in Finland. In 1930, Jacobsen who had visited "Stockholm International Exhibition" once, completed his own house, which incorporated symbols of functionalism, a flat roof and a white box-like shape. Jacobsen was about to make his mark as the standard-bearer of Modernism after he became an independent architect in 1929.

However, Asplund, Aalto and Jacobsen left Modernism behind and changed their style to domestic expressions that had roots in their own country. For them, to express Modernism was only short period. It was short duration that they accept functionalism and revalue wood materials and craftsmanship peculiar to Scandinavian. That is exactly the way to achieve "the total work of art emphasizing architecture" that Gropius aimed for in the beginning of the Bauhaus period.

4 | The Royal Danish Academy of Fine Arts | 1924–1927

In 1924, Jacobsen, at 22 years of age, enrolled in The Royal Danish Academy of Fine Arts, and studied under Professor Kay Fisker (1893-1965), an architect in the Department of Architecture. In the same year, the Furniture Department was established and Kaare Klint (1888-1954) assumed the position of lecturer in it. Klint was a designer-architect who standardized to the dimensions of the furniture by ergonomics research, which measures human action and daily necessities. Also, after an exhaustive study of past designs, he established a process to make modern shapes. While Bauhaus ignored the past and developed materials and techniques from scratch, Klint found beauty in the furniture that was made in the 18 century. He considered the process of function and form and then refined the furniture into sophisticated shapes. This way to design was called "redesign." This became mainstream for later Danish designers, although there it involved a risk of being perceived to be copying. Jacobsen was one of Klint's first students so that later he often attracted this problem of design similarity.

At 23 years of age, Jacobsen joined the Paris Exhibition of 1925 in "Danish Pavilion," which was designed by Kay Fisker. He won a Silver medal for his first designed chair. It was an armchair of good quality, under a redesign initiated by Klint that emphasized sharpness by straight line and edges and was free of ornamentation.

It's not too much to say that an architect's graduation work at university expresses his style of future direction. In 1926, Jacobsen, now 24 years old, chose Klampenborg for his local site for design of a "National Museum." It was a long and low building along the beach, which reminds us of "Rodovre City Hall," "Munkegard Elementary School"

「国立ミュージアム」(1926) 先史時代展示部門の室内透視図。

A perspective of the prehistoric age exhibition room at the "National Museum" (1926).

ヤコブセンはクリントの1期生として学んだ。後にヤコブセンの作品にまつわる類似性の批判は、往々にしてこの問題に起因する。

　23歳のヤコブセンはカイ・フィスカ設計の「パリ万国博覧会デンマーク館」(1925)のプロジェクトに参加し、自身の設計した椅子が銀メダルを受賞する。ヤコブセンの処女作は、クリント直伝のリ・デザインの下、装飾を省き、直線とエッジを強調したシャープかつ上質な仕上がりの肘掛け椅子だった。

　大学での卒業設計が、建築家の将来の作風を方向付けるといっても過言ではない。1926年、24歳のヤコブセンは地元のクランペンボーを敷地に選び、「国立ミュージアム」を設計した。それはビーチに沿ってひたすら低く長い建築で、後年の「ロドオア市庁舎」や「ムンケゴー小学校」、「セント・キャサリンズ・カレッジ」のイメージを彷彿とさせる。植物が好きなヤコブセンらしく、外観透視図には大きな樹木と、建物の奥にある森のような公園を丁寧に描いている。内部の展示室にはガラス製の展示ケースと、その中の展示物を克明なタッチで描き出した。断面図には「SASロイヤルホテル」を思わせる美しい螺旋階段が現れている。勾配の付いた屋根と、煉瓦の外壁には、師であるカイ・フィスカ設計の「オーフス大学」の影響が見られる。「オーフス大学」をモチーフとして正統な古典建築の秩序を生かしながらも、現代的にアレンジするリ・デザインの手法を読み取ることができる。ヤコブセンはこの設計案でアカデミーのゴールドメダルを受賞した。1927年、25歳の明るい未来を予感させる卒業であった。

5 ｜ フンキス ｜ 1927–1937 ｜

1927年、25歳のヤコブセンはコペンハーゲン市の建築課に就職し、技術学校時代に知り合ったマリー・イェストロップ・ホルムと結婚した。ふたりの息子を授かるが、マリーの奔放な性格とヤコブセンの内向的性格のギャップから長くは続かなかった。マリーは才気あふれる女性で、芸術的な友人と交流があった。そのうちのひとりが、「PHランプ」で成功を収めていたポール・ヘニングセン(1894-1967)だ。ヘニングセンは『クリティスク・レヴュー』誌(1926-1928)を編集し、積極的にデザイン評論を行い、機能主義だけでなく伝統やクラフトマンシップを尊重した北欧モダニズムの重要性を説いていた。ヤコブセンは一時的には機能主義の建築家(フンキス)と呼ばれたが、独自の北欧モダニズムに移行していく。転換点は1943年にポール・ヘニングセン夫妻と2組で決行したスウェー

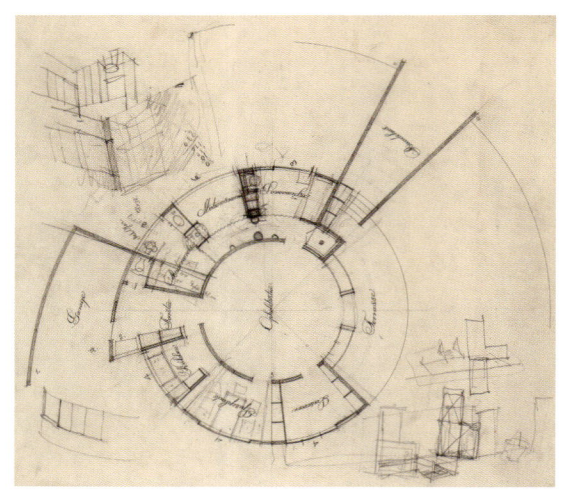

デンマーク美術図書館に保管されている、「未来の家」の平面図。
A floor plan of "House of the Future" in the care of The Danish National Art Library.

デンへの亡命だった。ヤコブセンは1946年にデンマークに帰国したのを境に、母国の伝統や気候風土に適した建築へと変貌を遂げていく。

　とはいえ、ヤコブセンは「フンキス」として鮮烈なデビューを飾った。1929年、27歳で「未来の家」のコンペに幼なじみのフレミング・ラッセンと共同で勝利し、受賞案の実物モデルがコペンハーゲンの「フォーラム住宅展示会」(1929)で展示されて話題となった。また、ル・コルビュジエやミースに続き、フラットルーフの白い箱を思わせる自邸も完成させた。装飾を一切排除した機能主義スタイルの建築はメディアにも大きく取り上げられた。ヤコブセンは独立し、一躍デンマークのモ

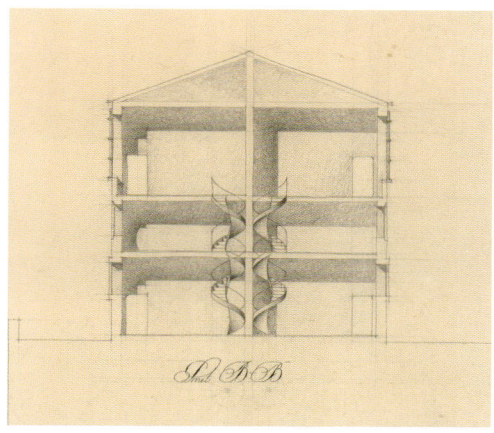

「国立ミュージアム」(1926) 主翼棟の断面図。
A cross section of the main wing of the "National Museum" (1926).

and "St Catherine's College," which were built in his later years. As he liked plants, he sketched fine large trees and a forest-like park behind the building in a perspective. He also described indoor displays and their glass cases in great detail. Beautiful winding stairs, which were suggestive of "SAS Royal Hotel," appeared in a sectioned drawing. A sloping roof and exterior walls of block show the influence of "Aarhus University," which Fisker designed. Although the motif from the orthodox and traditional order of classic architecture was used, it was modernized in the redesign method. Jacobsen won the Golden medal for this work in the Academy. In 1927, a graduate of 25 years of age seemed to be destined to have a bright future.

5 | Funkis | 1927–1937

In 1927, Jacobsen, at 25 years of age, started work in the construction division of the City of Copenhagen and married Marie Jelstrop Holm whom he met in engineering school. They had two sons, but their marriage did not last because of the difference between Marie's freewheeling character and Jacobsen's introversion. Marie was a talented woman and had many artistic friends. One of them was Poul Henningsen (1894-1967), who was successful at the PH-lamp. He edited *Critical Review* magazine (1926-1928) and actively reviewed designs: He had preached the importance of Nordic Modernism that respects craftsmanship and tradition, as well as functionalism. Although Jacobsen was once called the architect of functionalism (Funkis), but he changed his style to Scandinavian modernism. His turning point came when he sought refuge in Sweden with his wife and Mr. and Mrs. Henningsen in 1943. Immediately on his return to Denmark in 1946, Jacobsen's style has undergone changes to architecture that was suited for the land, climate and tradition of his home country.

However, Jacobsen brilliantly debuted with Funkis. In 1929, the 27-year-old won "House of the Future" design competition with his childhood friend, Fleming Lassen. Their winning model was displayed at "Housing Exhibition at the Forum" and became a topic of conversation in 1929. He also built his own house, which was reminiscent of the white box with the flat roof that Le Corbusier and Mies van der Rohe had achieved. The building in a Functionalism style, which eliminated any ornamentation, was widely reported in the media. Then Jacobsen established his own studio and suddenly became renowned as a bearer of Modernism in Denmark.

In 1931, he won a nomination competition

1929年にコペンハーゲンで開催の「フォーラム住宅展示会」に展示された「未来の家」(1927) の実物大モデル。
A life-sized model of the "House of the Future" (1927) was exhibited at the "Housing Exhibition at the Forum" in Copenhagen in 1929.

ダニズムの担い手として名を馳せた。

　1931年、29歳でクランペンボー地区の「ベルビュー海水浴場」の指名コンペで勝利したのをきっかけに、ベルビュービーチのリゾート開発にかかわっていく。ビーチのキオスク、更衣室、監視塔、そしてビーチを望むようにシアター、レストラン、集合住宅、乗馬クラブ、さらにスタッフのユニホームに至るまで、共通のコンセプトに基づき総合的にデザインした。まさに現代でいうところのCI計画の実践である。

　1932年、更衣室、シャワー、クローク機能をもつコスタル・バスと白と水色のストライプのさまざまなキオスクがヤコブセンによってデザインされ、「ベルビュー海水浴場」がオープンする。1934年、「マットソン乗馬クラブ」(1933-1934)、「ベラヴィスタ集合住宅」(1931-1934)が竣工。1937年、「ベルビューシアター」(1935-1937)、「テキサコ・ガソリンスタンド」(1937)が竣工。そして、「カヤッククラブ」(1938)が竣工し、一連の白い建築群のリゾート開発が完成する。

　「未来の家」、「自邸」、ベルビュー地区の白い建築群はヤコブセンの「フンキス」としての名声を確かなものとした。

6 ｜ アスプルンド・スクール ｜ 1937–1940

　ヤコブセンから見るとエーリック・グンナール・アスプルンドは17歳年上の憧れの存在であった。ヤコブセンがまだ建築を学ぶ学生だった頃から、アスプルンドは「森の礼拝堂」(1918-1920)、「スカンディア・シネマ」(1921-1923)、「ストックホルム市立図書館」(1921-1928)といった作品で北欧を代表する建築家の地位を確立していた。「ストックホルム国際博覧会」の翌年、1931年にアスプルンドは母校であるスウェーデン王立工科大学に教授として就任し、「われわれの時代の建築は日本建築に近付く」と記念講演で論じた。折しもヨーロッパにジャポニスムのブームが到来し、日本建築や工芸に関する情報が広まっていた。アスプルンドは日本建築がもつ空間の流動性、可変性、そして自然素材とクラフトマンシップにこれからの北欧の建築の在り方を見出していた。この時期からふたりの交流は密度を増す。ヤコブセンは頻繁にスウェーデンの

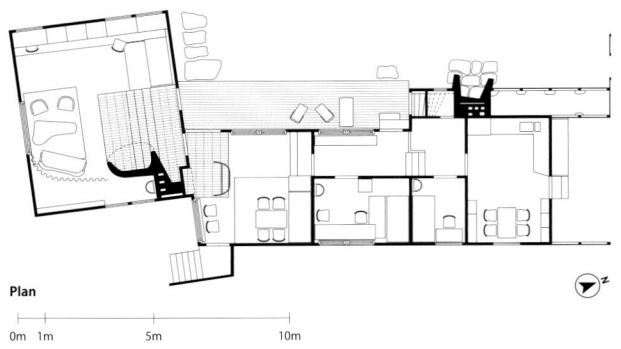

「アスプルンドの夏の家」(1936-1937)の平面図。
A floor plan of "Asplund's Summer House" (1936-1937).

アスプルンドの下を訪れては建築談義に花を咲かせた。アスプルンドが学生を連れてヤコブセンの事務所に訪れることもあった。

　1937年、ヤコブセンは建築家のエリック・ムラー(1909-2002)と共同で「オーフス市庁舎」(1937-1942)のコンペに勝利する。ちょうどアスプルンドが「イェーテボリ裁判所」の増築(1934-1937)を完成させた翌年のことだった。ヤコブセンは、アスプルンドの裁判所を手本に市庁舎を手掛けた。メインホールの上部トップライトからの光天井、木をふんだんに用いた内壁、内部の手摺の繊細な縦桟のデザイン、階段の蹴上げと踏み面の断面を連続的に見せるささら板のデザイン、随所に設置した木の文字盤の大きな壁掛け時計に類似点が散見される。ヤコブセンは外壁のファサードや時計塔の設置に関しても逐一アスプルンドに相談した。そしてアスプルンドもヤコブセンを若き教え子とみなして、快く指導した。

　「ヤコブセンの夏の家」(1938)と、「アスプルンドの夏の家」(1936-1937)にも交流の跡を垣間

for "The Bellevue Beach" and was involved in a resort development. He designed completely everything based on a coherent concept: the kiosks on the beach, changing rooms, guard towers, a theater, a restaurant, apartments fronting on the beach, an equestrian club, and even the uniforms of the staff. What he had done was to achieve a so-called corporate Identity of the modern age.

In 1932, kiosks painted in stripes of light blue and white and a seaside bathhouse, which included changing rooms, showers and a cloak room, were opened at Bellevue beach. The "Riding School Hall for Mattson" (1933-1934) and "Bellavista Housing Complex" (1931-1934) were completed in 1934, "Bellevue Theater" (1935-1937) and a "Texaco Service Station" were completed in 1937. The resort development that consisted of a series of white buildings was finished with completion of "Kayak Club" (1938).

Thus, "House of the Future," "Arne Jacobsen's own house" and the white buildings at the Bellevue Area ensured his fame as a devotee of Funkis.

6 | Asplund's School | 1937–1940 |

Jacobsen looked up to Erik Gunnar Asplund, who was 17 years older than him. When Jacobsen was a student who majored in architecture, Asplund has already renowned as an architect who represented Scandinavia for such works as "Woodland Chapel" (1918-1920), "Skandia Cinema" (1921-1923) and "Stockholm Public Library" (1921-1928). In 1931, a year after "Stockholm International Exhibition," Asplund became a professor of architecture at the Royal Institute of Technology and conducted a special lecture entitled "Architectures in our modern age become similar to Japanese architecture." Just then, there was the Japanism boon in Europe, and information about Japanese architecture and crafts was widespread. Asplund found a way to construct Scandinavian architecture in future into Japanese architecture, which makes use of flexibility and a variety of spaces, natural materials and craftsmanship. From then on, Jacobsen and Asplund kept in touch. Jacobsen frequently visited Asplund in Sweden and enjoyed lively discussions of architecture. Sometimes, Asplund took his students with him to visit Jacobsen.

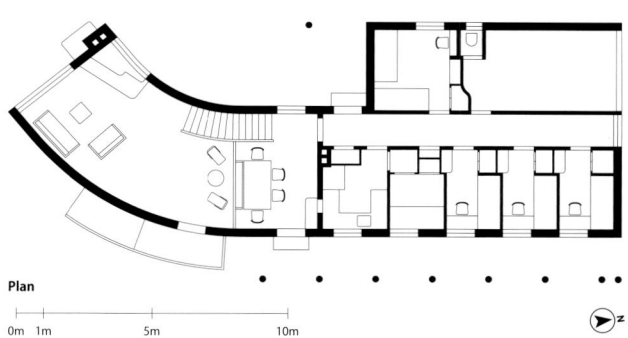

「ヤコブセンの夏の家」（1938）の平面図。
A floor plan of "Jacobsen's Summer House" (1938).

In 1937, Jacobsen entered and won "Aarhus City Hall" (1937-1942) competition with an architect named Erik Møller (1909-2002). A year after that Asplund completed "Gothenburg Law Court extension" (1937-1942). Jacobsen followed Asplund's law court extension and designed the city hall. We can find similarities between the two. They include: a top-lit luminous ceiling in the main hall, lavish use of wood on interior walls, an elaborate design of vertical crosspieces for a handrail, the continuous design of cut stringers that connect risers and treads, and the large wall clocks with their wooden faces that hang in several places. Jacobsen consulted with Asplund at length in deciding how to construct the outside facade and tower with a clock. Asplund regarded Jacobsen as his young student and willingly guided him.

"Jacobsen's Summer House" (1938) and "Asplund's Summer House" (1936-1937) suggest to us that the two men had a very close friendship. They might have exchanged opinions on the

見ることができる。意見を交換しながら設計を進めたのだろう。個室からリビングまでの廊下を、ふたりとも地形の傾斜に沿って軸線上に配置し、リビングルームだけ海に向けて軸を傾ける構成を試みている。アスプルンドが1室だけ傾けたのに対し、ヤコブセンは連続的に先端を湾曲させた。

アスプルンドが1940年に短い生涯を閉じるまで、ふたりの交流は続いた。師匠亡きあと、ヤコブセンはアスプルンドの面影を追いつつ、独自に空間を展開していく。

7 | スウェーデン亡命と帰還 | 1943–1946 |

デンマークは1940年にドイツに占領されて、ドイツ軍による取り締まりが厳しくなっていた。1943年、テキスタイル職人のヨナ・ムラーと再婚したヤコブセンは、「スモーク・ハウス」(1943)の完成を待って中立国スウェーデンへの亡命を決断する。ユダヤ系のヤコブセンにはゲシュタポの迫害が迫りつつあった。事務所の経理を弁護士に任せ、自分の留守中にも少数の所員で継続する体制を整えた。友人のポール・ヘニングセンは、レジスタンス運動に協力していたため亡命の必要に迫られていた。同年9月30日、ヤコブセン夫妻とポール・ヘニングセン夫妻、そして漕ぎ手の5人は小さなボートを漕いでコペンハーゲンから船出し、対岸の街の明かりを目指した。ナチス警備艇のサーチライトをかいくぐっての決死の逃亡劇である。約4時間をかけて国境であるエーレスンド海峡を渡り、対岸のランズクルーナにたどり着いた。

10月初めにはストックホルムに移動して、スヴェン・マルケリウス(1889-1972)に迎えられた。マルケリウスはスウェーデンのモダニズムを代表する建築家で、「ストックホルム国際博覧会」の主要メンバーのひとりである。マルケリウスと親交があり、ストックホルムにも事務所があったアルヴァ・アールトがヤコブセンに小さなアパートを手配した。また、スウェーデン最大の住宅協同組合(HSB)の設計事務所での仕事も世話してくれたが、長くは続かなかった。その後ヤコブセンは幾つかの住宅コンペに参加し、一軒の住宅(1944-1945)を手掛けるが、主にファブリックや壁紙等のテキスタイルデザインに専念した。ヤコブセンが草花の水彩画を描き、シルクスクリーンに熟練していたヨナがプリントした。彼らのテキスタイルデザインは、ノーディスカ・コンパニーをはじめとするスウェーデンのデパートで販売され、ナショナルミュージアムの買取となることもあった。亡命期間中、ヤコブセンはスウェーデンの植生を徹底的に研究した。その甲斐もあって、ヤコブセンは植栽に関する高度な専門性を獲得した。

自邸の植物の写真を撮る1960年頃のヤコブセン。ヤコブセンは花や植物を愛して膨大な数の写真を撮影した。その中には壁紙やテキスタイルデザインのモデルとして撮影したものもある。

Jacobsen was taking pictures of plants in his house around 1960. He loved flowers and plants so that took a great number of photographs. Some of them were used to illustrate his wall papers and textiles.

1946年、終戦を受けてヤコブセンは祖国デンマークに帰還する。戦後第一作として「ベラヴィスタ集合住宅」の隣の敷地に計画したのは、「スーホルムⅠ」(1946-1950)という低層のテラスハウスである。ヤコブセンは祖国デンマークの伝統や風土に回帰し、デンマーク伝統の黄色い煉瓦と、セメント瓦の勾配屋根を用いた。専用の玄関と庭付きの5棟の住居ユニットを、海への視界を確

design of each house while planning and constructing each. Both of them have a corridor that connect private rooms and the living room on an axis along the geographical slope, and have the living room positioned on the rotated axis.

Their relationship lasted until Asplund's death ended his short life in 1940. In the years after the death of his master, Jacobsen often thought of Asplund, as he developed his own architecture.

7 | Refuge in Sweden and repatriation to Denmark | 1943–1946

Denmark was occupied by Germany in 1940. The Germans soon were cracking down on the Jewish people. In 1943, Jacobsen, who was then remarried to Jonna Møller, completed "Fish Smokehouse" (1943) and decided to seek refuge in Sweden, a neutral country. Persecution by the Gestapo of Jacobsen, a Danish Jew, was imminent. He arranged that a few members of his staff take over his business and left the financial aspects of his studio to his lawyer. His friend, Poul Henningsen had, of necessity, fled the country because of his cooperation with the resistance movement. On September 30th of 1940, Mr. and Mrs. Jacobsen, Mr. and Mrs. Henningsen and an oarsman left Copenhagen in a small row boat. It was a desperate escape by five people in which they headed to the city lights on the opposite shore, without being spotted by the searchlight of Nazi patrol boats. It took about four hours to cross Oresund Strait and to reach the opposite shore of Landskrona.

In the beginning of October, Jacobsen and his wife moved to Stockholm where Sven Markelius (1889-1972) welcomed them. Markelius was one of the architect representatives of Swedish Modernism and an important member of "Stockholm International Exhibition." Alvar Aalto, who had a close relationship with Markelius and an office in Stockholm, arranged for a small apartment for Jacobsen. Jacobsen also was introduced to a new job at HSB, Sweden's largest housing association, but did not work there for long. Instead, Jacobsen applied some competition and realized a house (1943-1945). Then, he concentrated on textile design, such as wallpaper and fabric. Jacobsen painted flowers in watercolors and Jonna, who was skillful in the silk screen process, printed them. Their textile designs were sold in department stores throughout Sweden, including Nordiska Kompaniet and even National Museum, which purchased some of them. During his exile, Jacobsen studied thoroughly the vegetation of Sweden. Consequently, he acquired a great deal of knowledge about planting.

ヤコブセン自身が撮影した自邸の庭の写真。
Jacobsen's garden at his house. This photograph was taken by him.

In 1946, Jacobsen returned to Denmark, his native land after the war ended. His first work after the war was "Soholm I" (1946-1950), a low-rise terraced house that he built next to "Bellavista Housing Complex." Jacobsen returned to Danish traditions and culture, and used traditional, yellow bricks for walls and cement tiles for pitched roofs. He arranged five buildings, which have separate porch and garden, in a line, shoulder-to-shoulder, in order to secure a view of the sea. The layout plan featured a kitchen and a dining on the first floor and a living room on the second floor. This is similar to a layout that he used once in "Jacobsen's Summer House." He bought the closest building to the sea

保するため雁行に並べた。キッチンとダイニングを1階に配してリビングルームを2階に置く構成は、かつて「夏の家」で試みた空間構成と共通する。ヤコブセンは最も海側の住戸を自宅とした。そして、地下に新しい設計事務所を構えて再出発の体制を整えた。専用の庭には300種以上の植物を植えて亡命時からの植物研究を継続した。さらに第2期工事として「スーホルムⅡ」（1949-1951）、第3期工事として「スーホルムⅢ」（1953-1954）を建設した。

8 │ 学校建築のトータルデザイン │ 1948-1964

ヤコブセンは4つの校舎を手掛けている。「ホービュー・セントラルスクール」（1948-1950）、「ムンケゴー小学校」（1948-1957）、「ニュエア小学校」（1959-1964）そしてイギリスのオックスフォード大学「セント・キャサリンズ・カレッジ」（1959-1964）である。これらの建築では、材料選定、自然採光、植栽、インテリアエレメントに共通した理念が感じられる。特に細部まで気を配った「ムンケゴー小学校」の出来映えが、後に「セント・キャサリンズ・カレッジ」の設計者として選ばれる決定的理由となった。

「ムンケゴー小学校」（1948-1957）の航空写真。廊下、教室そして中庭の構成が分かる。

An aerial view of "Munkegard Elementary School" (1948-1957) that shows the construction of corridors, classrooms and courtyards.

「ホービュー・セントラルスクール」と同時期に着手した「ムンケゴー小学校」は1957年に完成する。東西に4列の教室棟を平行に並べ、南北に5列の廊下を垂直に貫通する格子状の構成である。教室の南面にはそれぞれ中庭がある。壁は黄色い煉瓦積みで、屋根はアスファルトルーフィングの上にアルミシートを葺いた。教室棟には屋根勾配のずれを利用して上部から光を採り込む「スーホルムⅠ」の断面形状を応用した。2重の窓ガラスにはルーバーが仕込んであり、夏場の南の光を遮断する仕組みだ。教室を仕切る煉瓦の壁も2重で、間には砂を充填し遮音性を高めている。格子状プランで単調に反復してつくった中庭には、異なる舗石パターンと植栽と彫刻を施し、空間に変化を与えた。また、学校生活の道具すべてをデザインした。小学生の体格に応じた3段階の大きさのプライウッド・チェア、ステージの緞帳とカーテン、照明器具、透明な樹脂製のスピーカー等である。中でも照明器具は「ムンケゴー」という名でルイスポールセン社から商品化されて、以降のさまざまなプロジェクトに用いられた。

ここで、ヤコブセンがイギリスで大学の校舎を手掛けるまでの経緯を紹介する。1957年、オックスフォードでは「セント・キャサリンズ・カレッジ」の新キャンパス計画が始まる。敷地を決め、基金を立ち上げ、新キャンパスのための建築家選定委員会が設立された。彼らは多くの現代建築を視察するため、イギリスとアメリカを巡り、最終的にデンマークの建築家も視野に入れた。「ルイジアナ美術館」を設計したヴィルヘム・ヴォラート（1920-2007）、「シドニー・オペラハウス」をつくったヨーン・ウツソン（1918-2008）、「オーフス大学」を手掛けたC・F・ムラー（1898-1988）、そしてヤコブセンがリストアップされた。1958年11月、コミッティはデンマークを訪問した。竣工したばかりの「ロドオア市庁舎」と「ムンケゴー小学校」の仕事ぶりが決め手となってヤコブセンが最有力候補になった。委員会の中心となり活動したのは、後に学長となるアラン・ブロッ

for his residence and set up his studio on the basement floor to start over again. He planted more than 300 species of plants in his garden and continued his study of them that he had begun in Sweden. Then he built "Soholm II" (1949-1951) as a second phase and followed this with "Soholm III" (1953-1954) as a third phase of the construction.

8 | The total design of school buildings | 1948–1964 |

Jacobsen designed school buildings in four locations. They are "Harby Central School" (1948-1950), "Munkegard Elementary School" (1948-1957), and "Nyager Elementary School" (1959-1964) in Denmark and "St Catherine's College" (1959-1964) in Oxford, England. In these buildings, we can see common a philosophy in material selection, natural lighting, planting and interior elements. He was chosen as an architect of "St Catherine's College" because "Munkegard Elementary School" demonstrated his superb execution of details. It was the decisive reason that he was chosen.

He launched "Harby Central School" and "Munkegard Elementary School" at the same time, but the latter was completed in 1957. It was a latticed pattern-shaped building that contained four classrooms, which extend east and west, and five corridors, which run north and south. Courtyards were attached to each classroom on the south side. The wall was constructed of yellow brick and the asphalt roofing was covered by aluminum sheet. The structure of the classrooms was an application of "Soholm I," in which a gap in the sloped roof forms a top light. He designed a mechanism whereby a louver between the double panes of glass can block the light from the south, especially in summer. The double walls that divide the classrooms contained sand to improve sound insulation. He normally made the courtyards in a latticed pattern, but he used different paving stones, plants and sculptures in each to produce different spaces. He designed everything for the students, including three sizes of plywood chairs that corresponded to the sizes of students, curtains for the class and a drop curtain for the stage, lighting fixtures and transparent speakers made of resin. In particular, the lighting was named "Munkegard Lamp" and commercialized at Louis Poulsen. He later used this lighting in many buildings.

Here, I will introduce why Jacobsen was chosen as the architect to design a university in England. In 1957, the University of Oxford introduced a new campus plan for "St Catherine's College" and decided the site, accumulated the necessary funds and established an architect selection committee. The committee travelled around England and the USA to inspect the works of a number of modern architects and finally settled on Danish architects. Three architects were nominated. They were Jorn Utzon (1920-2007) who designed the Sydney Opera House, C. F. Møller (1898-1988) who built Aarhus University and Jacobsen. In November, 1958, they visited Denmark. Jacobsen became the leading candidate because he had just completed "Rodovre City Hall" and "Munkegard Elementary School" in great architectural performances. The committee's foremost member was Alan Bullock, who later became Vice-

「ムンケゴー小学校」（1948-1957）の1956年頃の普通教室の授業風景。椅子、机、照明器具そしてスピーカーに至るまでヤコブセンがデザインした。

A regular class in session at "Munkegard Elementary School" (1948-1957). He designed everything, including chairs, desks, lighting fixtures and speakers.

クである。彼は「ムンケゴー小学校」を視察した感想を次のように述べている。「一目見て気に入った。スケール、素材と色、中庭の植栽までもが完全に調和している。子供たちはまるで自分の家にいるようだ。ムンケゴー小学校を歩きながら、私たちは2年間探し続けた建築家をついに見つけたと確信した」

　1959年、ヤコブセンは新キャンパスの正式な設計者としてオックスフォードに招待された。プロジェクトについて打ち合わせた際に、ランドスケープデザイン、インテリアデザイン、家具と什器のデザインを含む総合的な設計を手掛けることも受諾した。イギリスの大学の設計に他国の建築家を選ぶにあたり大きな議論があったが、学内のみならず『タイム』誌などの世論の擁護があったことが幸いした。数か月後、ヤコブセンは完成予想模型をロンドンに持参し、委員会を大いに満足させた。かくして1960年10月、ヤコブセンの計画案は最終的な合意に達し、ロンドンにてプレス発表が行われた。11月4日、女王陛下とエジンバラ公爵とオックスフォード大学長が定礎式を執り行った。

9 ｜ 建築を彩るプロダクトデザイン ｜ 1952-1960

　1952年、ヤコブセンは世界で初めて背と座を一体化して3次元成形したプライウッド・チェアの開発に成功する。かの有名な「アントチェア」の誕生である。1955年には改良版として「セブンチェア」を発表した。成形技術や接着剤の進化がより難しい形状の成形を可能にし、座り心地を高め、不安定であった3本脚から4本脚に変更した。「アントチェア」と「セブンチェア」は商業的に大成功を収め、ひいてはヤコブセンのプロダクトデザイナーとしての信頼性を高め、以降の製品開発と量産に拍車がかかった。

　ちょうどこの頃、ヤコブセンはデンマーク初の高層ビルとなる「SASロイヤルホテル」(1955-1960)の設計に着手する。スカンジナビア航空(SAS)がコペンハーゲンの中央駅前に北欧の玄関口として最新鋭の旅客ターミナルと近代的ホテルをヤコブセンに依頼したからだ。「ロドオア市庁舎」(1952-1956)の設計においてデンマーク初のカーテンウォールを経験していた

「SASロイヤルホテル」(1955-1960)の北側からの遠望（2012年）。
A distant view from the northern side of "SAS Royal Hotel" (2012).

ヤコブセンは、いよいよ先駆的なカーテンウォールの高層ビルに挑戦する。高層のカーテンウォールは、シカゴでミース・ファン・デル・ローエが設計した26階の「レイク・ショア・ドライブ・アパートメント」(1951)とニューヨークでSOMが設計した24階の「レバーハウス」(1952)がすでに実現していた。ヤコブセンが1956年に発表した「SASロイヤルホテル」の完成イメージは後者に酷似していた。ただし、デンマーク芸術図書館のアーカイブには、ヤコブセンが高層ブロックのレイアウトに数多くのオルタナティブをスタディしたドローイングが残されている。結果的に低く長い低層棟の上にガラスの箱が直立するイメージに落ち着いたのであれば、これもまたリ・デザインの末の結論だと言えるだろう。確かに外観イメージは似ていたが、建築の細部はオリジナリティに満ち溢れていた。外装ではカーテンウォールのアルミ枠の見付けにこだわり、極限までの細さを追求した。インテリアでは、ドアノブ、電気のスイッチ、照明器具、椅子、テーブル、フォーク、ナイフ、調味料入れ、キャンドルスタンド、グラス、絨毯、カーテンなど、最先端のホテルライフを彩るあ

Chancellor of Oxford University. He gave his impression of "Munkegard Elementary School" as follows. "I liked it at first sight. Scales, materials, colors and even planting in the courtyard were in perfect harmony. The children seemed to be in their own home. As I strolled through the elementary school, I was convinced that I had finally found the one that we had sought for two years."

In 1959, Jacobsen was invited to Oxford as the official architect to design the new campus. He agreed to design the landscape, interior, furniture and fixtures after meeting with the committee. The selection of a foreign architect to design a university in England generated a lot of discussion. However, people in the university and public opinion, including *Time* magazine, supported Jacobsen. A few months later, he brought the expected completion model to London and, to a great extent, satisfied the committee. Thus, the university reached final agreement on Jacobsen's plan and announced it in London in October of 1960. On November 4th, Her Majesty the Queen, the Duke of Edinburgh and Vice-Chancellor of Oxford University, laid the cornerstone.

9 | Product design that enhances Architecture | 1952–1960

In 1952, Jacobsen succeeded in becoming first in the world to develop a molded plywood chair that integrates the seat and the back of the chair. It became famous as "The Ant." In 1955 he released its fully developed version, "The Seven." The evolution of adhesive agents and molding technology enabled more difficult shapes to be molded and more comfortable sheets to be made. He changed the design of unstable three-leg chairs into four-leg chair. "The Ant" and "The Seven" achieved great commercial success, which increased Jacobsen's reputation as a designer of reliable products. In turn, this spurred the development of his product design and mass production of it.

Around this time, Jacobsen undertook design of "SAS Royal Hotel" (1955-1960), which was Denmark's a first high-rise building. He did so because Scandinavian Airlines System (SAS) asked Jacobsen to build a state-of-the-art terminal building and a modern hotel. Jacobsen once designed curtain wall for "Rodovre City Library" (1952-1956). He finally decided to accept the challenge of pioneering the use of curtain walls in high-rise buildings. As previous examples, Mies already had built "Lake Shore Drive Apartments" (1951) in Chicago and SOM had created a twenty-four-story building, "Lever House" (1952), in New York. In 1956, Jacobsen completed "SAS Royal Hotel." Its form was very similar to that of "Lever House." However, there are many drawings that Jacobsen studied as alternative layouts for the high-rise block in the archive of the Danish National Art Library. As a result, he created a final shape of an upright glass box on a long low-rise building. It can be said that this was the conclusion to the process of the redesign. It is true that appearance closely resembled "Lever House," but architectural details were full of originality. Around the outside, sheets of glass plate were attached to the extremely thin aluminum frame of the curtain walls. Around the inside, to achieve a feeling of a state-of-the-art hotel, he developed every interior element from scratch.

「SAS ロイヤルホテル」(1955-1960) の今は改装されてなくなったウィンターガーデン。2枚のガラスの間に蘭の花が吊るされたウィンターガーデン越しにバーカウンターを望む。

The winter garden at "SAS Royal Hotel." It does not exist now because of renovation. A bar counter can be seen through the winter garden in which pots of orchids are suspended between two sheets of glass.

りとあらゆるインテリアエレメントをオープンに向けて次々とゼロからデザイン開発していった。

1958年、パリ装飾芸術美術館で「北欧のかたち展」が開催された。ヤコブセンは「SASロイヤルホテル」のために開発したさまざまなプロダクトを展示し、建築とインテリアのトータルデザインをアピールした。中でも、同年開発に成功した「エッグチェア」と「スワンチェア」が衆目を集めた。「エッグチェア」に腰掛けると左右の視界が遮られ、体は丸い背もたれにすっぽりと包み込まれる。喧騒の中にあっても個室のようなパーソナルスペースを創出するこの椅子は、「SASロイヤルホテル」のロビーに欠かすことのできない一品に仕上がった。

1960年、「SASロイヤルホテル」はデンマーク初の高層ビルを受け入れるか否かの激しい議論の中で完成した。新しい建築を揶揄する一方で、人びとは競うようにエレベーターで20階のロビーに昇り、地上70mからの展望を楽しんだ。繊細な窓枠のファサードがコペンハーゲンの空に溶け込んだように、ヤコブセンの意欲的な試みは次第に市民に受け入れられていった。「SASロイヤルホテル」は「エッグチェア」と「スワンチェア」と並び、デンマークのモダンデザインのアイコンとなった。

10 | トータルデザインの集大成 | 1961–1971

1961年、ヤコブセンは「デンマーク国立銀行」（1961-1971, 1972-1978）の指名コンペに参加した。歴史的建造物である旧銀行をどう扱うか、また、銀行業務を中断せずに増築することが設計の要点であった。カイ・フィスカを含めた4名の建築家は、いずれも歴史的建物を保全する案を考え

「デンマーク国立銀行」（1961-1971, 1972-1978）の航空写真。
Aerial photograph of "Danmarks Nationalbank" (1961-1971, 1972-1978).

たが、ヤコブセンは唯一残さない案を提示してコンペに勝利した。銀行業務を滞らせることなく、紙幣印刷所を含む建物全体を3段階で建設するフェイジングが勝因となった。第1段階で紙幣印刷所と事務棟の北側、第2段階でエントランスホールと事務棟の南側、そして第3段階で西側の低層棟に着手する。1965年に事務棟の北側に取り掛かり、1970年4月に第一段階の工事が完了した。1971年2月には行員が北側に引っ越し、新銀行での業務の開始を見届けたところで、ヤコブセンは3月24日に突然死去する。多くの仕事を抱え、働き詰めだった中での心臓発作だった。

その後の工事を、ヤコブセン事務所のパートナーであったハンス・ディシング（1926-1998）とオットー・ヴァイトリング（1930-）が引き継いだ。ディシング＋ヴァイトリング建築事務所は1972年に第2、第3段階の工事に着工し、1978年に竣工した。彼らは同様に、同年に「ドイツのマインツ市庁舎」、1977年にはロンドンに「デンマーク大使館」を完成させた。

こうして「デンマーク国立銀行」はヤコブセンの遺作となった。これまでのプロダクトデザインを総動員し、さらに混合水栓「ボーラ」、「バンカーズ・クロック」、「セブンチェア」を進化させた「エイトシリーズ」を新たにデザイン開発した。また、これまでの設計で培ったガーデニングの手腕も存分に発揮した。銀行西側の低層棟の屋上全体をルーフガーデンとし、事務棟にはふたつの中庭を作った。さらに室内には植物の鉢を吊るすガラスケースを導入し、思う存分に植物を建築

These included: doorknobs, lighting switches, lighting fixtures, chairs, tables, forks, knives, seasonings containers, candle stands, glasses, carpets, curtains, etc.

In 1958, the Museum of Decorative Arts in Paris held an exhibition of "Scandinavian Forms." Jacobsen displayed various products that he had developed for "SAS Royal Hotel" and demonstrated his total design of architecture and interior. In particular, the just-completed "The Egg" and "The Swan" attracted public attention. When you sit on "The Egg," right and left visual fields are blocked and the body is wrapped comfortably in a round backrest. This chair became essential in the lobby of the "SAS Royal Hotel" because it creates a personal space-like private room, even if the lobby is exposed to hustle and bustle.

In 1960, the completion of "SAS Royal Hotel" led to heated discussions of whether or not accept Denmark's first high-rise building. While critics ridiculed the new building, they took the elevator to the 20th observation floor and enjoyed the view from a height of 70 meters. As the new facade with elaborate window frame blended with the Copenhagen sky, they gradually became accustomed to Jacobsen's ambitious attempt. Hence, "SAS Royal Hotel" became an icon of Danish modern design, as well as "The Egg" and "The Swan."

10 | Culmination of total design | 1961–1971

In 1961, Jacobsen took part in a nominated competition of designs for "Danmarks Nationalbank" (1961-1971, 1972-1978). The points of design were how to deal with the bank's present historical building and how to construct the building without interrupting the banking. While all four architects, including Kay Fisker, planned to preserve the historical building, Jacobsen proposed a design that did not preserve it and won the competition. The deciding factor was his planned gradual construction in three phases of the entire, new building, including the banknote printing works, without interrupting the business. The plan was to undertake the north side of the office building with the printing works in the first stage, the south side of the office building with the entrance hall in the second stage, and the low-rise building on the west side in the third stage. In 1965, the bank began the construction on the north side of the office building. In February, 1971, part of the banks staff began to conduct business in the new building. Jacobsen unfortunately died from a heart attack on March 24th. Hans Dissing (1926-1998) and Otto Weitling (1930-), who were partners in the Jacobsen studio, took over the rest of the building activities. The Dissing and Weitling studio finished the second stage in 1976 and third stages in 1978. They also completed "Mainz City Hall" in Germany and "Denmark Embassy" in London.

Thus, "Danmarks Nationalbank" became a posthumous work of Jacobsen. In this building, he used many of the products that he had designed so far. Moreover, he developed a new combination faucet "Vola," "Bankers Clock," and "Series 8" which evolved from "The Seven." Then he fully exercised his gardening skills. He created a roof garden on the roof of the low-rise building, which is located in the west side of the bank, and two courtyards in the office building, In addition, he developed glass cases in which plants pots are suspended to create plant spaces to his heart's content within the interior. Thus, "Danmarks

オードロップ墓地のヤコブセン夫妻の墓。左が妻のヨナ (1908-1995)、右がヤコブセン (1902-1971)。

The tombstone of Mr. and Mrs. Jacobsen in Ordrup Cemetery. On the left is Jonna (1908-1995). On the right is Jacobsen (1902-1971).

に取り入れている。国立銀行はまさにヤコブセンのトータルデザインの集大成となった。

現在、ヤコブセンは妻のヨナ(1908-1995)と共にオードロップ墓地に埋葬されている。何ともヤコブセンらしい丸い形の墓石は、「シリンダライン」や水栓を担当した元所員、テイト・ヴァイラント(1941-)がヤコブセンの庭の石を用いてデザインした。

11 おわりに

ヤコブセンのデザインの原点はふたつある。ひとつは卒業設計の「国立ミュージアム」、もうひとつは彼が愛してやまなかった植物である。

デンマーク王立芸術アカデミーの卒業時にヤコブセンはひとつのスタイルに行き着く。それは低層で水平に長い直線的な建築である。卒業設計の「国立ミュージアム」をはじめ、「ベルビューコスタル・バス」、「カヤッククラブ」、「ロドオア市庁舎」、「ムンケゴー小学校」、「セント・キャサリンズ・カレッジ」、「SASロイヤルホテル」低層部、「デンマーク国立銀行」では、そのスタイルを追求した。

一方で、ヤコブセンはプロダクトデザインに曲線を多用している。「ベルビュービーチ監視塔」、「シリンダライン」は円筒で表現し、「アントチェア」、「エッグチェア」は有機的な弧で構成している。

植物を好んでスケッチしたヤコブセンは、植栽そのものにも熱心に取り組んだ。「SASロイヤルホテル」と「デンマーク国立銀行」では植物の鉢をガラスケースに吊るし、温室を作った。また、「ムンケゴー小学校」や「ロドオア市庁舎」では廊下の端に土の区画を設けて緑地を作った。北欧の冬は長い。ヤコブセンは、室内に緑のオアシスを切望したのだ。そして、ヤコブセンにとって家具もまた枯れることのない植物だったのではないか。「エッグチェア」や「スワンチェア」の丸みを帯びた形状は植物にインスパイアされたものだ。それらの形はヤコブセンがこの世で一番美しい植物と称賛したサボテンや、好んで「SASロイヤルホテル」の各室に置いた蘭の花の形にも見えてくる。

建築の直線的な構成と、プロダクトデザインのオーガニックな形状という対比が、ヤコブセンのトータルデザインを特徴付けている。彼は建築という不変のプロポーションに永遠性を託し、プロダクトデザインという再生産される製品に色あせない未来を託した。21世紀となった今日、ヤコブセンの魅力は古びるどころか、むしろ今日的なデザインのアイコンとして人びとに認識されている。本稿は「今、なぜヤコブセンなのか」という問い掛けから始めたが、結論としては「今もなお、ヤコブセンである」という答えに達するのである。

Nationalbank" became the culmination of Jacobsen's total design.

Now Jacobsen and his wife, Jonna (1908-1995), are buried in Ordrup Cemetery. The circular tombstone, which is suggestive of Jacobsen, was designed by Teit Weyland (1941-), a former member of the staff of Jacobson's studio and the person who was responsible for the water faucet and "Cylinda Line." He used garden stone from Jacobsen's house for the tombstone.

11 | Conclusion

Jacobsen's design originality was aroused by two influences. One was his graduation work, "National Museum." Plants, which he loved, was another.

When he graduated from The Royal Danish Academy of Fine Arts, he realized his particular style, which is low-rise, horizontal, long and straight construction. This style is reflected in "National Museum," "Bellevue Costal Bath," "Kayak Club," "Rodovre City Hall," "Munkegard Elementary School," "St Catherine's College," and the low-rise section of "SAS Royal Hotel" to "Danmarks Nationalbank."

On the other hand, Jacobsen frequently introduced curves into his product design. He used a cylinder form at the "Guard Towers" at Bellevue Beach, and the "Cylinda Line" and organic arc forms at "The Ant" and "The Egg."

He liked to draw plants and to plant them as well. He created a greenhouse with the glass case in which he suspended pots for plants at "SAS Royal Hotel" and "Danmarks Nationalbank." In addition, he created flower beds at the end of the corridor at "Munkegard Elementary School" and "Rodovre City Hall." The winter in Scandinavia is so long that Jacobsen sought a green oasis in a room. I hypothesize that furniture was like plants for Jacobsen. He was inspired by plants and designed "The Egg" and "The Swan." These round shapes resemble cactus, which he admired and considered to be the most beautiful plant in the world, and the orchid, which he liked to plant in a pod in each room at "SAS Royal Hotel."

A comparison of the straight structure and the organic shape of product design characterizes Jacobsen's total design. He entrusted perdurable proportion of the building with permanency and conducted reproduction of product design as timeless design. Now, in the 21st century, the Jacobsen's design has not become old, but rather is regarded as a modern design icon. In beginning to write this article I sought to answer the question that asks "Why should we consider Jacobsen now?" I concluded my article with an answer that "Jacobsen is still worth considering."

ベルビュー地区　1930年〜／クランペンボー
The Bellevue Area／Bellevue-området, 1930〜, Klampenborg

コペンハーゲン中央駅から電車で北へ15分のクランペンボー駅で降りると、「ベルビュー地区」という海辺の高級リゾートがある。ヤコブセンの家族は彼が小学生の頃にコペンハーゲンの中心部からこの地域の住宅地に引っ越した。ヤコブセンがデンマーク王立アカデミーで卒業設計を行う折りにここを敷地に選んだのは、勝手知ったる地元であったからだ。

建築家として独立して2年後、29歳でベルビュー地区の「コスタル・バス」の指名コンペで勝利したのをきっかけに、ヤコブセンはベルビュー地区のリゾート開発に関わっていく。

具体的には、1930年にオープンしていた海水浴場の再整備を手始めに、海岸沿いにリゾート関連施設を統一的なコンセプトに基づいて次々と実現していった。

まず1932年に、更衣室、シャワー、クローク機能を備えた「ベルビューコスタル・バス」、青と白のストライプで統一した「キオスク」と「監視塔」が整備された。その後、1934年に「マットソン乗馬クラブ」と「ベラヴィスタ集合住宅」、1937年に「ベルビューシアター＆レストラン」と「テキサコ・ガソリンスタンド」、そして1938年に「カヤッククラブ」が竣工して、一連の白い建築群から成る高級リゾートが完成した。

監視塔
Guard Tower

ベルビューコスタル・バス
Bellevue Coastal Bath

マットソン乗馬クラブ（竣工当時写真）
Riding School Hall for Mattson (photo taken upon completion)

Take a train from Copenhagen Central Station for 15 minutes to Klampenborg Station to find a luxury seaside resort, "The Bellevue Area." When Jacobsen enrolled in elementary school, his family moved from the center of Copenhagen to Klampenborg. When he did his graduation work at The Royal Danish Academy of Fine Arts, he chose this local site because he knew it well.

Two years later, he became an independent architect and won a nomination competition for "The Coastal Bath." Thanks to that, he was involved in development of The Bellevue Area as a resort.

In particular, he began the redevelopment of the beach that had been opened in 1930, and created the resort facilities along the coast, one after another, based on a coherent concept.

First, he developed "Bellevue Coastal Bath," which he equipped with changing rooms, showers and cloaks, a "Kiosk" and "Guard Towers," both in stripes of blue and white, in 1932. Then, he created "Riding School Hall for Mattson" and "Bellavista Housing Complex" in 1934, "Bellevue Theater and Restaurant" and "Texaco Service Station" opened in 1937. The "Kayak Club" was completed in 1938. Thus, a series of white buildings at the Bellevue area were developed as a luxury resort.

ベルビューシアター
Bellevue Theater

ベラヴィスタ集合住宅
Bellavista Housing Complex

テキサコ・ガソリンスタンド
Texaco Service Station

ベルビュー 海水浴場　1930年／クランペンボー

The Bellevue Beach／Bellevue Strandbad, 1930, Klampenborg

ベルビュー海水浴場の海岸に突き出た突堤の先端に立つ、電柱を利用した4本足の監視塔。

The guard tower that has four tele-graph poles for legs, stands on the pier at Bellevue Beach.

ベルビューリゾート地区の中心となるのが「ベルビュー海水浴場」だ。公園の海側に大量の砂を敷き詰めて造成した人工の海水浴場としてオープンした。予想以上に多くの人が詰めかけたため、更衣室、シャワー、クローク等の施設が必要となり、1931年に急遽「コスタル・バス」の指名コンペが行われた。敷地はヤコブセンがデンマーク王立芸術アカデミーの卒業設計で「国立ミュージアム」を設置しようと研究した公園のすぐ傍だった。地の利を知り尽くしていたヤコブセンはこのコンペに勝利する。

ヤコブセンは公園とビーチの高低差を生かすべく「ベルビューコスタル・バス」を設計した。白く低い建築の屋根の高さは公園の地面の高さに合わせてあり、芝生の公園とビーチを区切るように、複数の更衣室を連ねている。海から浜辺を見た時の左側に女性用の更衣室を並べ、その奥にビーチのメインエントランスの階段とスロープを構成した。ビーチの右側には男性用の更衣室を並べ、建物の右端はL型に曲げてビーチを囲むように配置した。

現在も夏季の「ベルビュー海水浴場」は海水浴、散歩、ビーチバレー、日光浴を楽しむ人びとでにぎわっている。浜辺にはヤコブセンがデザインしたキオスクはもうないが、桟橋の先端には「ベルビュー海水浴場」のシンボルたる青と白のストライプの監視塔がそびえている。

The center of the Bellevue resort area is "The Bellevue Beach." This artificial bathing resort was constructed and paved with large amounts of sand from the park's sea shore. When the resort opened, many people flocked to the beach unexpectedly. In 1931, a nomination competition for "The Coastal Bath" was held because facilities, such as changing rooms, showers and cloaks were needed immediately. The site was located next to the park for which Jacobsen once had intended to design "National Museum" for his graduation work. Thus, his knowledge of the topography of the area gave him an advantage and, consequently, he won this competition.

Jacobsen designed "Bellevue Coastal Bath" to take advantage of the difference in height between the park and the beach. It was white roof and low building that adapted to the height of the ground in the park. He located several buildings as changing rooms to separate the beach and park lawn. When you stand in the sea and look back towards the beach, the women's changing rooms, the main entrance to the beach, the stairs and the slopes are located on your left side. The men's changing rooms are located on your right side. The L-shaped right end of the building was arranged to follow the beach.

Even now, "The Bellevue Beach" is crowded with people who enjoy bathing, walking, sun-bathing and beach volleyball during the summer season. Although the kiosk that Jacobsen designed no longer exists, the guard towers painted in stripes of blue and white rise as symbols of the beach.

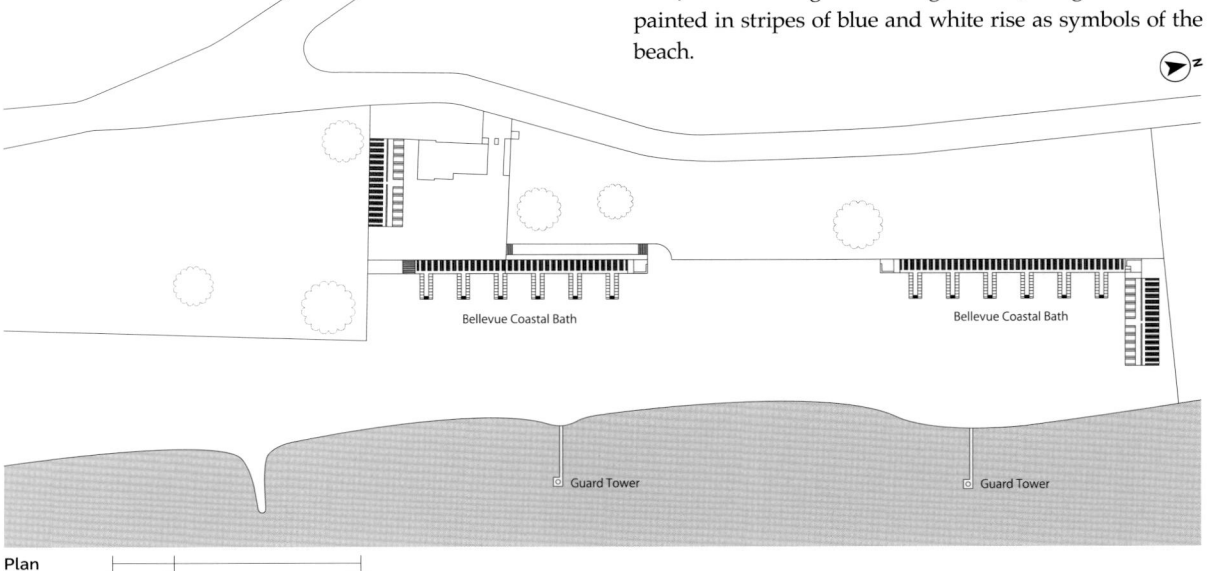

Plan

突堤先端の監視塔。竣工時、突堤の床は木製であった。監視塔腰部分の青と白のストライプ柄は、ビーチの売店やテントなどにも使われたテーマカラー。

The guard tower stands on the pier. The guard tower had a wood floor when it was completed. Its blue and white stripes were theme colors and also appeared on the kiosks and tents at the beach.

ヤコブセンによるアイスクリームのキオスクの水彩画。青と白のストライプとアイスクリームのISの赤い文字が特徴。

A watercolor of ice cream kiosk drawn by Jacobsen. It features stripes of blue and white and red letters. IS means ice cream.

ヤコブセンのスケッチの力を感じる監視塔のスケッチ。

A drawing of guard towers shows Jacobsen's drawing ability.

ベルビュー海水浴場全景。監視塔はビーチに２か所立てられている。

Full view of Bellevue Beach. The beach has two guard towers.

ベルビュー海水浴場全景。海岸線の向こうはスウェーデン。

Full view of Bellevue Beach. Across the ocean is Sweden.

シャワースタンドとベルビュー・コスタルバス。

Shower stalls and Bellevue Coastal Bath.

ベラヴィスタ集合住宅　1934年／クランペンボー

Bellavista Housing Complex ／ Bellavista Boligbebyggelse, 1934, Klampenborg

表通り（ストランドベーゲン）に面した南棟コーナー。階段の向こう側の通路の先はガレージ、道路側の住戸は１層低く抑えられている。右奥に北棟が見える。

A round corner of the south building that faces Strandvejen Street. A garage is on the other side of the staircases. The buildings facing the street are one-story shorter than the others. The north building on the right at the back.

この時期のヤコブセンは北欧の機能主義の旗手（フンキス）として、自邸や「ベルビューコスタル・バス」といった白い箱型の建築を次々と実現していった。「ベラヴィスタ集合住宅」もそのひとつである。しかし、ここでは建築の与条件もヤコブセンに味方したと言えるだろう。市当局の指導で、周囲の住宅地を考慮して3層以下の低層であること、他の建物と同様に白い建築であることが求められたのだ。
　バルコニー付きの2LDKの68戸の住棟配置は海側に開いたコの字型である。海に向かって東西に延びるふたつのウィングと駅側の南北のウィングで中庭を囲んでいる。すべての住戸のリビングルームと寝室から海を眺められるように、東西のウィングでは各戸の界壁でバルコニーの奥行き分を雁行させた。バルコニーの上部に設置したパーゴラは、晴れた日には白い壁面に黒いストライプの影を落とし、ファサードに表情をもたらす。東西のウィングの先端にあるバルコニーとパーゴラに見られるラウンドコーナーの手法は、のちの「ノヴォ治療ラボラトリウム」（p.64）や「ステリング・ビル」（p.72）に共通する。
　当時の住宅としては珍しく、バスタブのある浴室、電気コンロ、冷蔵庫、ステンレストップのカウンター、ダストシュート、ラジオのアンテナ等、ハイスペックの設備が各住戸に整っていた。裕福で社会的地位の高い客層を想定して売り出した結果、全戸の完成前に完売したという。

Elevation

西棟3階バルコニーからの眺望。各住戸を雁行させることにより、ベルビュー海水浴場の眺望とプライバシーの確保を両立させている。右に広がるのは1961年ヤコブセン設計の5戸からなるコートハウス。

A view from the balcony of the west building. The houses were so arranged in echelon that each would have privacy and a view of Bellevue Beach. Five courthouses designed by Jacobsen in 1961 appear on the right in the photograph.

In this period, as the architect of functionalism in Scandinavia (Funkis), Jacobsen built white, box-like shapes one after another, such as his own house and "Bellevue Coastal Bath." "Bellavista Housing Complex" is another. However, we could say that the architectural conditions are on his side. The city authorities asked him to design low-rise housing that did not exceed three stories in height and to make the structure white to harmonize with the surrounding residential areas.

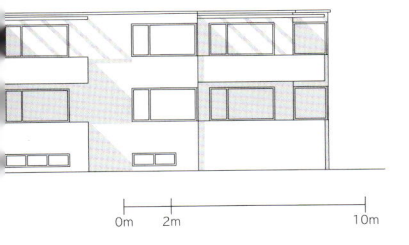

The housing complex of 68 units of 2LDK with balconies forms a C shape that faces the beach. Two east-west wings and one north-south wing surround a courtyard. In the east-west wing, he arranged for each partition wall to zigzag only for the width of the balcony, in order to obtain a view of the sea from the bedroom and living room of all of the dwelling units. A pergola on top of the roof casts black striped shadows on the white wall on a sunny day and accentuates the facade. The balcony and the pergola on the edge of the east-west wing form a round corner. We can see the same method of forming round corners in his later architecture, "Novo Terapeutisk Laboratorium" (p.64) and "The Stelling Building" (p.72).

It was unusual for each dwelling unit to be equipped with high-spec facilities, such as a bathroom with a bathtub, electric stove, refrigerator, stainless steel counter top, dust chute and a radio antenna. Wealthy and socially prominent people were the target. All houses were sold before completion.

Bellavista Housing Complex 41

クランペンボー駅前から見る北棟。手前の曲面壁は階段室。左のベルビューシアターを挟む道路の先はベルビュー海水浴場。

A view of the north building from Klampenborg Station. A curved corner contains staircase inside. On the left is Bellevue Theater. The road leads to Bellevue Beach.

北棟の道路に面した入口。

An entrance to the north building.

北棟コーナーの階段室見下ろし。4分の1円弧の不思議な空間。壁面は微妙な色遣い。

Look down a stairwell in the corner of the north building. The one-quarter arc is an amazing use of space. The wall was painted in a subtle color.

Arne Jacobsen

最上階からのトップライトで明るい北棟
コーナー階段室の見上げ。

Looking up the bright stairwell to the
top lights in the north building.

北棟コーナー階段室に面した住戸入口。
An entrance to the stairwell in the corner of the north building.

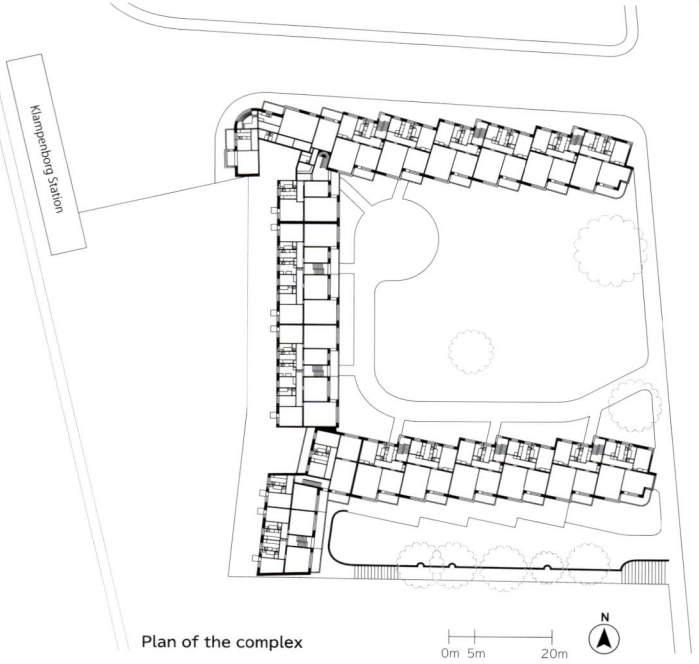

扇型トップライトで明るい北棟コーナー階段室。
The fan-shaped top right brightens the stairwell at the corner of the north building.

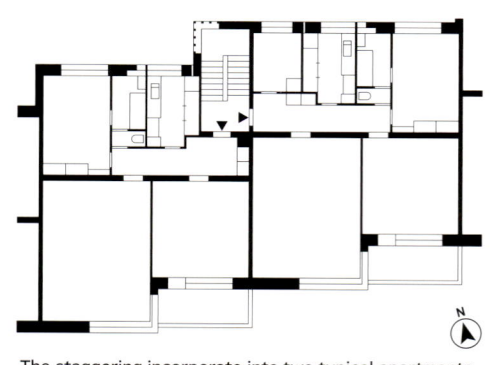

Klampenborg Station

Plan of the complex

0m 5m 20m

The staggering incorporate into two typical apartments

0m 2m 10m

44　Arne Jacobsen

道路からベルビュー海水浴場に下りる階段。
正面にベラヴィスタ集合住宅が見える。

The staircase in front of the Bellavista
Housing Complex connects the road
and Bellevue Beach.

西棟3階のリビングルームからベルビュー海水浴場を望む。

A view of Bellevue Beach from a third floor living room in the western building.

Bellavista Housing Complex 45

ベルビューシアター 1937年／クランペンボー
Bellevue Theater / Bellevue Teatret, 1937, Klampenborg

大きくうねる庇が特徴的なベルビューシアター。緩やかな凹面と凸面を組み合わせた構成のファサード。

The large undulating eave that typifies Bellevue Theater. A facade that combines gentle concave and convex surfaces.

表通り（ストランドベーゲン）からの外観。
左奥にベラヴィスタ集合住宅が隣接する。

A view of Strandvejen Street. Bellavista Housing Complex is behind the theater on the left.

「ベルビューシアター」は夏期に公演を行う劇場と、隣接するレストランから成るベルビューリゾート地区の基幹施設である。目の前には「ベルビュー海水浴場」の入口がある。

真っ白な劇場の正面で人目を引くのは青い大きなロゴタイプと広告である。湾曲した独特のファサード全体が広告塔としてデザインされた。長さ60mのレストランのウィングは海岸線に対して平行に、道路からは奥まっていくように、南へ延びていく。「ベラヴィスタ集合住宅」と同様に、高さは低く抑えられた。

劇場の内部は、海側からエントランス、ホワイエ、客席そして舞台が一直線状に並ぶが、客席に向かうにはホワイエから客席の両サイドのクロークがある広い廊下に出てから1階席、2階席に分かれていく。オーディトリアムの内部には開放的な海辺のリゾートのイメージが集約されている。開閉可能な可動屋根を開けると青空が見える。防火性と吸音性能を備えた布張りの壁は白と青のストライプ柄を踏襲した。また、波のように湾曲した椅子の背板が、客席に幾重もの波を作り出す。内装のところどころにふんだんに用いた竹の仕上げがオリエンタルな印象を醸し出す。

レストランの大半は集合住宅に改修された。シアターに隣接してオリジナルの暖炉があった場所は「レストランヤコブセン」として営業していた。

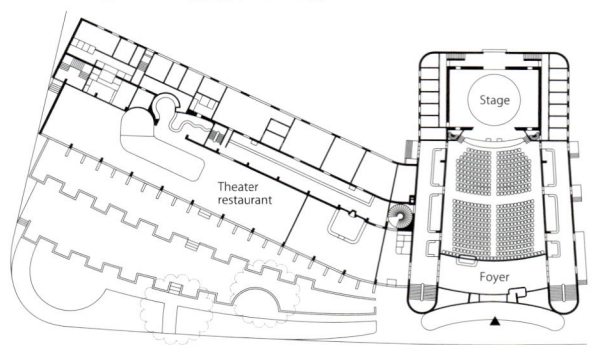

First floor plan

"Bellevue Theater" forms part of the infrastructure of the Bellevue resort area. It comprises a theater in which performances are held during the summer, and an restaurant. An entrance is facing "The Bellevue Beach."

In front of the white theater, the name in large blue letters and advertising attract the attention of tourists. Jacobsen designed the curved facade of the entire theater as a billboard. A wing that is 60 meters in length and contains a restaurant extends to the south, parallels the shoreline and is set back from the road. Jacobsen kept the height the same as the low-rise housing of "Bellavista Housing Complex."

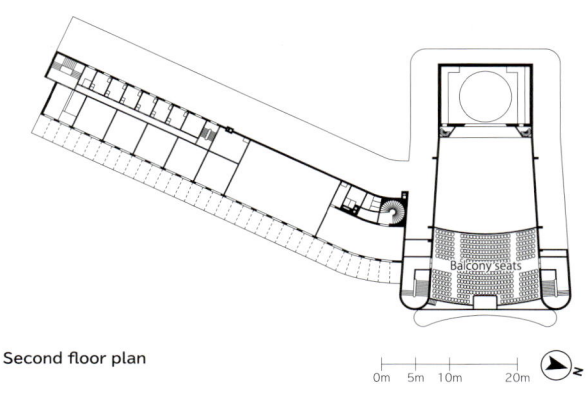

Inside of the theater, the entrance, the foyer, seats and a stage are arranged one after the other form the sea side. Corridors, which contain cloakrooms on both sides of the theater connect the foyer to the auditorium and the balcony. The portion of the roof that covers the auditorium can be opened to permit a view of the blue sky. The interior wall is upholstered in sound-absorbing and fire resistant material that is painted in stripes of blue and white. The curved backs of the chairs in the auditorium look like a succession of waves. The bamboo is used generously in some parts of the interior to give an Oriental touch. Today, most of the restaurant has been renovated into the housing complex. However, the original fireplace and the place next to the theater were used as "Restaurant Jacobsen."

Second floor plan

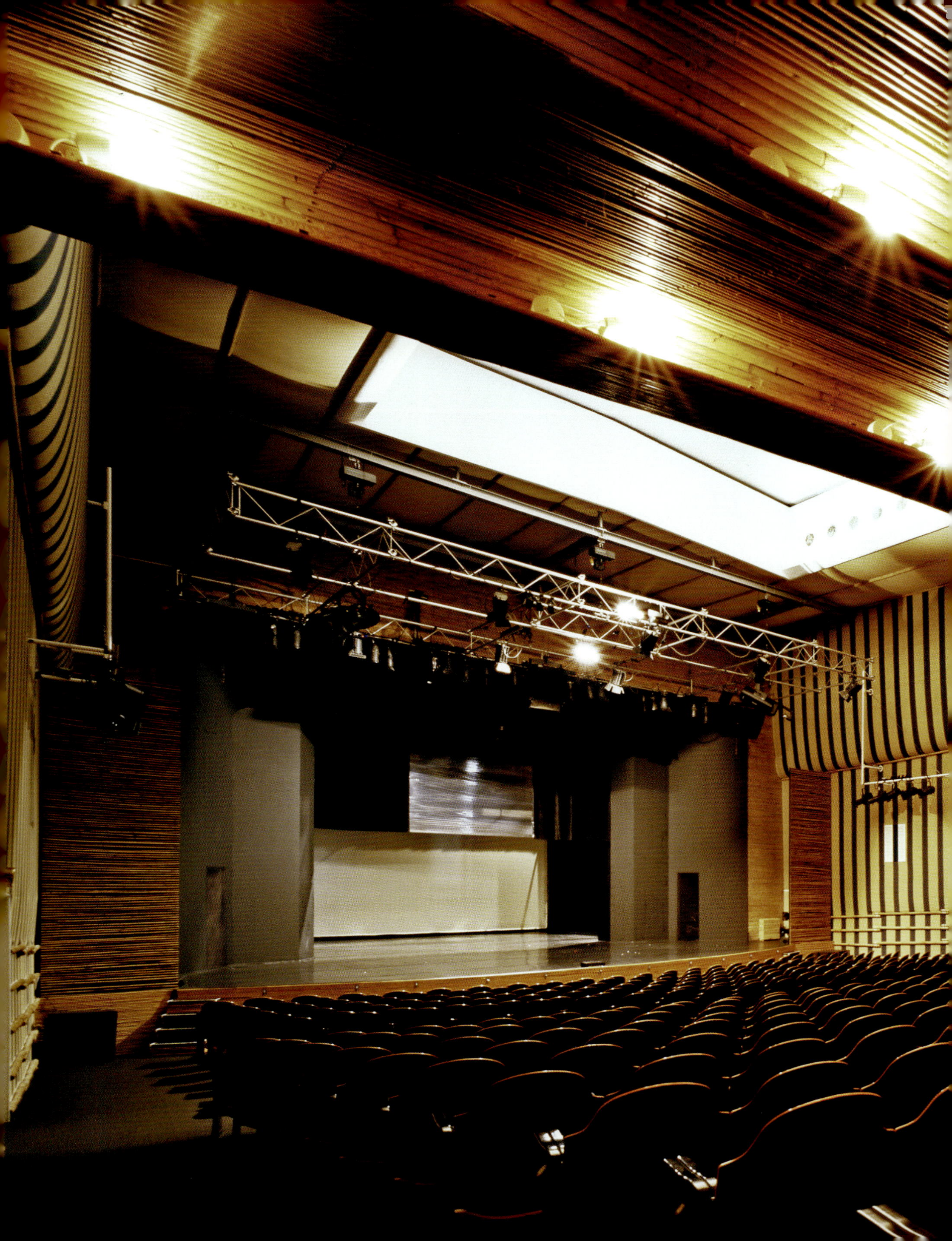

オーディトリアム1階。竹、ラタン、キャンバスなどが内装に使われ、サマーシアターらしい仮設的でカジュアルな印象を醸し出している。

The first floor of the auditorium. Bamboo, rattan, and canvas are used for interior decoration. They lend a feeling of informality and summer to the theater.

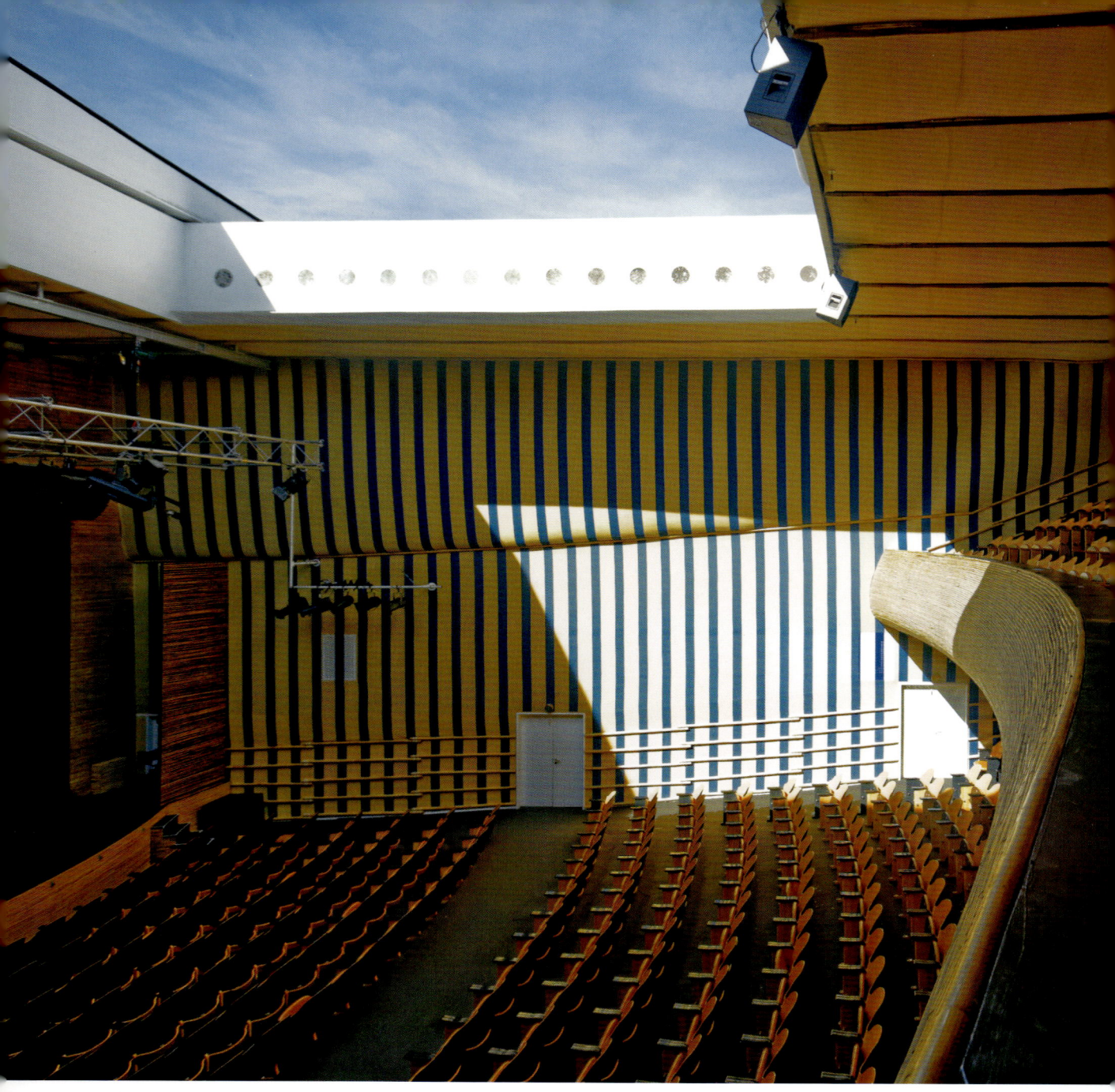

オーディトリアムのバルコニー席。天井は可動式で開放できる。ベルビュー海水浴場のテーマカラーである青と白のストライプ柄のキャンバスが壁に掛けられ、波のようなカーブを描く天井のキャンバスと呼応している。夏の公演では、天井を開放して星空の下での観劇も行われていた。

The balcony of the auditorium. The roof that covers the auditorium can be opened and closed. The interior wall is upholstered with canvas in stripes of blue and white, the Bellevue Beach's theme colors and in harmony with the ceiling canvas in its wave-like pattern. On summer nights, the audience attended the performance under the starry sky.

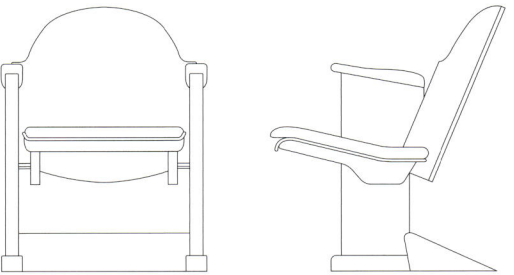

バルコニー席の腰壁は細い竹で仕上げられ、緩やかなカーブを描いて1階天井につながる。

The front of the balcony was finished with thin strips of bamboo in a gentle carve. The bamboo strips also covered the first floor ceiling.

壁を覆う青と白のストライプ柄キャンバスは、竹の横桟で無造作に押さえられている。

The blue-and-white-striped canvas was held in place by horizontal lengths of bamboo.

波の形をイメージさせる背が特徴の客席。

The distinctive curved backs of the auditorium chairs are reminiscent of a succession of waves.

Front view and Side view of the auditorium chair

Bellevue Theater

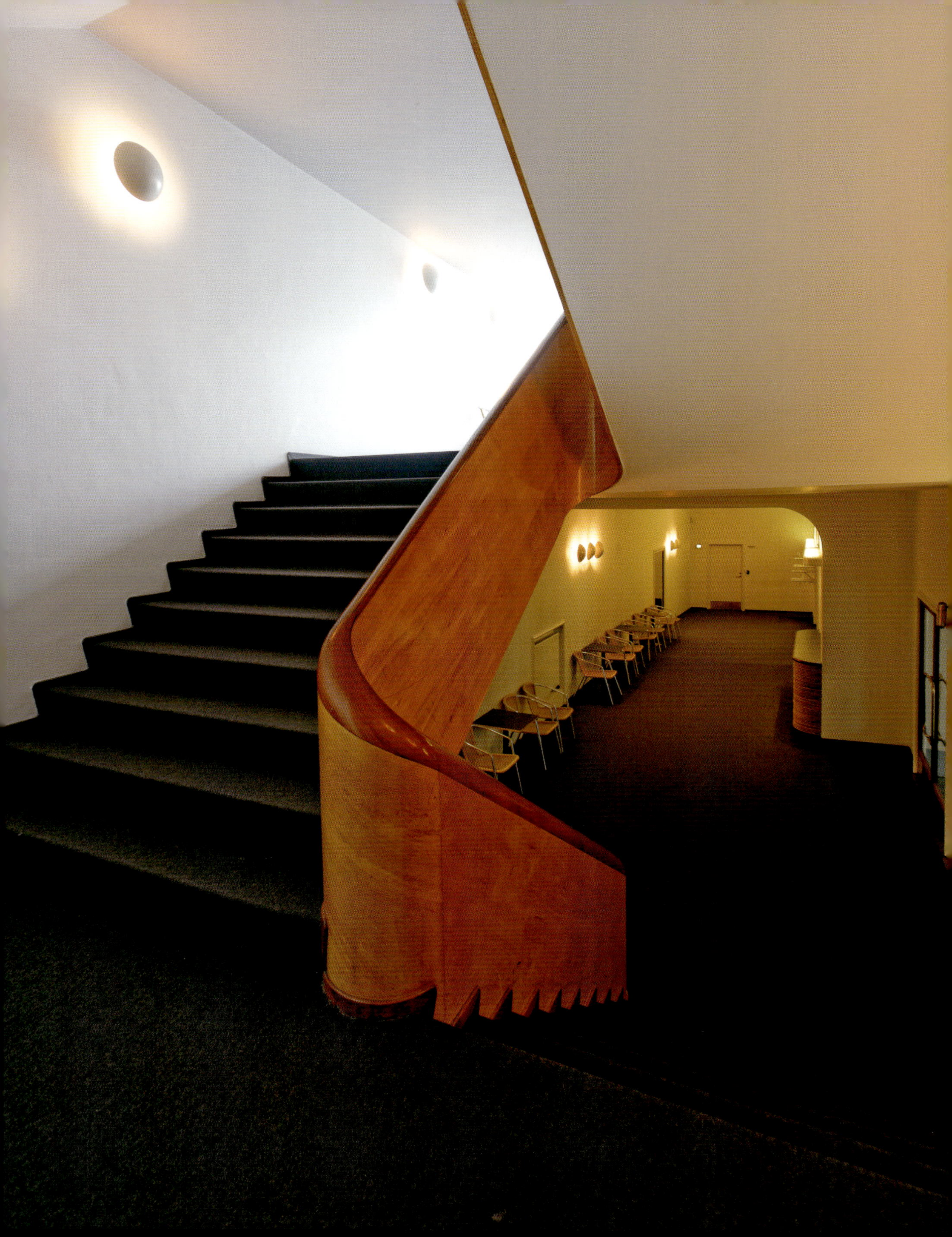

左頁：1階からバルコニー席に通じる階段。
右にエントランスホールへの扉が見える。

Left page: The staircase that leads from the ground floor to the balcony. The door to the entrance hall is on the right.

腰壁から天端まで木で仕上げられた階段手摺。白い壁と黒い床の中央にボリューム感のある木製の手摺が優雅なカーブを描いている。

The bannister and the handrail were finished in wood. The wooden bannister forms an elegant curve against the white walls and black floor.

木の質感が美しい手摺。樹種を変えた組み合わせがアクセントとなっている。

Beautiful textures of woods. A combination of different woods provides an accent.

バルコニー席へ上がる階段。踊り場で曲面を描いてつながる手摺が上昇感を与えている。

The staircase to the balcony. The curve in the handrail at the landing indicates tells us that the staircase is continuing upward.

Bellevue Theater

ヤコブセンによるベルビュー・レヴューのポスター。

A poster drawn by Jacobsen for the Bellevue Revue.

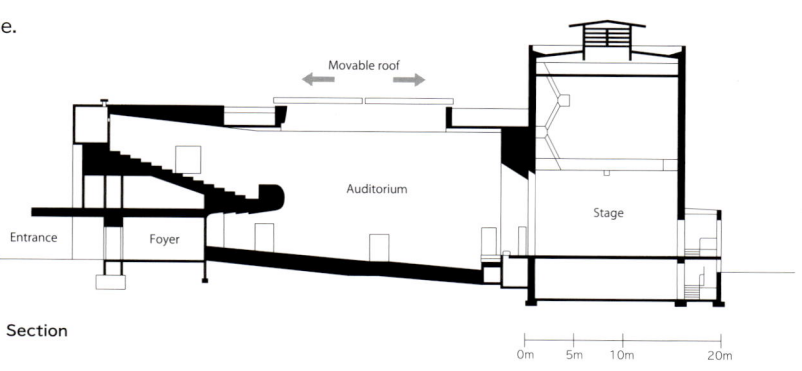

Section

Entrance | Foyer | Auditorium | Movable roof | Stage

0m 5m 10m 20m

56　Arne Jacobsen

ベラヴィスタ集合住宅側からの全景。シアターレストランだった手前部分の大半は、集合住宅に改修されている。

A view of the theater from Bellavista Housing Complex. Most of the theater restaurant has been converted to an apartment house.

シアター横には大規模なシアターレストランがあり、その後は規模を縮小して、「レストランヤコブセン」として営業していた。

At first there was a large theater restaurant. Later it was renovated and operated as "Restaurant Jacobsen."

ベルビューシアターおよびレストランの鳥瞰スケッチ。

A bird's eye view of Bellevue Theater and Restaurant.

レストランの内観スケッチ。

A perspective of the restaurant's interior space.

Bellevue Theater   57

緩やかな円弧を描く劇場のホワイエ。
The gently curving foyer.

レストラン奥にある、オリジナルの姿をとどめる暖炉回り。うねる煉瓦壁面が特徴的。
Original fireplace remains inside the restaurant. Distinctive, undulating, brick wall.

「レストランヤコブセン」の店内。竣工時は正面のグレーの壁の奥までレストランが続いていた。

An inside view of "Restaurant Jacobsen." When the restaurant opened, it had more space in place of the gray wall.

道路側の大きな開口部の先にはベルビュー海水浴場が広がる。

Bellevue Beach can be seen past the road through the large windows.

Bellevue Theater

テキサコ・ガソリンスタンド 1937年／スコウブスホウブ
Texaco Service Station ／ Texaco Tank, 1937, Skovshoved

建物から大きく突き出したマッシュルーム形の庇が目印のテキサコ・ガソリンスタンド。

The mushroom-shaped structure attached to the building marks Texaco Service Station.

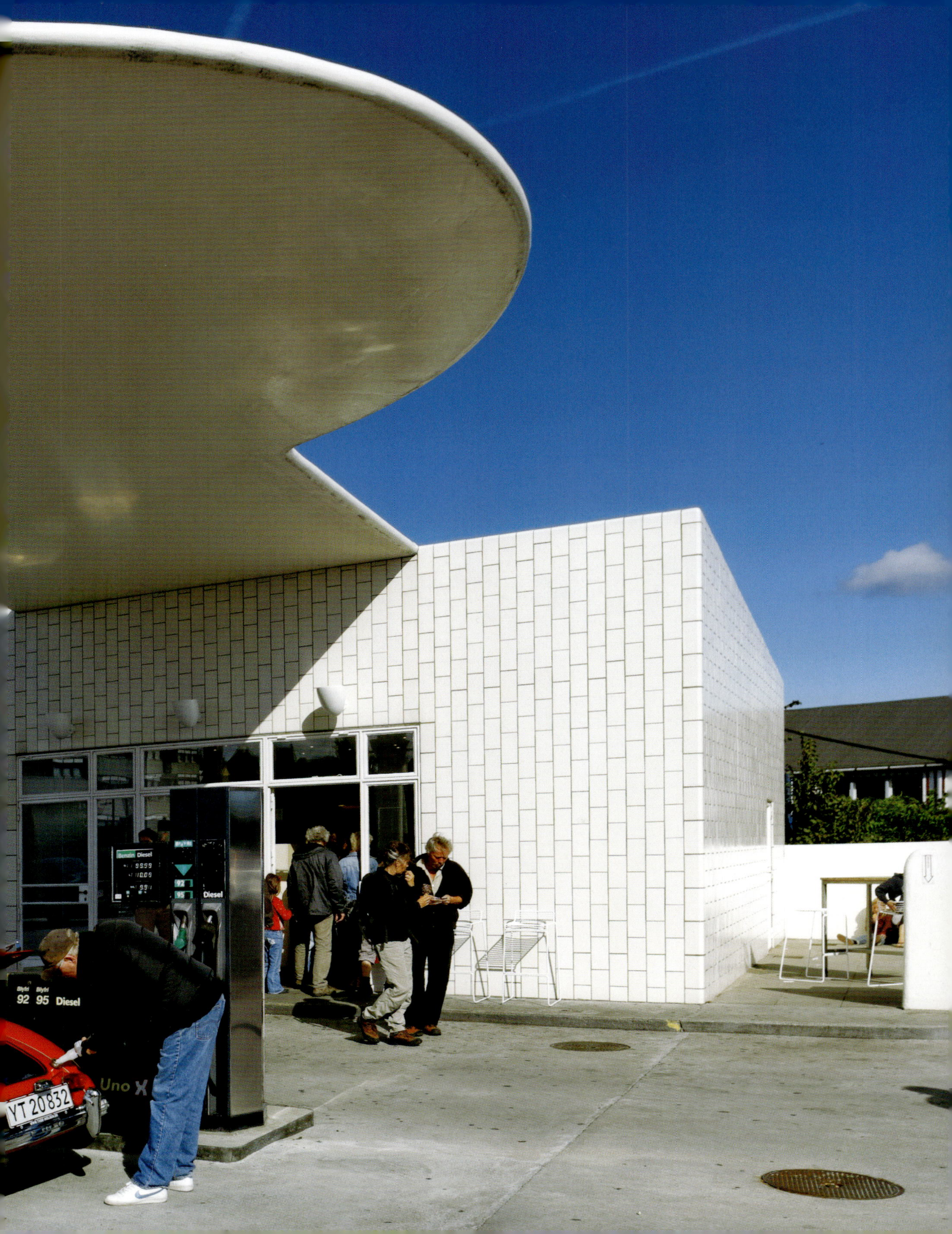
92 95 Diesel
Diesel
Uno X
YT 20832

コペンハーゲンから海岸沿いにベルビュー地区に向かう途中、道の海側に小さなガソリンスタンドがある。洗車機能、オフィス、ボイラー室、休憩室を備えた小さな箱状のボリュームから1本の柱で支えた「アントチェア」の背板のような形状のキャノピーが付き出している。造形のもたらす妙なのだろう。この造形を見ると、誰もがほのぼのとした気持ちになる。柱の周囲には4台、建物には3台のスポットライトがあり、夜間はキャノピーを下から照らし出して、給油スペースの間接照明として利用者の手元の視認性を高めている。特筆すべきは、建物、屋根、柱のすべてのエッジと接合コーナーに滑らかなアール加工が施されているため、何とも言えない一体感を醸し出していることだ。建物、キャノピー、柱ともにRC構造で、建物は白いセラミックタイル仕上げ、キャノピーとそれを支える1本の柱は白の塗装で仕上げている。

現在、テキサコの看板はないが、屋外はセルフ式のガソリンスタンド、店内のオフィススペースはジェラート売り場、洗車スペースは軽食のイートインスペースとして機能しており、ヤコブセン詣でに来た外国人や、小腹を満たしに立ち寄った地元の人びとでにぎわっている。

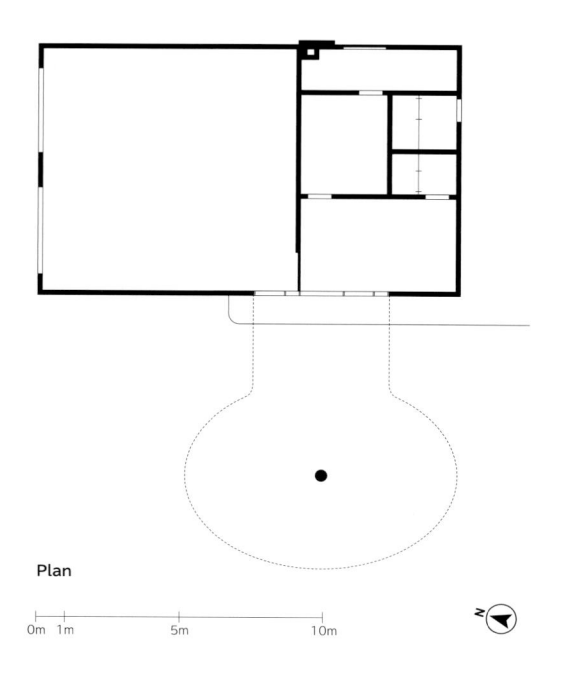

There is a small gas station on the way from Copenhagen to the Bellevue area along the shore. The building, which resembles a small box, was once equipped with a car washing machine, an office, a boiler room, and a rest room. A canopy, which projects from the building and is supported by one post, seems like a backboard of a giant "The Ant." It has a magical form. Looking at it, everyone feels uplifted. There are four spotlights mounted on the post and three on the building. At night, the canopy is lit up and its reflection illuminates the refueling space. This helps drivers to refuel their vehicles. It should be noted that all edges and corners of the building, its roof and the post, have round and smooth in shape. Therefore, we feel an indescribable sense of unity. The building, the canopy and the post are made of reinforced concrete construction. Then, the building was finished in white ceramic. The building, canopy and post ware painted white.

There is no longer a Texaco sign. However, it still functions as a gas station and has gas pumps that operate in the shelter of overhang. The inside space that once was used as an office has been turned into a gelato shop and the former car washing space has been converted to a fast food restaurant. Thus, the former gas station is still active and frequented by tourists who come to see Jacobsen's architecture and local people who drop in to purchase take-out food.

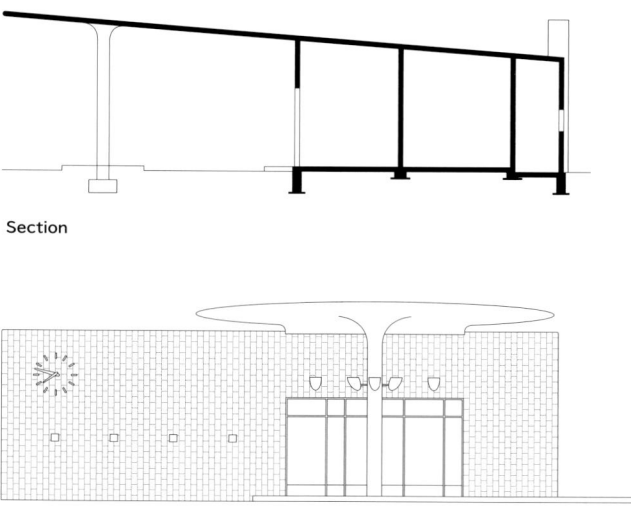

Plan

Section

Elevation

楕円形の庇とアッパーライト。少し上に傾斜した庇は、夜間は中心柱に取り付けられたアッパーライトで明るく浮かび上がる。

The oval-shaped roof projecting is slightly inclined. At night, it is brightly lit.

テキサコ・ガソリンスタンドの水彩画(1936年)。

A watercolor of Texaco Service Station.

西側からの全景。

A view from the west side of the site.

Texaco Service Station

ノヴォ治療ラボラトリウム

1935年〜／コペンハーゲン

Novo Terapeutisk Laboratorium, Now: Novozymes, 1935〜, København

従来様式の本館（左側の赤い屋根の建物）に接続して1935年に建てられた。モダンな解釈による3層構造のファサード。右奥に戦後に建てられた増築部分が見える。

In 1935, Novo was built next to the old, red-roofed, main building on the left. Its facade is a three-story Modern interpretation. The extension that was constructed after the war is behind at the right.

「ノヴォ治療ラボラトリウム」はコペンハーゲン中央駅から数km北にある。全体は、基部1層の生産部門と上部2層の研究所とオフィス部門から成る。この2層のファサードは、設計時期を同じくした「ステリング・ビル」(p.72)のファサードと酷似する。特に曲面のコーナーに正方形の窓が整然と並ぶファサードを、ヤコブセンは「ステリング・ビル」で繰り返す。その際には上部3層が基部の壁面線の外側に張り出しているのに対して、「ノヴォ治療ラボラトリウム」では1層の連続水平窓が柱をよけるように外側に張り出している。

戦後、屋上に増築した食堂に注目してほしい。この食堂の設計をしていた1952年、ヤコブセンはチャールズ＆レイ・イームズのプライウッドチェアをリ・デザインし、スタッキング可能なダイニングチェアを考案した。直ちに当時デンマークで唯一、プライウッドの成形技術をもったフリッツ・ハンセン社に商品化を持ちかけたが、開発費が掛かりすぎるという理由で受け入れられなかった。そこでヤコブセンはこの食堂の椅子として300脚の生産を依頼する。それでも渋るメーカーに、売れ残ったら買い取ると豪語して量産化の設備投資を引き出したのである。かくして「アントチェア」は誕生し、世界初の座面と背板が一体化した3次元成形のプライウッドチェアとして商品化され、成功を収めることになった。

"Novo Terapeutisk Laboratorium" is located several kilometers north of Copenhagen Central Station. The building contains a production division on the ground floor and a laboratory and an office division on the upper two floors. The facade of these two floors resembles closely the facade of "The Stelling Building" (p.72). In particular, Jacobsen repeated the pattern of square windows that are systematically arranged on the curved corner of the building. In "The Stelling Building," the upper three floors projected outward in a line. However, at Novo, the horizontal windows on the ground floor project around a pillar.

In 1952, when Jacobsen designed the canteen that extended from the top floor, he redesigned the plywood chair that was made by Charles and Ray Eames and created a stackable dining chair. He immediately consulted Fritz Hansen, the only company in Denmark that had a plywood-molding technique, to commercialize the product. However the company had no interest in doing so because the cost to produce it was too high. Still, Jacobsen asked that 300 chairs be produced for the canteen. He claimed that he would buy any unsold chairs and so succeeded in raising the capital necessary for mass production of the chair. Thus, "The Ant" debuted as the world's first molded plywood chair to integrate the seat and the back. It finally succeeded.

入口。NOVOのロゴタイプもヤコブセンのデザイン。
An entrance. Jacobsen also designed the NOVO logo.

入口扉のドアハンドル。
The entrance door's handle.

建物外壁にはヤコブセンの名前が記された銘板が取り付けられている。
The plaque bearing the name of Jacobsen was attached to the building's outside wall.

Novo Terapeutisk Laboratorium

戦後に建てられた増築部分の透明な円筒型ケースに納まった非常階段。

An emergency staircase from the building extension constructed after the war. It is shielded in a transparent cylindrical case.

ノヴォの階段室。

Stairwell in the Novo.

戦後の増築部分。1952年、中央奥に見える建物の屋上に社員食堂がつくられた。

The building extension constructed after the war. In 1952, a canteen added in the center building's top floor.

左：階段室の見下ろし。壁床ともに多孔質大理石の均質な仕上げ。

Left: Looking down a stairwell. The walls and the floor are finished similarly with porous marbles.

右：階段室の勾配に合わせた開口部。

Right: The form of the openings is coordinated with the slope of the staircases.

ノヴォ用にデザインされたブラケット。

A bracket designed for Novo.

Novo Terapeutisk Laboratorium

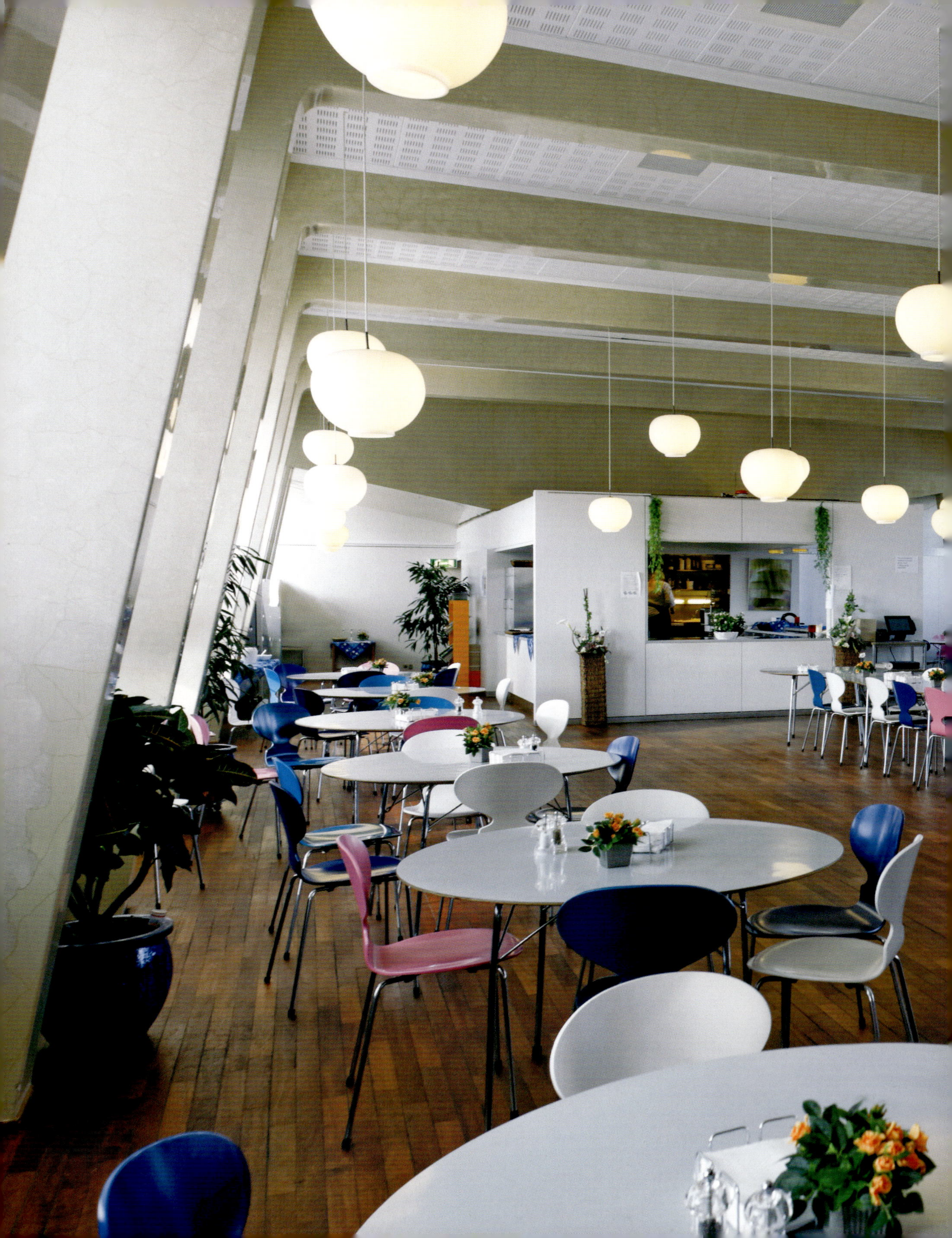

1952年、既存建物の屋上につくられた社員食堂。アントチェアはこの食堂のためにデザインされた。当時は3本足。

The canteen was built on top of the old building in 1952. The Ant that was originally a three-legged chair was designed for this canteen.

ステリング・ビル 1937年／コペンハーゲン
The Stelling Building／Stellings Hus, 1937, København

ガメルトーフ広場に面した角地に建つステリング・ビル。
The Stelling Building stands at the corner of Gammeltorv Square.

コペンハーゲン市庁舎から歩行者天国のストロイエ通りをニューハウンの方向へ250mほど歩き左折すると市内で最も歴史のあるガメルトーフ広場の噴水が見えてくる。「ステリング・ビル」はこの噴水の先の右端の角地にある。伝統的な建築群に囲まれた広場の一角にモダニズム建築がある様は、異彩を放っているが、同時にうまく収まってもいるようにも見える。ヤコブセンは、隣の建物のファサードの窓やコーニスの高さを意識しながら、「ステリング・ビル」のファサードをデザインした。

現在は飲食店や事務所が入っているが、建設当時はステリング画材店の本社ビルであった。大きな窓がある1、2階は画材店、正方形の窓が並ぶ3〜5階にオフィス、5階建ての屋上にペントハウスがあり、住居として使用されていた。ヤコブセンは、家具、照明、看板、インテリアを含めて建築のすべてをデザインしたが、現在の内部はほとんど改装されており当時の片鱗はない。

右隣の伝統的な建築に倣い、低層部の2層と上層部3層ではファサードを明確に区分している。低層部の仕上げは鋼板の塗装だが、上層部は壁面を20cm程度外側に張り出した上で、正方形のセラミックタイルのグリッドの中に正方形の窓を整然と並べている。

If you walk through the pedestrian precinct of Strøget Street 250 meters from Copenhagen's city hall to Nyhavn and turn left, you will find an historical square, Gammeltorv, and a fountain on your left. "The Stelling Building" is located on the corner lot on your right. The modernism architecture on the corner stands out from the historical buildings, but appears suited to its location. While Jacobsen was aware of the windows of the facade and the height of the cornice of the next building, he designed the facade of "The Stelling Building."

Today, "The Stelling Building" contains a restaurant and an office, but was the headquarters of Stelling Art supplies shop when it was first completed. On the ground and second floors, which have wide windows, was an art supplies shop. On the third to fifth floors, which have square windows, were offices. A penthouse on the fifth floor was used as a residence. Although Jacobsen designed everything, including furniture, lightings, signboards and the interior design, little of the original interior remains due to remodeling.

Jacobsen clearly designed the facade of the lower two floors and the upper three floors after a model of an historical building. The lower levels were finished in painted steel plate, but the upper levels were finished was with a systematic arrangement of square windows in a grid of square ceramic tiles, which projected 20 centimeters out from the wall.

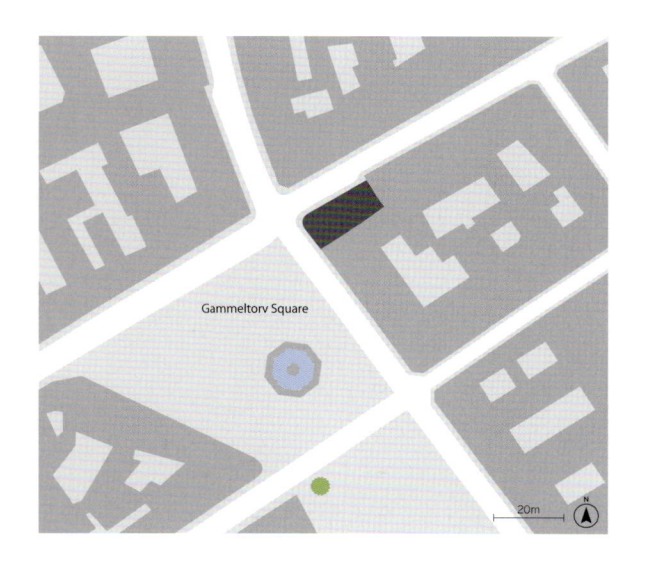

コーナーにある元画材店の入口。

The entrance to the building, the former art supplies shop.

ガメルトーフ広場に面した角地に建つ立地条件から、コーナーを大きなアールで構成し、店舗入口を設けている。1、2階の店舗外壁はペールグリーンのスチールパネル、3階から上のオフィス外壁は、明るいグレーのセラミックタイル張り。

The building stands at the corner of Gammeltorv Square. Because of this location, its entrance is in the round corner of the building. The exterior walls of the shops, first floor and second floor were finished in pale green, steel panels. The exterior walls of offices, the third floor and the upper floor were covered in bright gray, ceramic tiles.

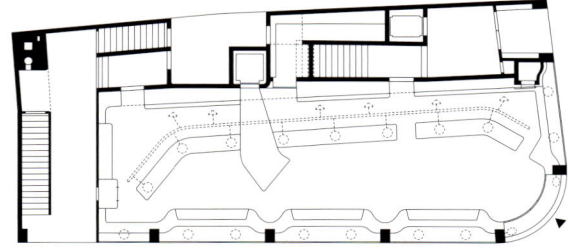

First floor plan

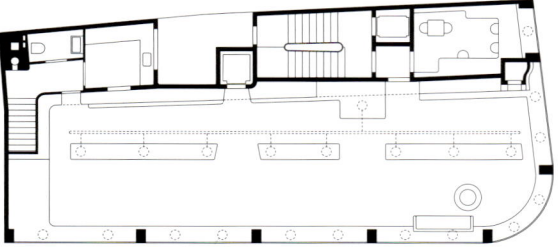

Second floor plan

Arne Jacobsen

北側外観見上げ。最上階にセットバックしたペントハウスが見える。ファサードを構成する3層構成のモダンな解釈。

Looking up at the building's north facade. A setback penthouse can be seen on the top floor. The combination of three types of facade was a modern interpretation.

ガメルトーフ広場から見る。ブロックの左端(西角)に現れたモダンデザインに、当時批判の声が上がったといわれる。

A view of Gammeltorv Square. The modern finishing of the west end of the building at its left corner was criticized immediately.

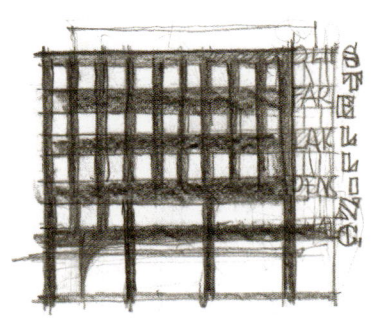

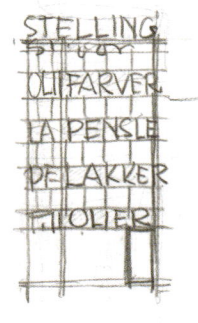

ファサードのスタディ。

A study of the facade.

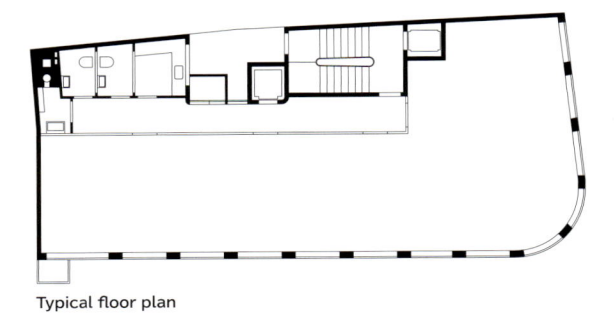

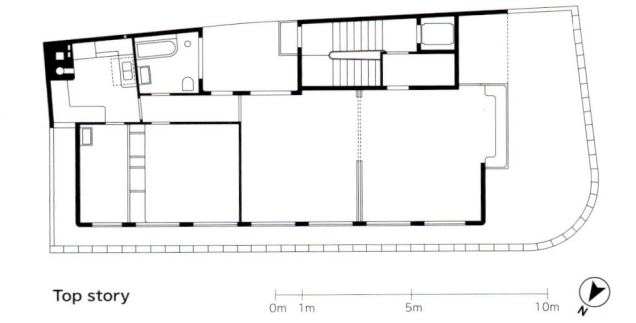

Typical floor plan

Top story

0m 1m 5m 10m

The Stelling Building 77

オーフス市庁舎 1942年／オーフス

Aarhus City Hall ／ Århus Rådhus, 1942, Århus, Design collaboration: Erik Møller

南側外観全景。オーフス駅から道路を上りきったところに建つ。建物は機能上3つのブロックからなり、中央に時計塔がそびえる。

A view of the south side. From Aarhus Station, the road leads to the city hall, which consists of three parts with different functions. The center building has a clock tower.

オーフス市はコペンハーゲンに次ぐデンマーク第2の都市である。コペンハーゲン中央駅からデンマーク国鉄DSBのインターシティ特急ICに乗って3時間弱でオーフスに到着する。この駅の目と鼻の先に「オーフス市庁舎」がある。細いフレームで輪郭をかたどった時計塔が目印だ。この塔には物語がある。

1937年、35歳のヤコブセンは28歳のエリック・ムラー(1909–2002)と共同でオーフス市制300年を記念して行われた「オーフス市庁舎」のコンペに勝利した。マーティン・ニーロップ(1849–1921)が「コペンハーゲン市庁舎」(1892–1905)のコンペに勝った時よりも、大規模なコンペに若い建築家が勝利したので当時の新聞の一面を飾った。しかし、やがて大きな議論が巻き起こった。ヤコブセンらのコンペ案には時計塔がなかったからだ。コンペでは、新しい民主主義を体現する建物が求められていたため、ヤコブセンは時計塔を余計なコストが掛かる権威の象徴だと考えた。工事はすでに進み、外壁のノルウェー産の大理石も発注済みだった。しかし、市民は時計塔を作ることを要求した。ヤコブセンは最後まで抵抗したが、結局、塔を付加する設計変更を受け入れざるを得なかった。

「オーフス市庁舎」以降に建てられたデンマークの市庁舎で、時計塔のある市庁舎はひとつもない。

Aarhus City is the second city in Denmark after Copenhagen. The trip from Copenhagen Central Station to Aarhus station by the Inter City Limited Express of the Danish national railways, DSB, takes less than three hours. "Aarhus City Hall" is within earshot of the Aarhus station. Its landmark is a tower clock in the shape of a contour with a thin frame. The tower has a story.

In 1937 at the age of 35, Jacobsen won the "Aarhus City Hall" design competition, which commemorated the 300th anniversary of Aarhus City with Erik Møller (1909–2002) who was 28 years of age. The news of the competition's

北面議場棟入口のエントランスホール。天井の低いエントランスホールを抜けると、光天井の開放的なアトリウムが現れる。その先は直線的なトップライトをもつ事務棟。

The north entrance hall of the City Council building. Visitors leave the entrance hall with its low ceiling and enter the open atrium with its luminous ceiling. An office building with rectilinear top lights appears on the center at the back.

outcome was emblazoned across the front page of the newspaper, because compared to the competition for the design of "Copenhagen City Hall" that Martin Nyrop (1849–1921) won, much younger architects had won a larger competition. However, soon a big debate arose. The plan of Jacobsen and Erik did not include a tower clock. The theme was a building that embodied the new democracy; Jacobsen regarded a tower clock as a symbol of authority that would involve extra costs. The construction work began and he already had ordered Norwegian marble for the outer wall. However, the citizens demanded that a tower clock be built. Jacobsen resisted. However, in the end, he had to accept a change in the design in order to add the tower.

After "Aarhus City Hall" was completed, no other city hall had a clock tower.

エントランスホールから3段上がったレベルにあるアトリウム。光天井からの均質な光で満たされた柔らかな空間。その奥には多目的ホールが隣接する。

The floor of the atrium is three steps up from the entrance hall. Light from the luminous ceiling unobtrusively fills the space. There is a multipurpose hall adjacent to the atrium.

アトリウム側から見た多目的ホール。正面のガラス面からは公園の緑の景色が取り込まれる。

A view of the multipurpose hall from the atrium. The greenery outside from the windows at the front.

エントランスホールのベンチ脇にある大型の灰皿。

A large ashtray on the bench side of the entrance hall.

エントランスホールにある角をアールで処理した十字形の柱と階段、モザイク模様の大理石床。

A cross-shaped pillar with rounded corners, a staircase, and a marble floor in a mosaic pattern.

Aarhus City Hall

多目的ホール西側のバルコニーから望む。櫛形のトップライトからの採光は、空間に方向性を与えている。6角形の行燈形ペンダントもヤコブセンのデザイン。奥のアトリウムに面した青い壁画の裏が市議会の議場。

A view from the west side balcony of the multipurpose hall. Round comb-shaped top lights indicate direction in the space. The hexagonal-shaped hanging lights were also designed by Jacobsen. The other side of mural in blue that adorns the atrium embellishes the City Council Chamber.

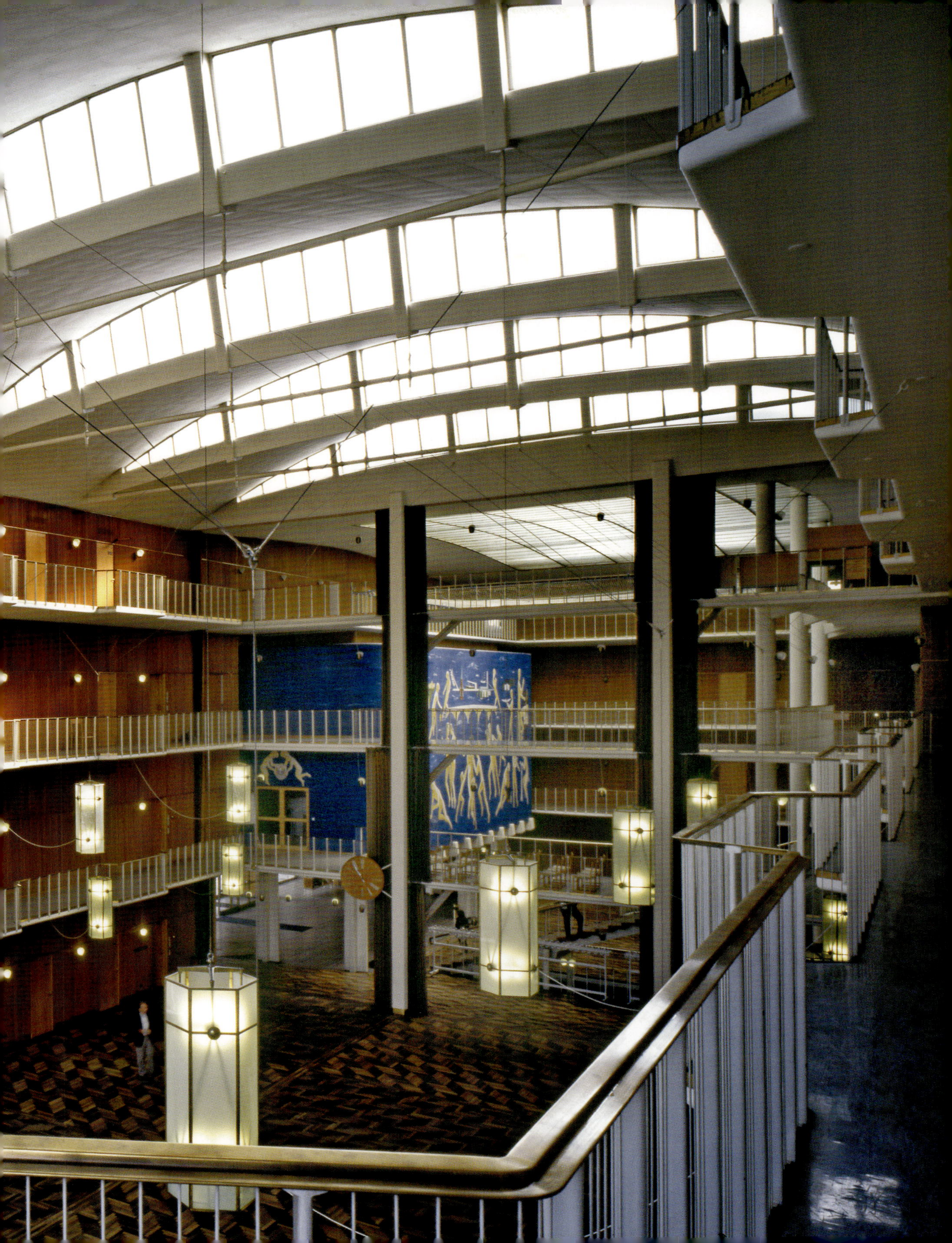

右頁：螺旋階段ディテール。建物内の手摺の笠木はすべて真鍮で統一され、空間にアクセントを与えている。

Right page: Details of the spiral staircase. The upper surface of the handrails in this building is brass, another feature of the structure's impressive design.

アトリウム見下ろし。螺旋階段と直階段の組み合わせ。螺旋階段下の床にある黒い石は定礎石を示す。

Looking down into the atrium. The combination of a conventional staircase and a spiral staircase. The black stone beneath the spiral staircase indicating a cornerstone.

螺旋階段下よりアトリウムを見上げる。

Looking up into the atrium from beside the spiral staircase.

86　Arne Jacobsen

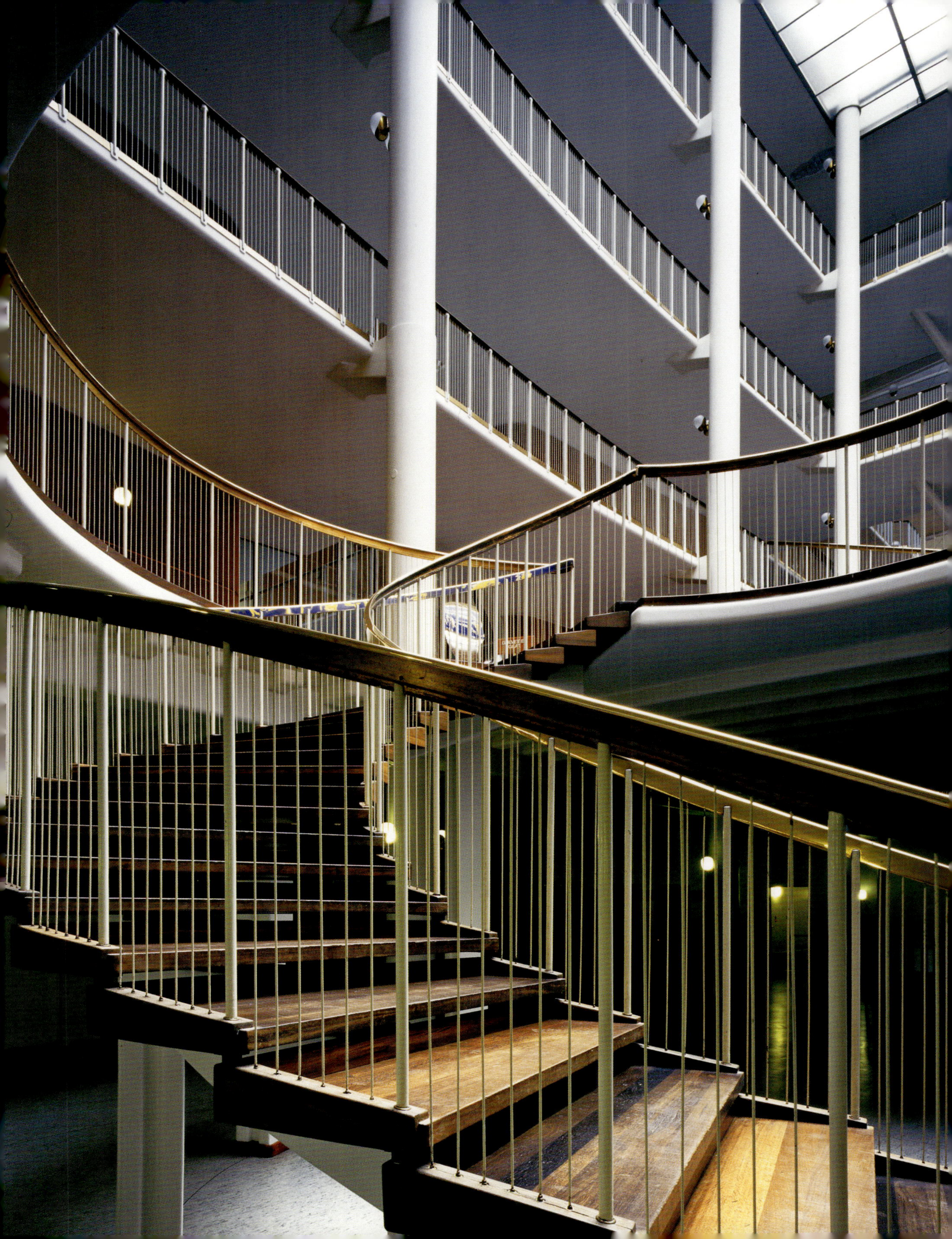

議場側よりアトリウムを見る。アトリウムの光天井とバルコニーの先端は緩やかな円弧を描き、すべてのディテールは角が丸く納められている。中央奥に延びるのは事務棟の中央通路。

A view of the atrium from the City Council Chamber. The luminous ceiling and edge of the balcony form a gentle arc. Every corner is rounded. There is a row of offices in the center of the photograph.

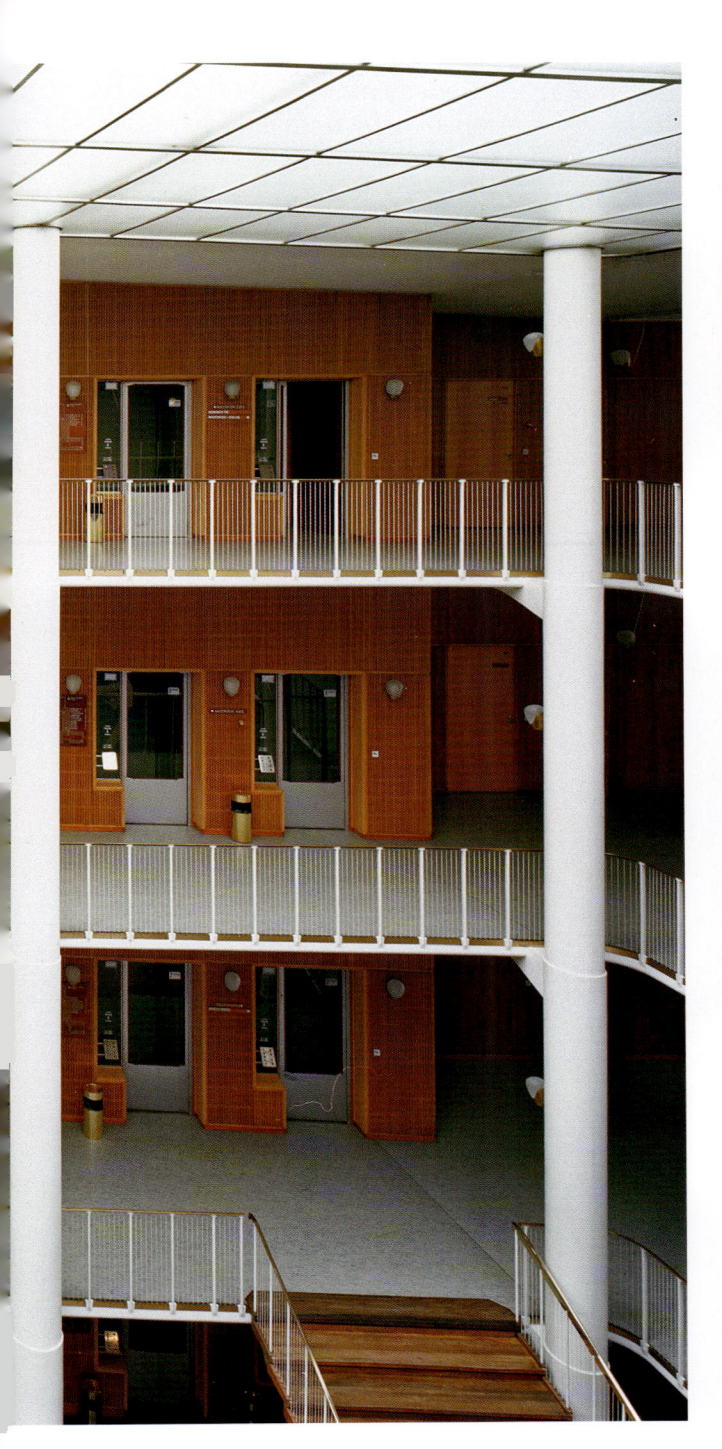

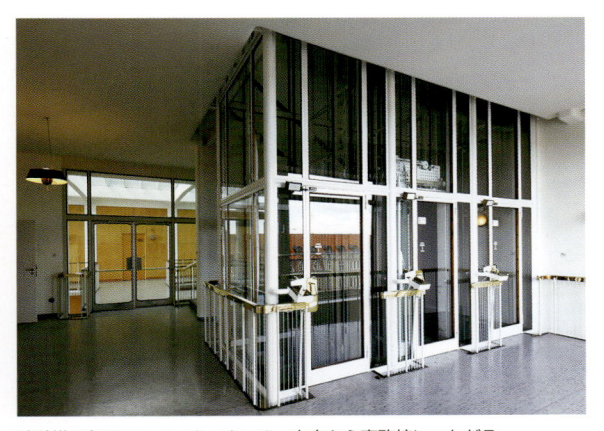

時計塔下部のエレベーターホール。左奥から事務棟につながる。
An elevator hall in the tower clock building. It connects to the office building on the left.

エレベーターの真鍮製操作盤。
An elevator brass control board.

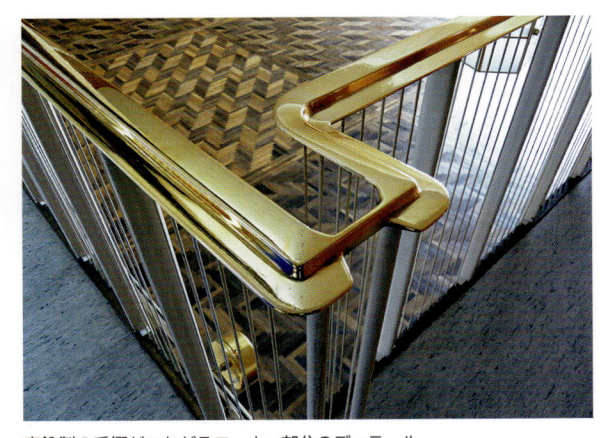

真鍮製の手摺がつながるコーナー部分のディテール。
Detail of the connection of the corner of the brass handrail.

Aarhus City Hall

通路の壁付き灰皿。

Hanging ashtrays in the passage.

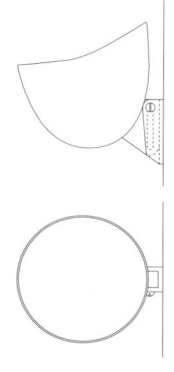

Drawings of a wall mounted ashtray

右頁：トップライトからの採光で明るい事務棟の中央通路。正面奥はアトリウムと議場、下にエントランスが見える。

Right page: Top lights illuminate the main aisle of the office building. In the center building is the atrium and the City Council Chamber. The entrance is located beneath them.

フロストガラスのブラケット照明。ペンダントタイプや議場用のバリエーションもある。

A bracket with a piece of frosted glass. Other variations to be suspended and the City Council Chamber.

アトリウムを囲む壁の一部は細い曲面リブの透かし張りで、裏側のトイレへの採光としている。

Part of the wall of the atrium was made of thin curved ribs. This semitransparent wall admits light to the lavatory.

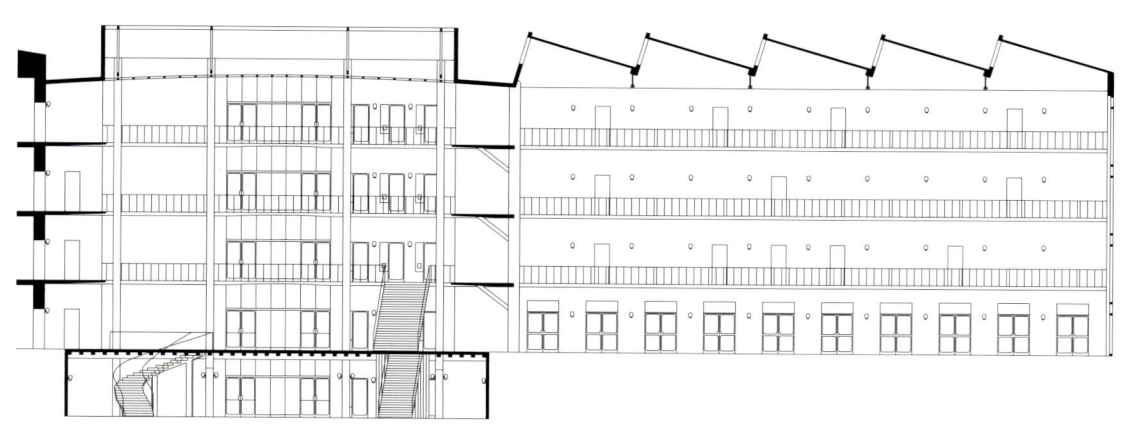

Section

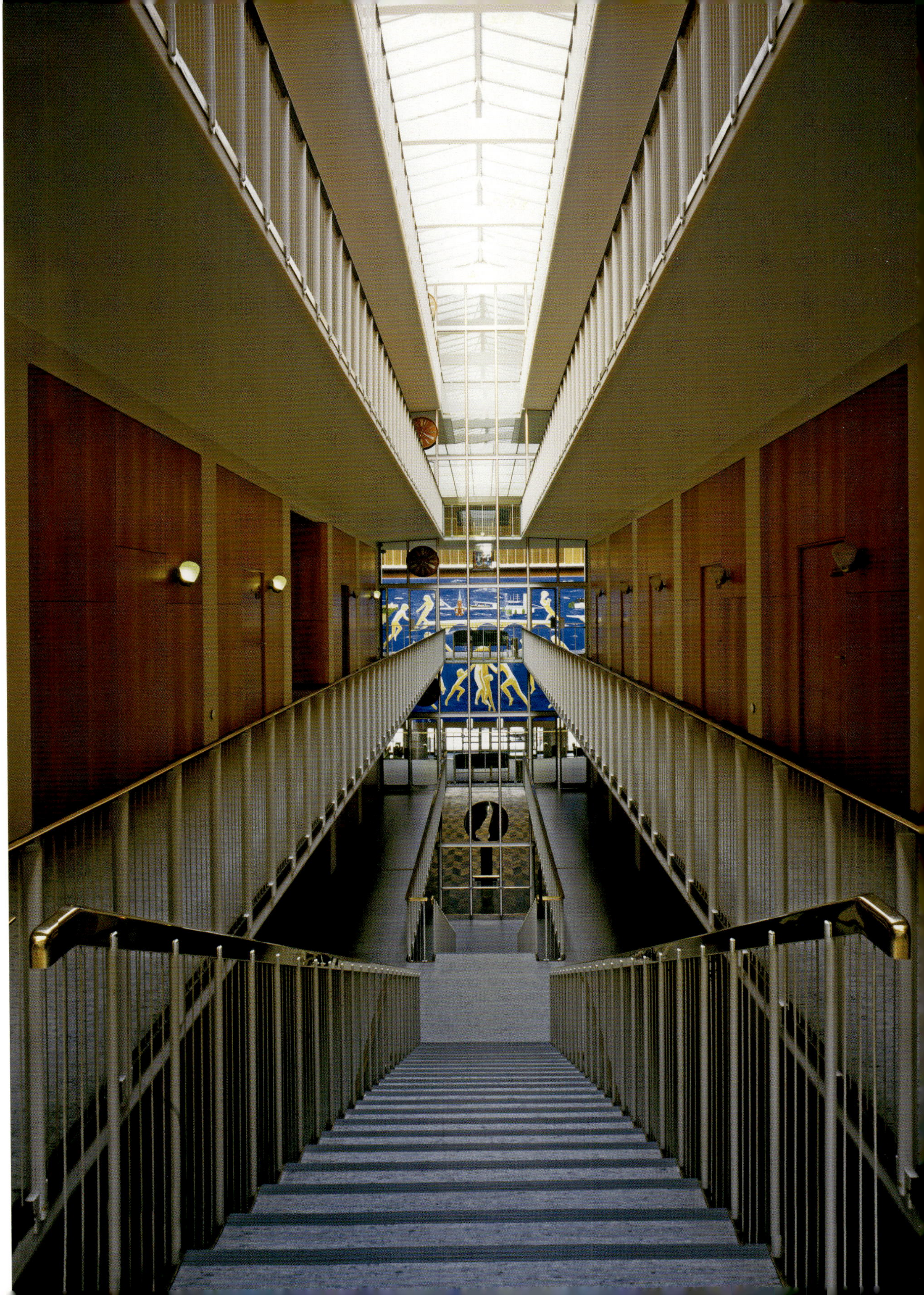

傍聴席より議場を見下ろす。床にはオーフス市の地図が描かれている。壁の入隅、壁と天井の取り合い部分は曲面でつながる。

A view of the City Council Chamber from the public gallery. A map of Aarhus City appears on the floor. The internal juncture of two walls and the ceiling is rounded.

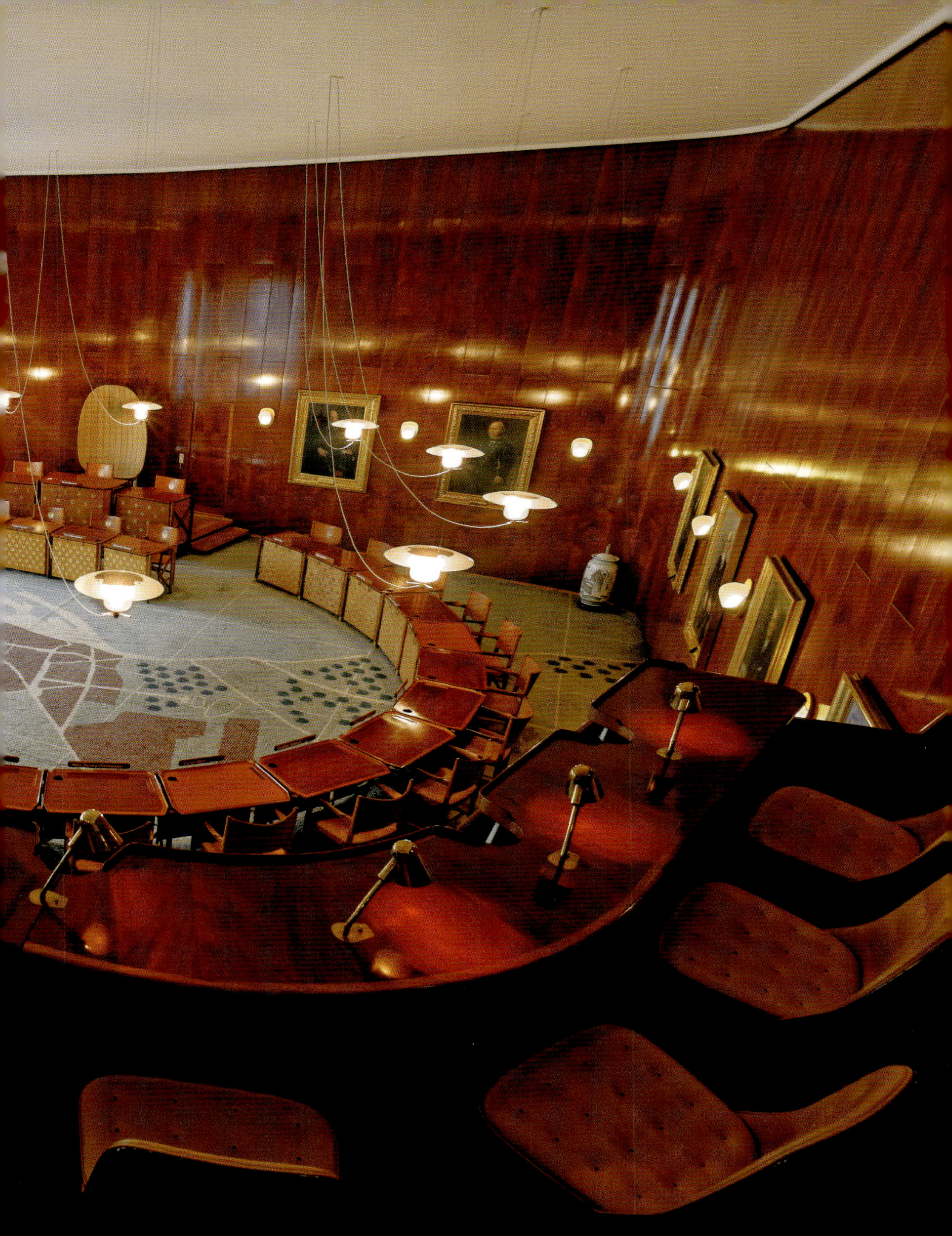

議場。天井から吊られた照明器具は、コードがカーブを描いて宙を舞い、優雅な浮遊感を与えている。

The City Council Chamber. The code of the hanging lamps form elegant curves and add a floating sensation to the space.

議長席。議場の壁・家具はマホガニー製。
The chairman's seat. The furniture and walls were done in mahogany.

傍聴席に上がる階段。壁面が湾曲して続く。
The staircase to the public gallery with its curved walls.

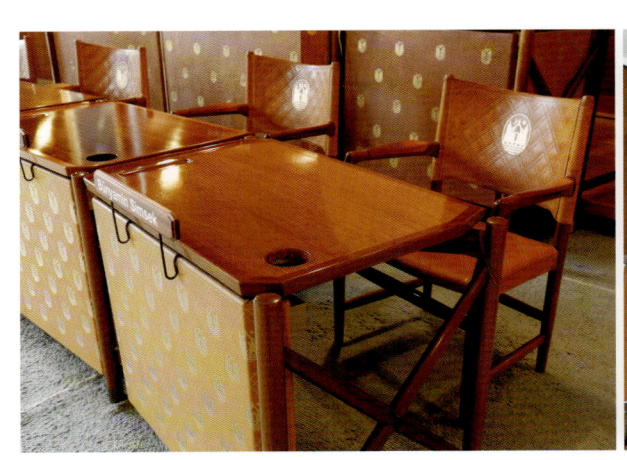

ハンス・J・ウェグナーのデザインによる議員席。
An councilor's chair designed by Hans J. Wegner.

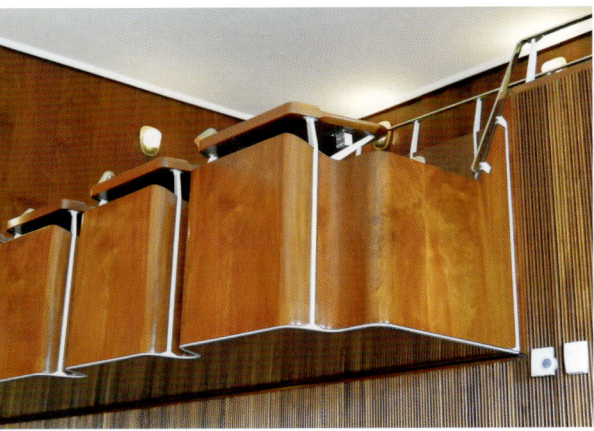

壁から飛び出したプレス用傍聴席。
Sticked out seats in the public gallery for the press.

Aarhus City Hall 95

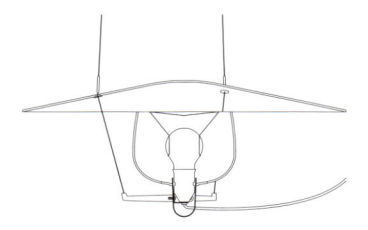

A lamp in the City Council Chamber

議場の掛け時計。文字盤はマホガニー製。

A wall clock in the City Council Chamber. The clock face was made of mahogany.

議場のペンダント型照明。

A pendant light of frosted glass in the City Council Chamber.

議場のベースプレート付きブラケット照明。

Bracket lighting with base plate in the City Council Chamber.

プレス席の真鍮製テーブルランプ。

A brass table lamp in the press area.

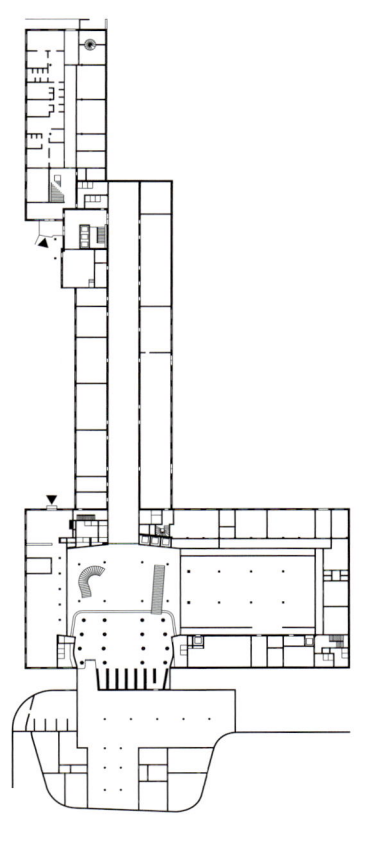

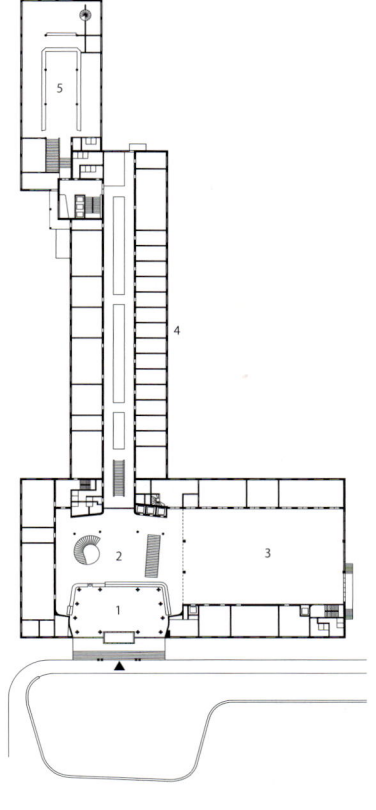

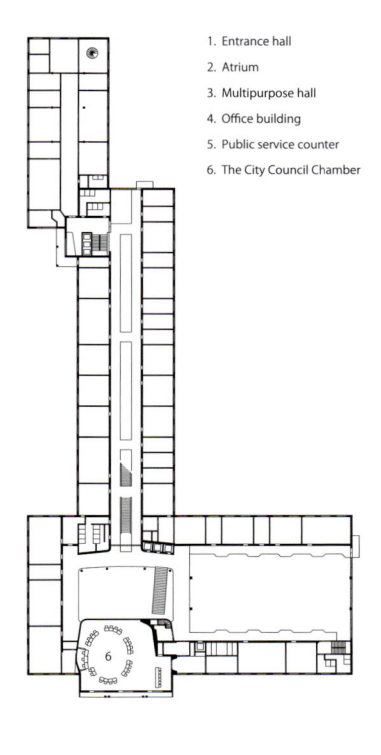

1. Entrance hall
2. Atrium
3. Multipurpose hall
4. Office building
5. Public service counter
6. The City Council Chamber

Basement plan　　First floor plan　　Second floor plan

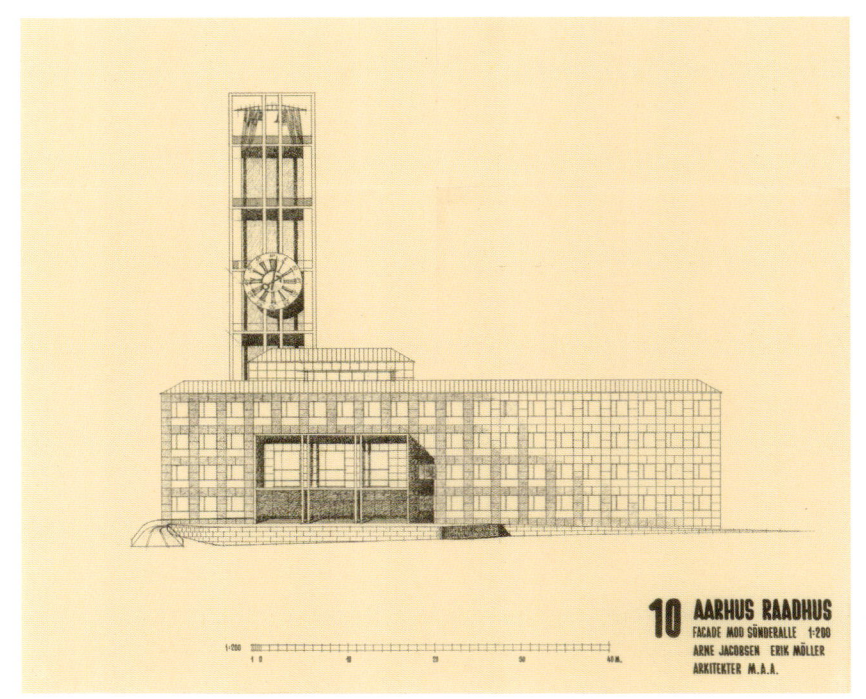

10 AARHUS RAADHUS
FACADE MOD SØNDERALLE 1:200
ARNE JACOBSEN   ERIK MØLLER
ARKITEKTER M.A.A.

市庁舎広場側のファサード。
Facade facing plaza of Aarhus City Hall.

Aarhus City Hall 97

議場横の議員控室。
A waiting room for the councilors adjunct to the City Council Chamber.

ABCDEFG
HIJKLMNØ
PRSTUVXYZÆ
1234567890

オーフス市庁舎のためにデザインしたロゴタイプ。
Typeface designed by Jacobsen for Aarhus City Hall.

右頁：多目的ホールに面したウェディングルーム。壁に描かれた植物の板絵が優しい。
Right page: A wedding room next to the multipurpose room. The reproductions of plants on wood are beautiful.

Aarhus City Hall

北側の議場棟。中央の突出した部分がエントランスと議場。

The north part of the City Council building. The entrance and City Council Chamber are the prominent parts.

右頁：事務棟西面と議場棟とのコーナー。正方形の窓下の腰部分がわずかに沈む繊細なディテール。

Right page: A corner of the west side of the office building and the City Council building. Delicate details: the rectangular part beneath the square windows was dented a little.

西の公園側から見る議場棟。多目的ホールの櫛形トップライトが見える。

A view of the City Council building from the west side park. Round comb-shaped top lights can be seen through the glass.

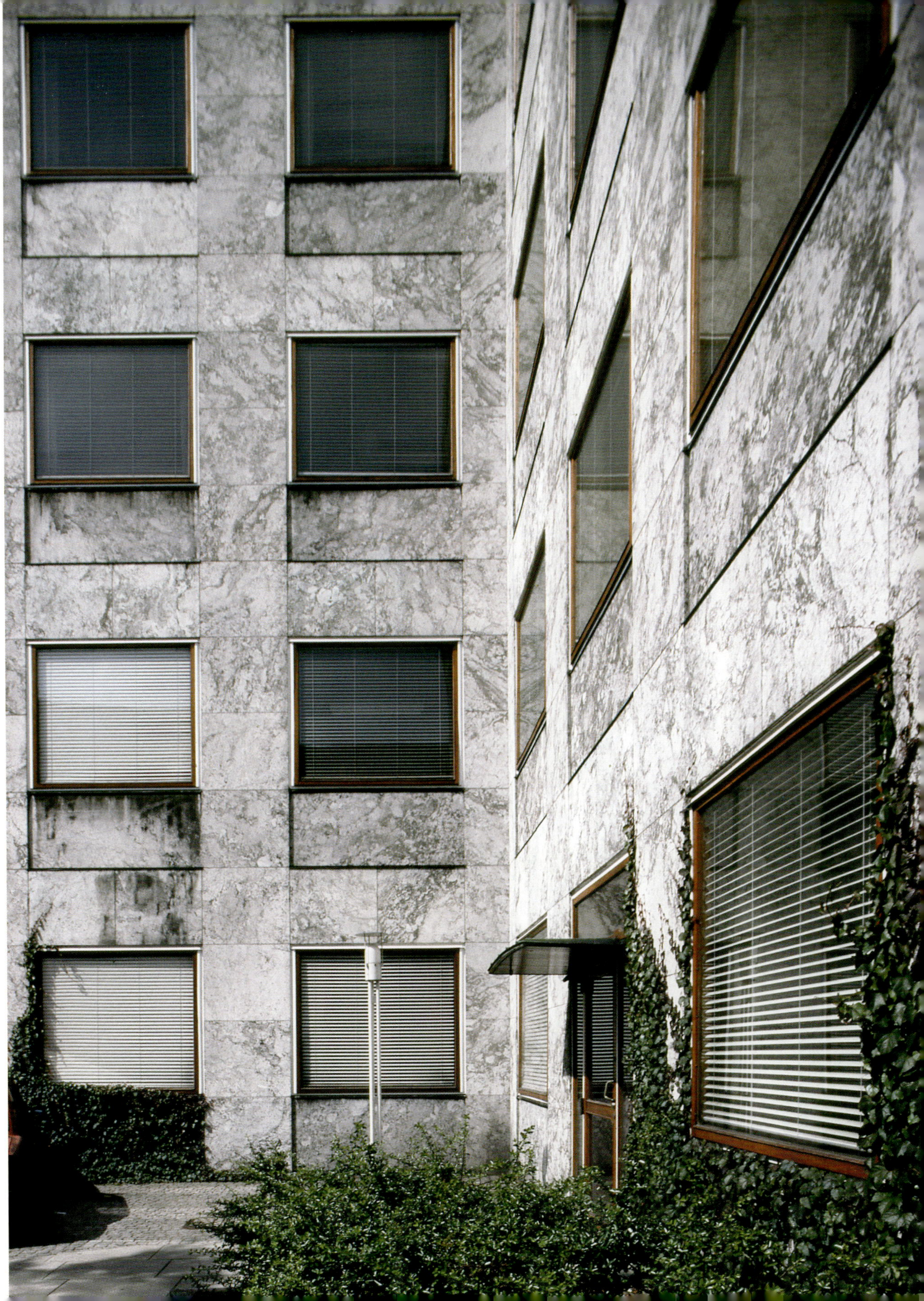

スレロド市庁舎 1942年／ホルテ

Sollerod City Hall／Søllerød Rådhus, Now: Rudersdal Rådhus, 1942, Holte, Design collaboration: Flemming Lassen

西側からの市庁舎全景。エントランスのある議場棟（左）と事務棟（右）が半階ずらして接続されている。

Full view of City Hall from the west side. The City Council building containing the entrance (left) and the office building (right) are connected by skip floors.

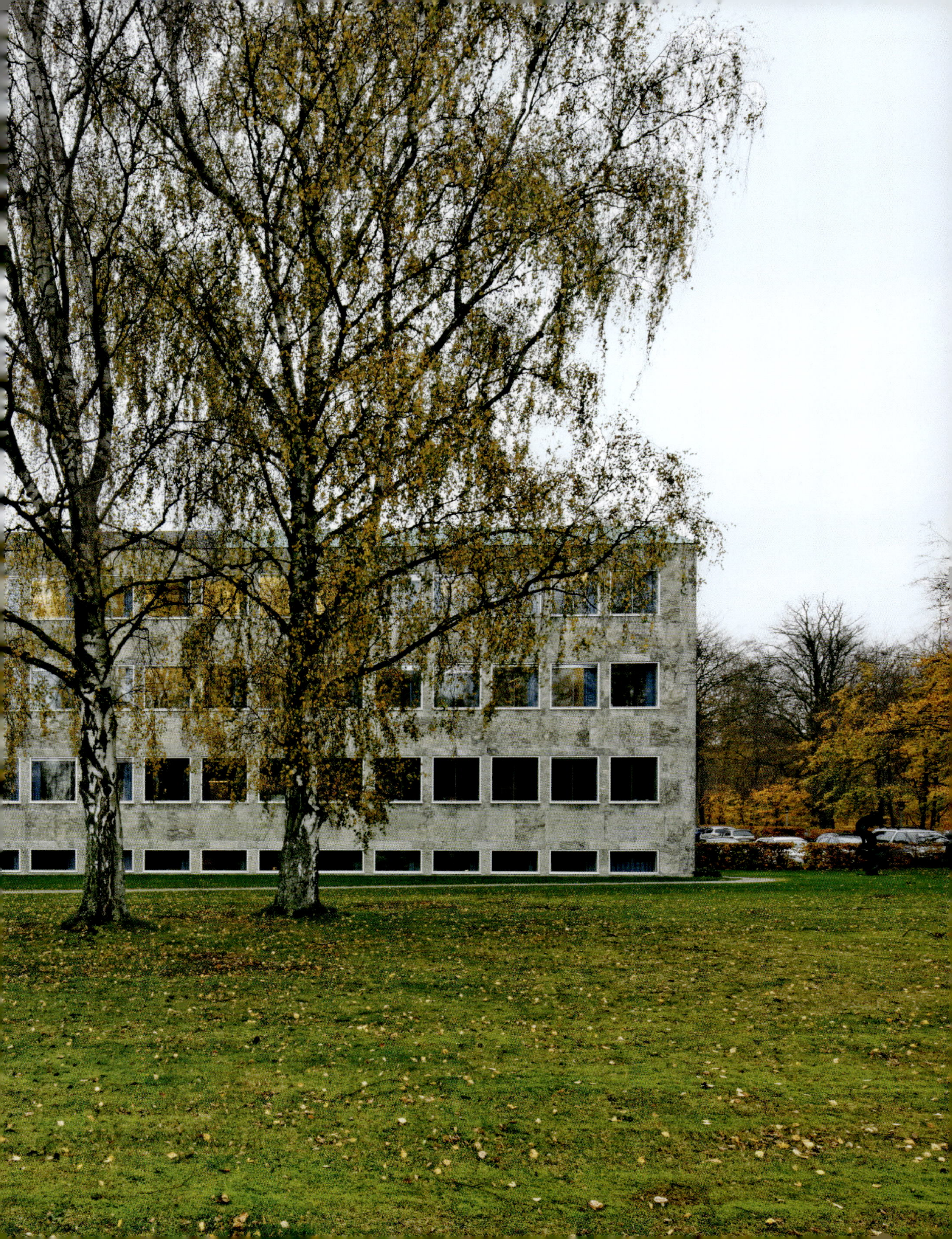

この市庁舎はコペンハーゲンから19km北にある。エントランスと市議会の議場がある３層の建物と、事務室がある４層の建物はガラスのエレベーターコアを中心にスキップフロア形式で結合している。

ヤコブセンは「オーフス市庁舎」(p.78)のコンペにエリック・ムラーと共同で勝利した２年後、旧友のフレミング・ラッセンと共同で「スレロド市庁舎」のコンペに勝利した。ふたつの市庁舎の工事は同時に進行し、1942年にそろって竣工した。したがって建物の規模こそ違うものの、似通った点が見受けられる。外観の大理石、正方形の窓、銅葺きの屋根形状は共通している。「オーフス市庁舎」に比べて「スレロド市庁舎」はコンパクトかつシンプルな仕上がりとなった。緑豊かなロビーや、作り付けの家具と彫刻があるエレベーターホール、議事堂内部の大きな壁画には工芸的な要素がちりばめられ、繊細な雰囲気の中、居心地の良さも感じられる。

当初のコンペ案では図書館と映画館を含む複合建築を予定していたが、最終的にはなくなった。また、「スレロド市庁舎」では時計塔を建てない代わりに、建物の北側に時計と鐘をあつらえた。スレロド市は2007年にルダスダル市に吸収合併されたため、現在では「ルダスダル市庁舎」を名乗っているが、ヤコブセンとラッセンが作り上げた空気感は大事に保たれている。

This city hall is located 19 kilometers north of Copenhagen. It consists of a three-storied building, which contains the main entrance and the City Council Chamber, and a four-storied building, which contains offices. The two buildings are connected by skip floors around the central elevator core, which is made of glass.

Two years after Jacobsen won the competition for the design of "Aarhus City Hall" (p.78) with Erik Møller, Jacobsen won a competition to design "Sollerod City Hall" with his old friend, Fleming Lassen. Constructions of both works proceeded at the same time and were completed in 1942. Consequently there are some similarities between the two projects, although the scale of the buildings differ. The outside of marble, square windows, and shape of roof's copper plates are common. In comparison to "Aarhus City Hall," the finishing of "Sollerod City Hall" is much simpler and more compact. The lobby features extensive greenery lobby, whereas the elevator hall contains sculptures and built-in furniture. In addition, a large mural adorns the interior of the city hall. Visitors to the complex are exposed to a soothing, but inviting, atmosphere.

In the end, the plans for the complex, which originally included a library and a movie theater, were abandoned. In place of a tower clock, the north side of the complex features a wall clock and a bell. In 2007, Sollerod was annexed by Rudersdal and became "Rudersdal City Hall." However the atmosphere that they created remains unchanged.

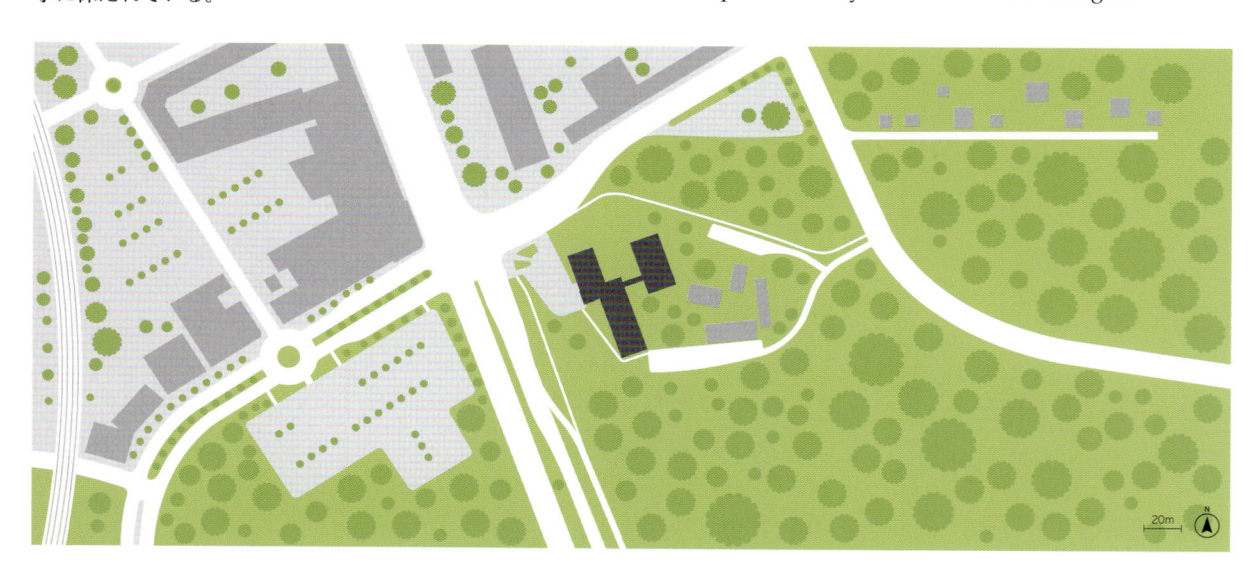

階段室踊り場よりエントランスホールを見る。
事務棟とは半階スキップして踊り場でつながる。
View of the entrance hall from the City Council building stair landing. The landing is offset by half a floor and connects to office building.

エントランスの風除室。
The windbreak room in the entrance.

2階エレベーターホール。階段室中央には透明ガラスのエレベーター。左はエントランスホール吹抜け。

Second floor elevator hall. A transparent glass elevator is located in the center of the stairwell. The entrance hall atrium is to the left.

2階エレベーターホールは議場へと通じる。

The second floor elevator hall connects with the City Council Chamber.

階段を上がったコーナーにあるラウンジスペース。薄緑色の壁にヤコブセンによるデザインの壁付きベンチが据え付けられている。

Lounge space located in the corner at the top of the stairs. A bench designed by Jacobsen is affixed to the pale green wall.

議場前通路からエレベーターホールへの扉。ドアハンドルが開き勝手を示してくれる。

Doors opening on the elevator hall from the City Council Chamber entrance corridor. The door handles indicate how the doors open.

Sollerod City Hall

議場全景。間接照明と音響拡散のための楕円形の反射板が緩やかなヴォールト天井に吊るされている。正面壁にはパステル調の風景が描かれ、議員の気持ちを和ませるかのようである。2階傍聴席も緩やかなカーブを描いている。

Full view of the City Council Chamber. An elliptical reflector panel for indirect lighting and sound diffusion is hung from the gently vaulted ceiling. The landscape painted in pastels on the front wall relaxes the councilors. The second floor public gallery is also gently curved.

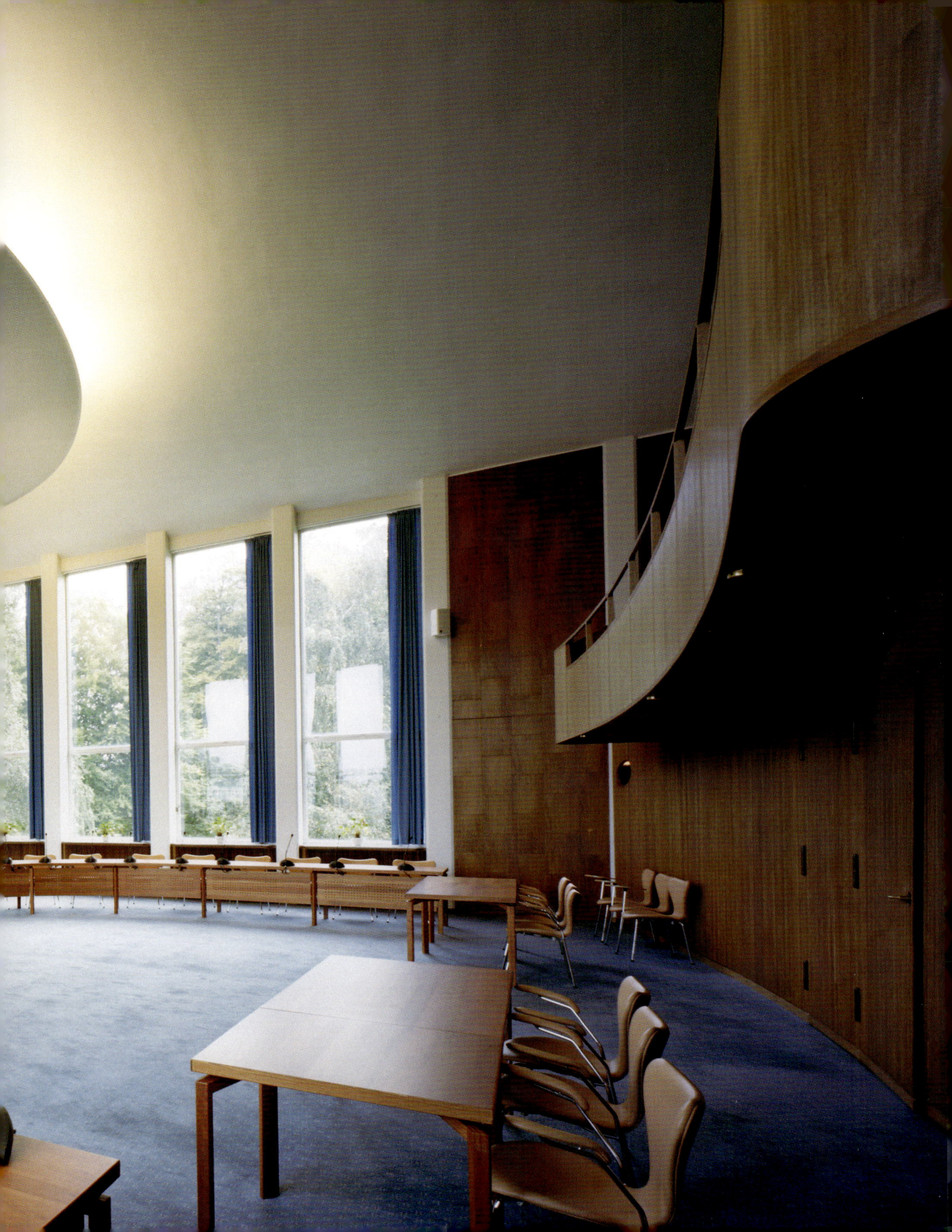

2階傍聴席。緩やかなヴォールト天井とともに傍聴席もカーブを描いている。ブラケット照明はスレロド市庁舎のためにデザインされたもの。

Second floor public gallery. Together with the gently vaulted ceiling, the public gallery is also curved. The lighting brackets were designed for Sollerod City Hall.

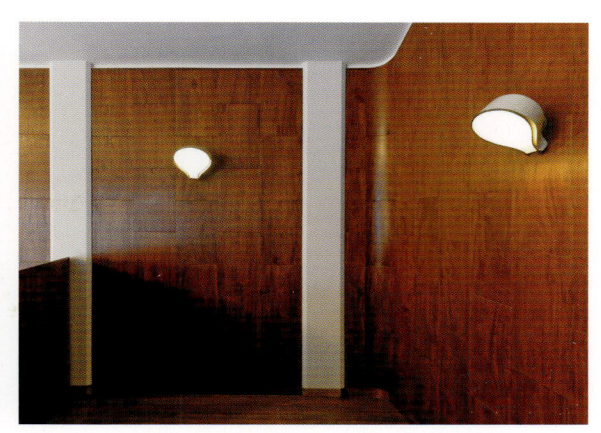

オーフス市庁舎同様、天井と壁の取り合い、壁入隅は曲面処理されている。
As in Aarhus City Hall, the internal juncture of two walls and the ceiling is rounded.

議員室通路のヤコブセンがデザインしたブラケット照明。
Lighting brackets designed by Jacobsen in the City Council Chamber corridor.

議場背面にある室の覗き窓。
An observation window in the rear wall of the City Council Chamber looking into the vestibule.

議場背面。上階は傍聴席。議員室通路への扉部分も壁と同じ曲面リブの縦張り。

Rear wall of the City Council Chamber. The public gallery is on the upper level. Both the door to the City Council Chamber corridor and the wall were made of curved ribs.

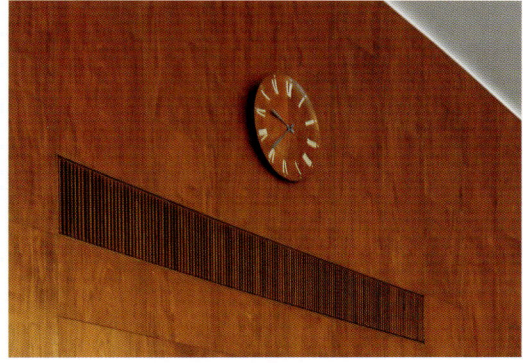

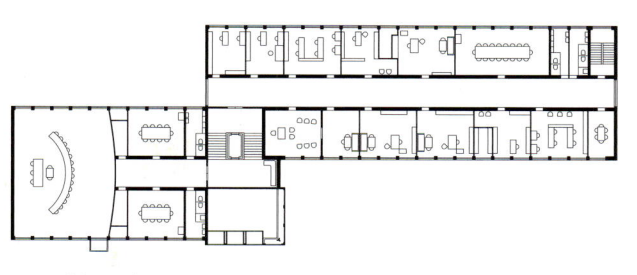

Second floor plan

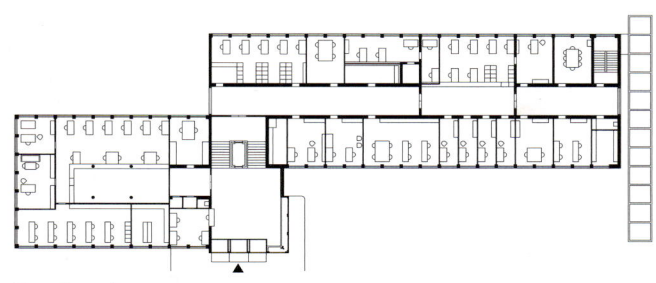

First floor plan

0m 5m 10m 20m

エントランスホール受付(上)と議場の掛け時計(下)。「シティホールクロック」と呼ばれている。

Walk clocks known as the "City Hall Clock". Located in the entrance hall receptions area (top) and the City Council Chamber (bottom).

議場棟外壁にレリーフ状に彫り込まれた時計と鐘(上)。議場内に設置された時報装置。外壁の鐘とはワイヤーでつながれている(右)。

A clock carved in relief on the exterior wall of the City Council building and the bell (top). The timekeeping equipment installed in the City Council Chamber is synchronized with the bell outside by wires (right).

Sollerod City Hall 113

西側からの全景。手前の議場部分を縦長の開口部とし、エントランスの吹抜け開口部と呼応させている。

Full view from the commons on the west side. The apertures in the City Council Chamber in the foreground are vertically long to align with the apertures of the entrance atrium.

本館事務棟(右)は戦後、渡り廊下で増築棟(左)と接続された。

The main office building (right) and the postwar extension (left) are linked by a connecting corridor.

本館と増築棟をつなぐ全面ガラスの渡り廊下。渡り廊下と増築棟(1969年)はフレミング・ラッセンとの共同設計。
An all-glass corridor connecting the main building and the extension. The connecting corridor and the extension were designed by Fleming Lassen in 1969.

スモーク・ハウス 1943年／シェランズ・オッデ
Fish Smokehouse / Fiskerøgeri, 1943, Sjællands Odde

北海を見下ろす高台に建つ。魚を燻製するための巨大な煙突の両側に作業場と事務所が平屋で接続される。

Standing on a hill overlooking the North Sea. A one-story workplace for smoking fish and a one-story office wing stands on each side of the gigantic chimney.

「スモーク・ハウス」はコペンハーゲンから100kmほど離れたシェラン岬の北側にある。岬の西側の付け根にある「ヤコブセンの夏の家」からもさほど遠くない。

　晴れた日の青空を背景に、真っ白な煙突が３本並ぶ様は壮観だ。３連の煙突が並ぶ燻製炉棟を中心に、東側に魚を洗うための作業棟、西側に事務棟がある。敷地の入口にある小さな建物は冷蔵倉庫だ。パンタイル瓦葺きの切り妻屋根の片面がそのまま外壁となる特殊な形状をしている。

　夏季には、燻製した魚をパンと飲み物と共に直売しているため、工場の隣の芝生にあるベンチに腰掛け、海の景色を楽しみながらピクニックをする家族連れでにぎわう。この工場で生産されるニシンの燻製やイクラやマスの卵の瓶詰めは日本でも販売されており、ヤコブセンがデザインした３本の煙突にSOFの文字を組み合わせたグラフィックを名刺や瓶詰めのパッケージに見ることができる。

　「スモーク・ハウス」の完成を見届けて、ヤコブセンはスウェーデンに亡命した。亡命時に唯一スウェーデンで実現した住宅は、ここの冷蔵倉庫のフォルムがベースとなった。

"Fish Smokehouse" is located 100 kilometers from Copenhagen on the north side of Cape Sjælland. It is not far from "Jacobsen's Summer House," which is located at the base of the cape's western side.

　The view of the three white chimneys in a line against a background of blue sky on a sunny day is spectacular. "Fish Smokehouse" is a complex that consists of a large white building. The fish are washed in the building on the east side; that on the west side contains offices. A small building located at the entrance to the complex is a warehouse for cold storage on which pantiles have been used for the gabled roof and the outside wall.

　During the summer, "Fish Smokehouse" sells smoking fish, bread and beverages directly to consumers. Many families can be seen are sitting on the lawn next to the factory and enjoying a picnic with a view of the sea. Smoking fish, salmon caviar and trout caviar are processed in this factory and sold in Japan, as well as elsewhere. We can see Jacobsen's graphic design work in the three chimneys and the SOF letters on the firm's business card and package design.

　After Jacobsen completed this project, he sought refuge in Sweden. While in Sweden, he only completed "Summer House for Ebbe Munck" in Arild. It was based on the form of this cold warehouse.

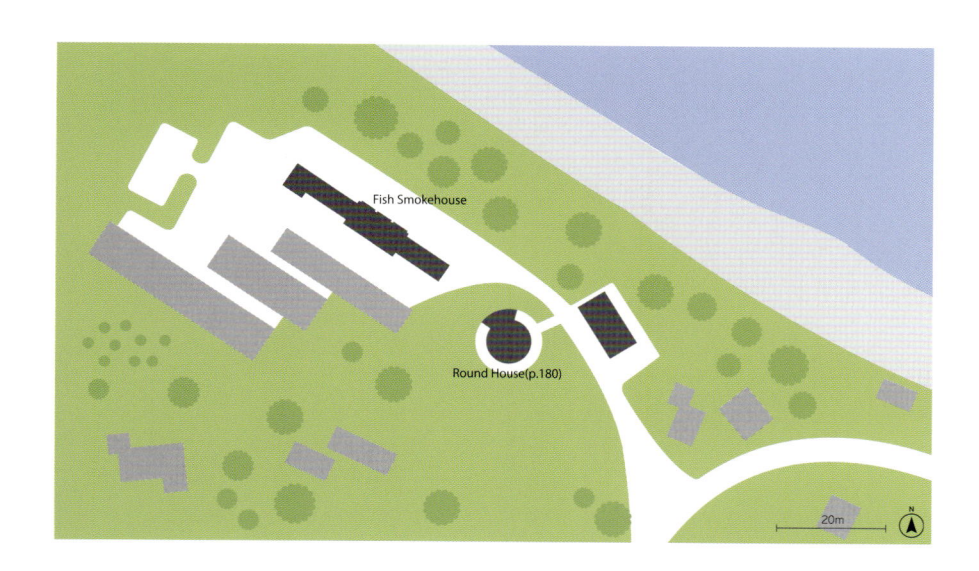

Fish Smokehouse

Round House(p.180)

20m

Section

巨大な煙突と対照的な事務棟の低い軒先。

The low eave of the office wing in contrast with the gigantic chimney.

Elevation

Plan

0m 1m   5m   10m

シンボリックな形態の煉瓦積の3本煙突。

Three brick chimneys for producing smoked food in a symbolic shape.

Fish Smokehouse 119

スーホルム I 1950年／クランペンボー
Soholm I / Søholm 1, 1950, Klampenborg

海岸道路側のアプローチ。手前の住戸はヤコブセンが晩年まで過ごした自邸。専用の門扉が左に見える。右奥がスーホルムⅡ（1951年）。

Approach from the ocean road. The house in the foreground was Jacobsen's own house in his latter years. The private gate can be seen on the left. To the right is Soholm II (1951).

「スーホルムⅠ」は、ヤコブセンが亡命先のスウェーデンから帰還後の最初のプロジェクトである。かつてベルビュー地区に実現したフラットルーフの白い建築群や、「ベラヴィスタ集合住宅」(p.38)の南側に隣接する敷地にヤコブセンが新たに出した答えは、黄色い煉瓦とセメント瓦の勾配屋根のタウンハウスだった。ヤコブセンはこの建築からデンマークの伝統や風土に回帰し、以降は白い建築を設計していない。

全体は、海への視界を確保するように東西に雁行して並べた5軒の地上2階建ての「スーホルムⅠ」と、西側の線路に沿って南北に並ぶ9軒の同じく2階建ての「スーホルムⅡ」(1949-1951)、そしてⅠとⅡの海への視界を遮らないように平屋に抑えた4軒の「スーホルムⅢ」(1953-1954)から成る。

「スーホルムⅠ」は地上2階地下1階建てのタウンハウスである。平面を見るとL型の住宅を雁行するように配置している。断面を見ると、伝統的な家型を踏襲しつつも、採光の高窓を設け、1階ダイニングと2階リビングをつなげる吹抜け空間を勾配屋根の下にうまく折り込んだ構成が秀逸である。

ヤコブセンは海側の1軒を自宅とし、地下に新しい事務所を構えて再出発の体制を整えた。専用の庭には300種以上の植物を植えて研究に余念がなかった。こうして亡命先のスウェーデンで磨きをかけたランドスケープの手腕をさらに進化させていった。

"Soholm I" was Jacobsen's first work after he was repatriated from his refuge in Sweden. Once had he built white buildings with flat roofs and "Bellavista Housing Complex" (p.38) on this site. However, as a new venture, he constructed town houses using yellow bricks and cement tiles for their pitched roofs on a site that adjoins the south side of "Bellavista Housing Complex." For this project, Jacobsen embraced Danish traditions and climate, discarding the use of white buildings.

The complete project consisted off five two-story house "Soholm I," which extended in zigzag fashion from east to west in order to obtain a view of the sea, nine two-story house "Soholm II" (1949-1951), which extended north and south along the railway tracks on the west side, and four one-story house "Soholm III" (1953-1954), which were designed as low buildings in order to avoid blocking a view of the sea from I and II.

"Soholm I" refers a two-storied town houses, including a basement first floor. A ground plan shows that the L-shaped houses were arranged in zigzag fashion. A cross section shows that he followed a traditional house type, but incorporated several innovations; a high window to provide daylight, an atrium to connects a dining room on the first floor and a living room on the second floor below a pitched roof.

Jacobsen set up his residence to the sea and his studio on the basement floor to begin anew. He planted more than 300 species of plants in his own garden and became absorbed by vegetation. Thus, he developed landscape designs more that he had when he first started in Sweden.

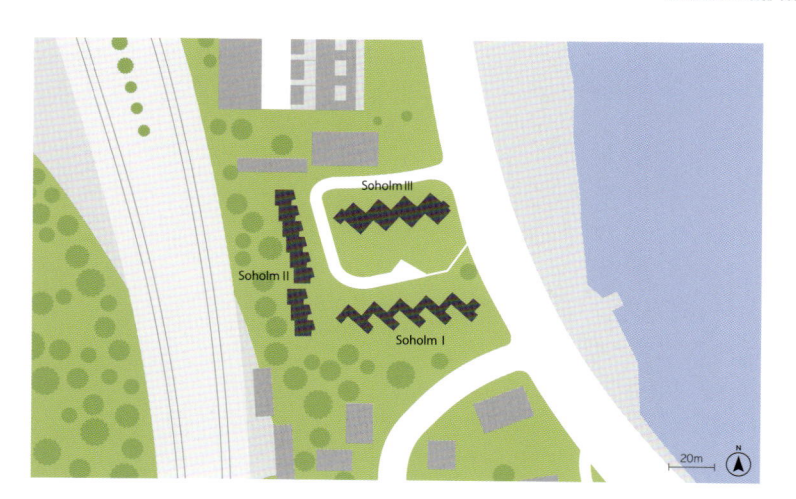

右頁上：アプローチ側から見た住戸。手前の階段は右側住戸の玄関に通じる。

Right page top: The house seen from the approach. The steps lead to the entrance of the house on the right.

右頁下：雁行した住戸配置により、プライバシーの確保と同時に魅力的な視界が得られる。ヤコブセンが力を入れた「庭付き核家族住宅」の典型。

Right page bottom: The layout of the houses in echelon creates both privacy and an attractive setting. This is typical of the "nuclear family home with garden" which Jacobsen focused on.

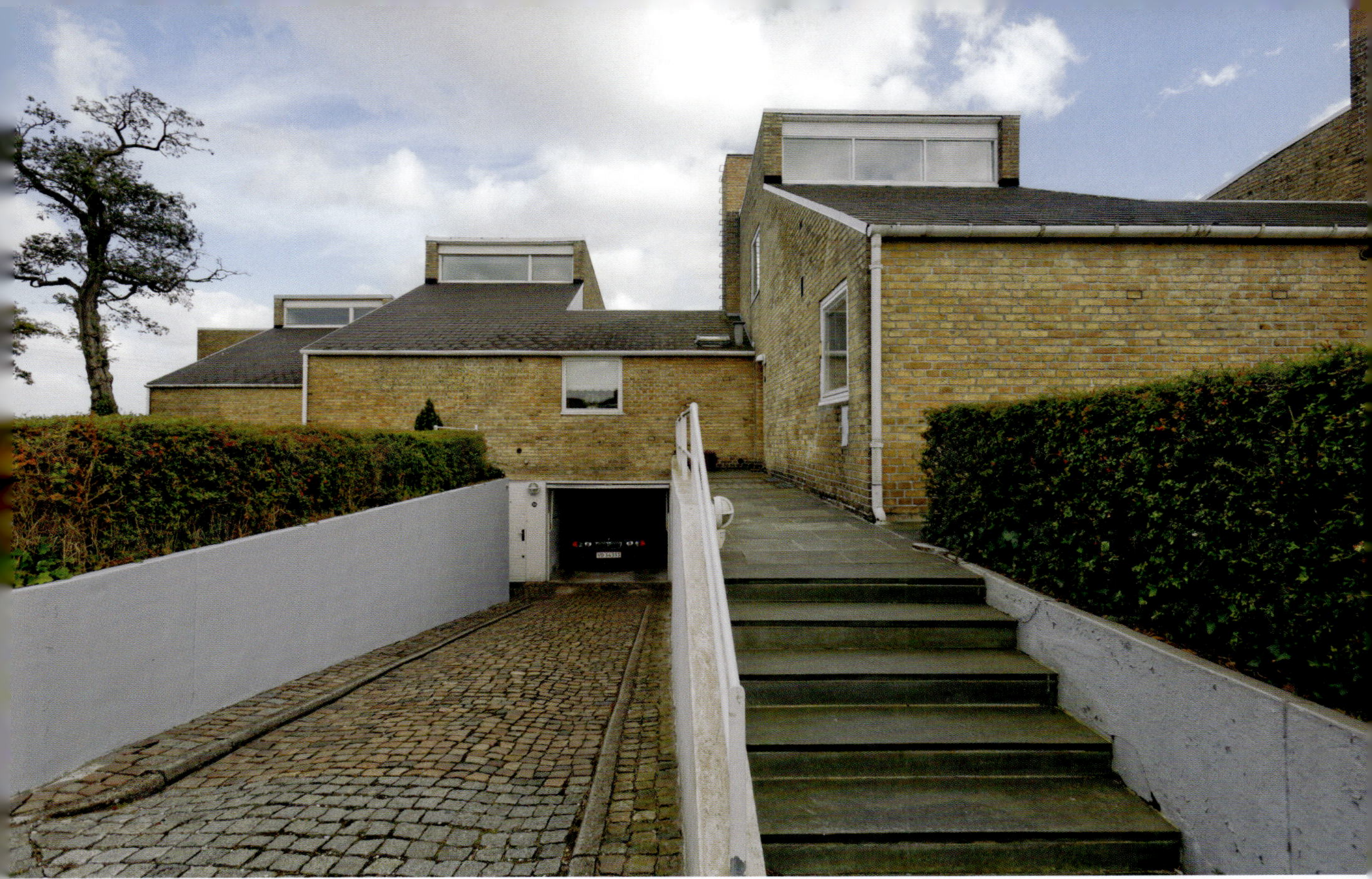

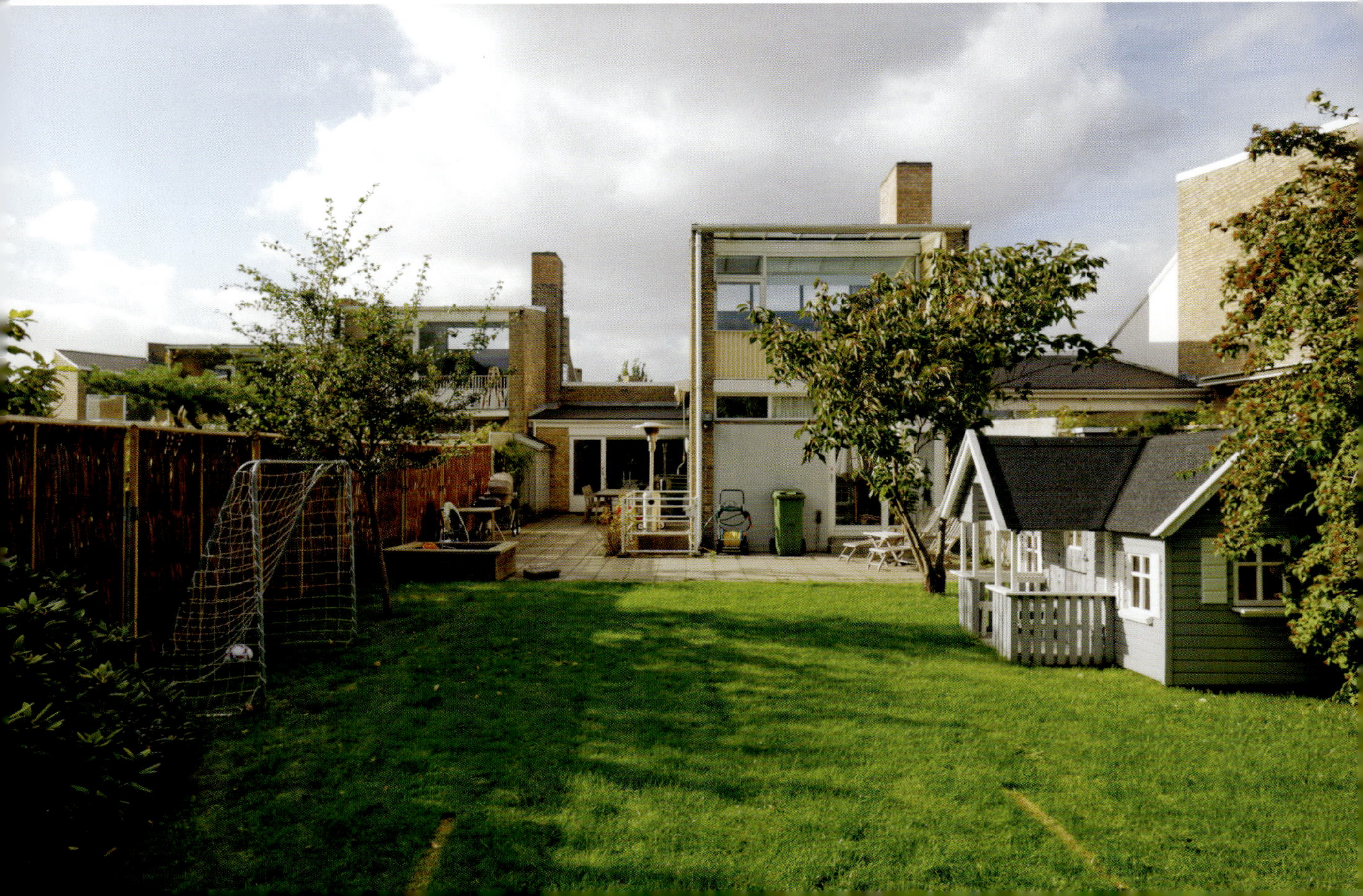

1階は個室が並び、2階リビングルームのバルコニーからはベルビュー海水浴場を見渡せる。

The first floor has a series of bedrooms, the second floor living room balcony affords views of Bellevue Beach.

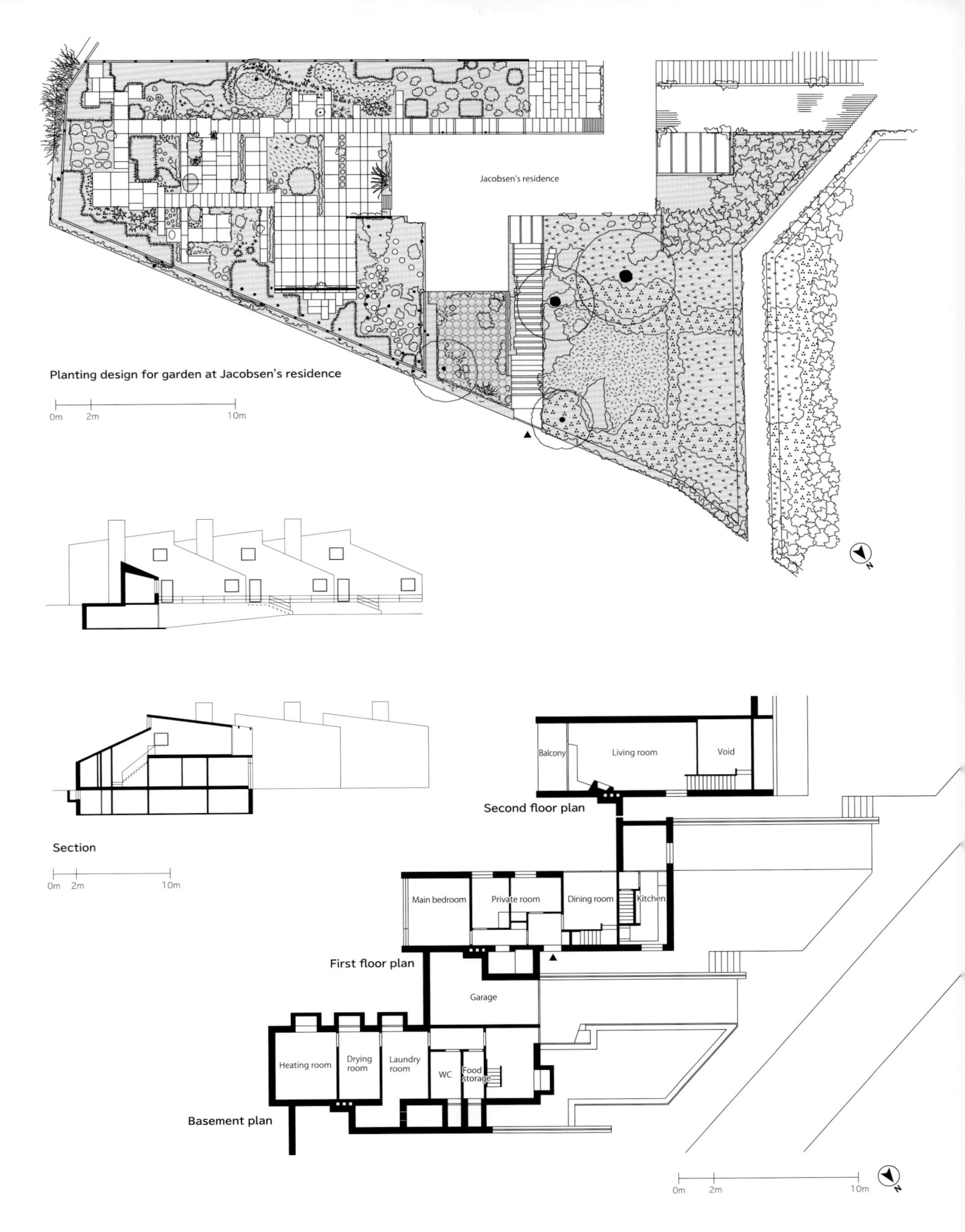

Planting design for garden at Jacobsen's residence

Jacobsen's residence

0m 2m 10m

Section

0m 2m 10m

Second floor plan

Balcony | Living room | Void

First floor plan

Main bedroom | Private room | Dining room | Kitchen
Garage

Basement plan

Heating room | Drying room | Laundry room | WC | Food storage

0m 2m 10m

Soholm I 125

吹抜け部分は本来ダイニングルームだったが、この住戸では右側に部屋を増築している。上にはリビングルームが見える。

The atrium area was originally to be a dining room, but in this house an additional was added to the right. The living room is visible upstairs.

階段途中から増築されたリビングルームを見る。

The extended living room as seen from the staircase.

2階リビングルーム。プランを海岸線に対して斜めに振っているため、2か所の窓からビーチの風景を楽しむことができる。

The second floor living room. The home is at an angle to the coastline, allowing beach views to be enjoyed from two windows.

バルコニー側からリビングルームを見る。北側の高窓からは、柔らかい天空光がリビングに入る。高窓下はダイニングルームの吹抜け。

The living room as seen from the balcony. The high north-facing window brings soft natural light into the living room. Below the skylight is the dining room atrium.

リビングルームにあるピクチャーウィンドウ。ビーチの風景が正方形に切り取られる。

The picture window in the living room. The beach view is framed in a square.

ホービュー・セントラルスクール 1950年／ホービュー
Harby Central School ／ Hårby Skole, 1950, Hårby

北側道路からの全景。3つの大きな窓のある部分は多目的ホール。

Full view from the north road. The building with three large windows is a multipurpose hall.

「ホービュー・セントラルスクール」は、デンマーク中央部のフュン島の南西部にある。第2次世界大戦後に亡命先のスウェーデンから祖国に帰還したヤコブセンのデザインは、祖国デンマークの伝統や風土に回帰したものだった。戦後の物資の不足もあって、伝統的な黄色い煉瓦とセメント瓦の勾配屋根を用いた作品が、この後しばらく続く。「ホービュー・セントラルスクール」は「スーホルムⅠ」(p.120)に続く、帰還後の第2作となる作品だ。設計と建設時期が重なっているため両者には類似点が数多く見受けられる。

全体のボリュームは、周囲の切り妻屋根の住宅とさほど変わらない大きさと形から成る。芝生の庭を、教室と多目的ホールから成るL型の校舎と、わずかに雁行して連なる3つの教職員住宅が囲む。芝生の庭と教職員住宅は生垣で仕切られている。敷地の南側に体育館と校庭が続く。

2層吹抜けの多目的ホールの光環境は自然光と人工照明がうまくバランスをとっている。北側の壁と屋根の境をかぎの手型にくり抜く3つの窓からベースとなる自然光が入る。2列の球形のペンダントライトは、片方の列の照明が高い位置から徐々に低くなるのに対し、もう片方の列は低い位置から徐々に高くなるように吊り下げてある。このようなちょっとした工夫が空間にリズムを与えている。

"Harby Central School" is located in the southwestern part of Fyn Island in the center of Denmark. After Jacobsen was repatriated from his refuge in Sweden to Denmark, his design taste returned to his native land's Danish traditions and climate. After the war, a lack of supplies forced him to use yellow bricks, cement tiles and pitched roofs for a while. "Harby Central School" was his second work that he completed after "Soholm I" (p.120) project. A number of similarities can be found in both buildings as Jacobsen designed and built them during the same period.

The entire project is similar in appearance to the many houses with gable roofs that border it. The project consists of a multipurpose hall, an L-shaped school building, which contains classrooms, and three faculty houses that surround a lawn in a zigzag fashion. A hedge divides the lawn and the faculty houses. The gymnasium and the schoolyard are located on the southern site.

An atrium that is two stories in height in the multipurpose hall provides natural light from three windows between the north wall and the roof. In addition, two rows of ball-shaped, hanging lamp fixtures add artificial light to the hall. The height of successive lamps in one row successively declines from, whereas the height of successive lamps in the other row rises from low to high. This minor arrangement contributes to a sense of rhythm to the space.

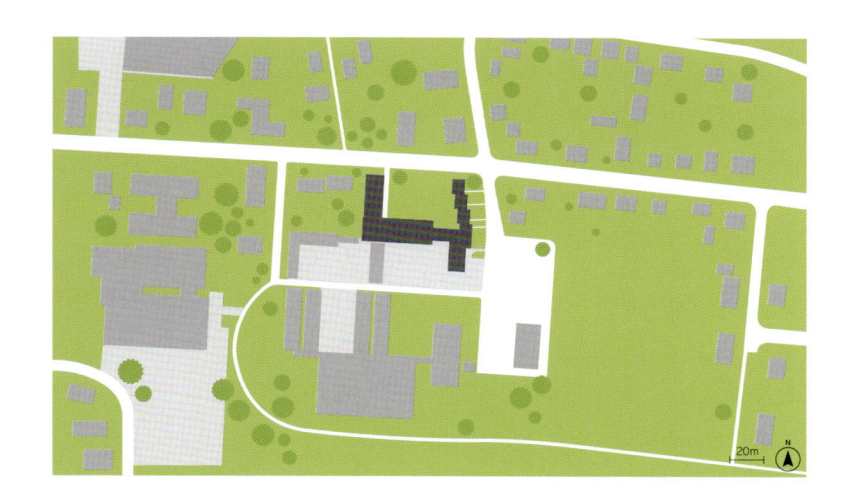

右頁上：北側の緑地広場。

Right page top: Open green space on the north side.

右頁下：学校入口へのアプローチ。白い木製のパーゴラが続く。

Right page bottom: Pathway to the school entrance. White wooden pergolas line the way.

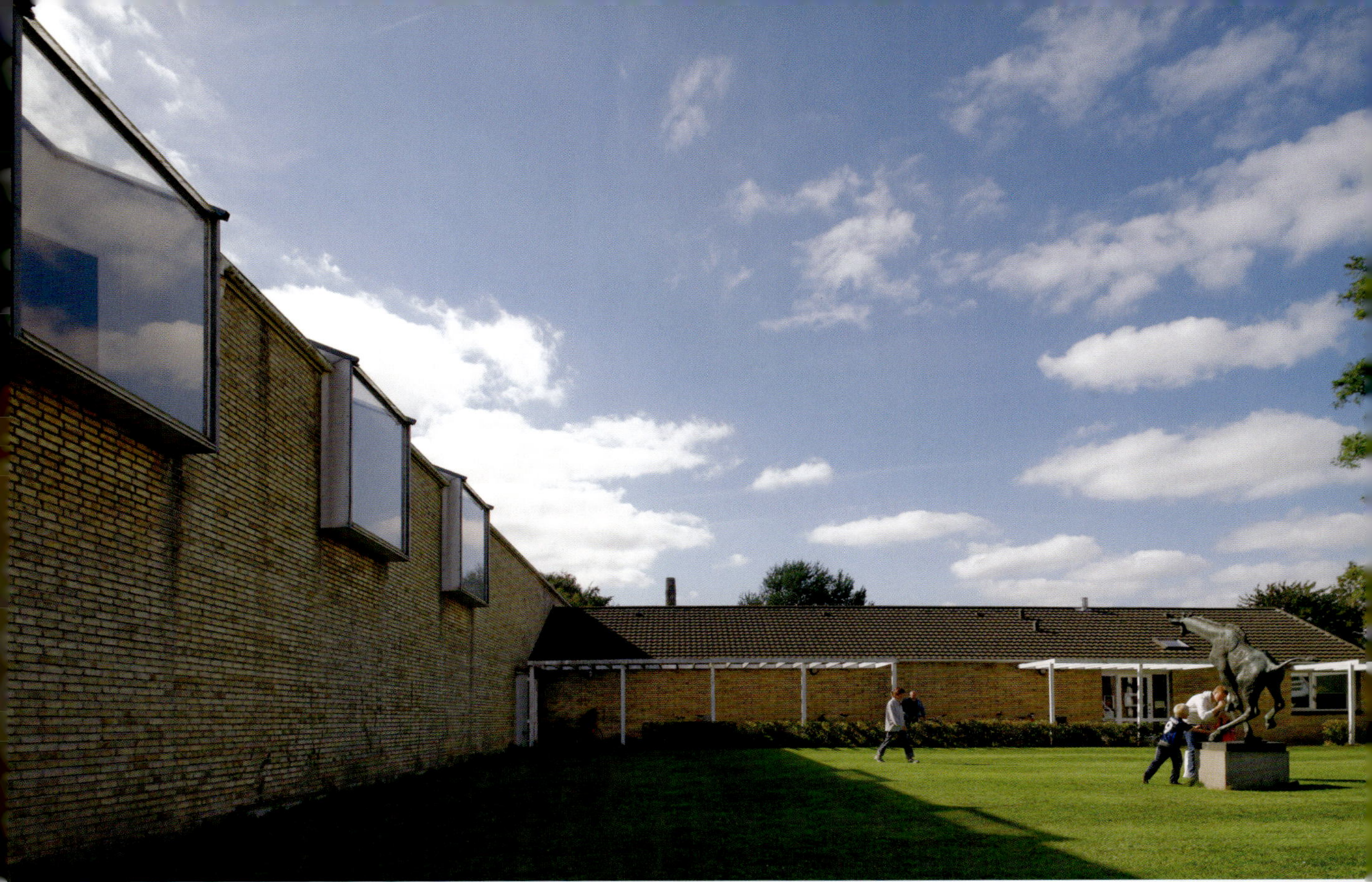

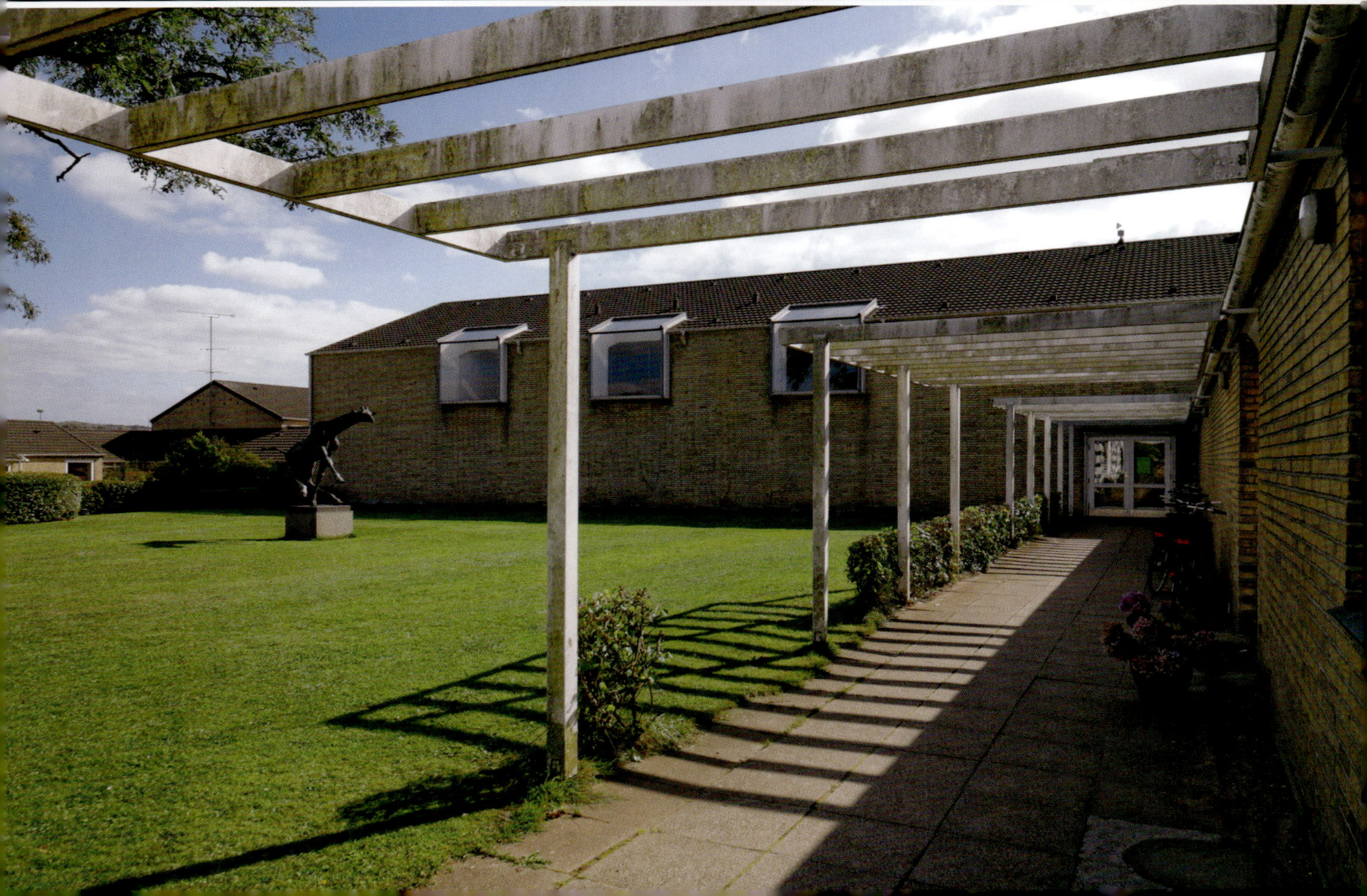

北東角の交差点からの全景。3軒の教職員住宅が並ぶ。

Full view from the northeast corner intersection. Three faculty houses are spaced around the corner.

更衣室と体育館がL型につながる。

Changing rooms and a gymnasium are connected in an L shape.

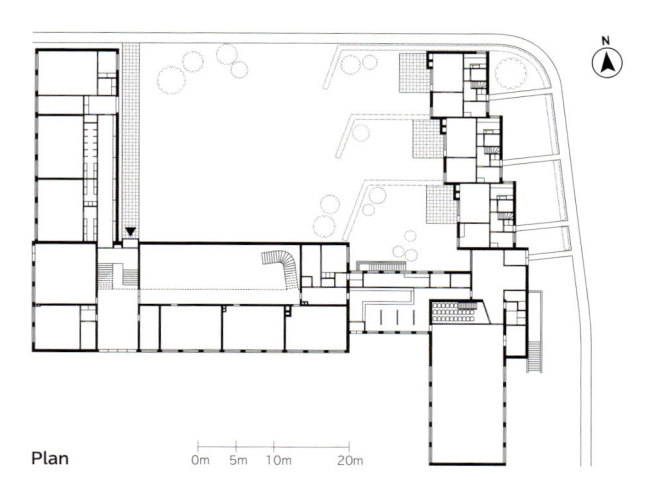

Plan 0m 5m 10m 20m

Arne Jacobsen

校庭から校舎全景を望む。右は更衣室の出入口。

Enjoying a view of a school building from the schoolyard. The entrance to the changing rooms is on the right.

Harby Central School

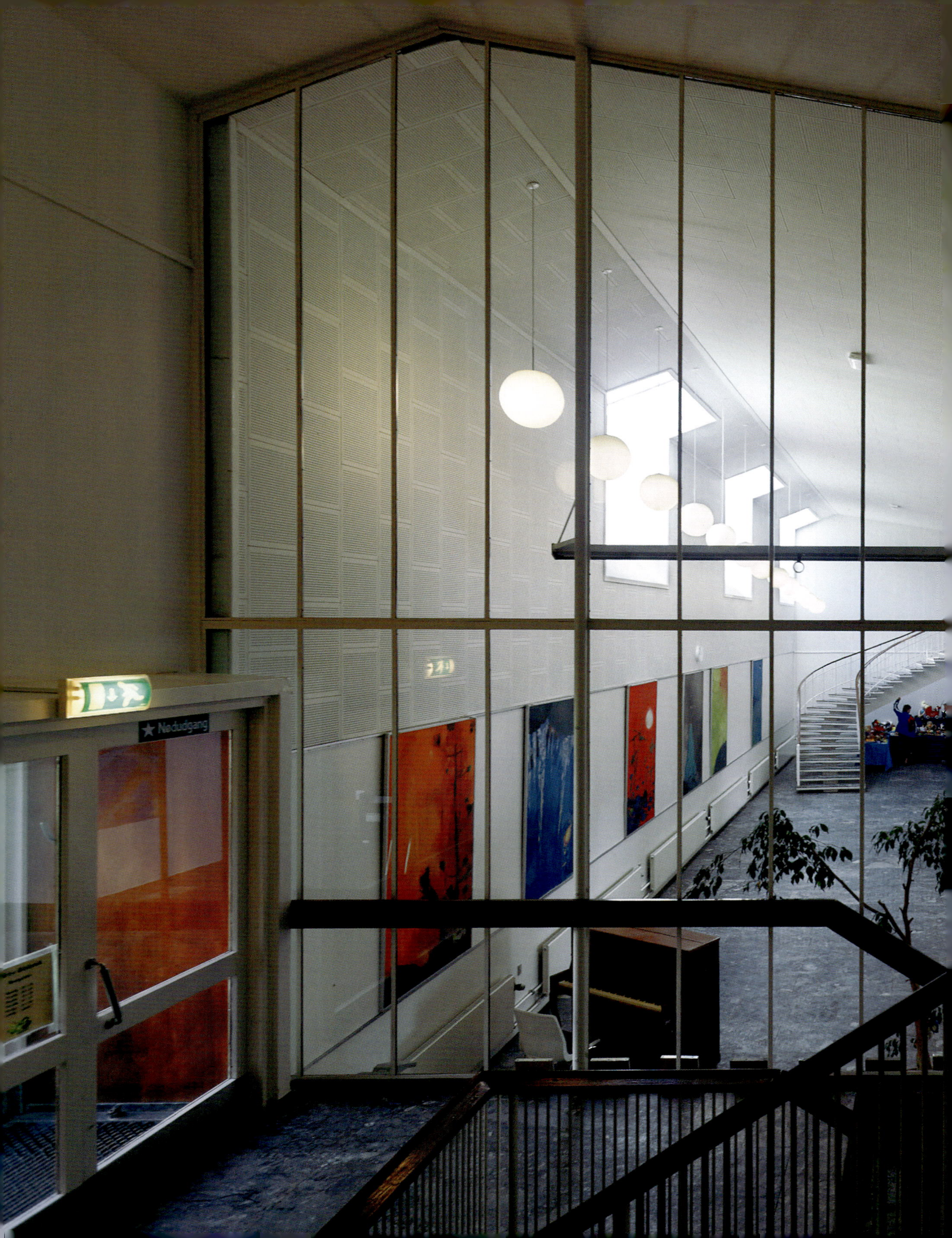
Nødudgang

多目的ホール。3か所の折れ曲がったトップライトから北側の天空光がホールを満たす。

The multipurpose hall. Natural sunlight fills the hall coming through the three two-faced skylights on the north side.

天空光を取り込みながら視界も確保するために折れ曲がったトップライトが風景を切り取る。

The two-faced skylight provides brightness inside and crops the beautiful outdoor scenery.

校舎入口から半階下がった多目的ホール。

The school entrance features a half floor stairway that leads to the multipurpose hall.

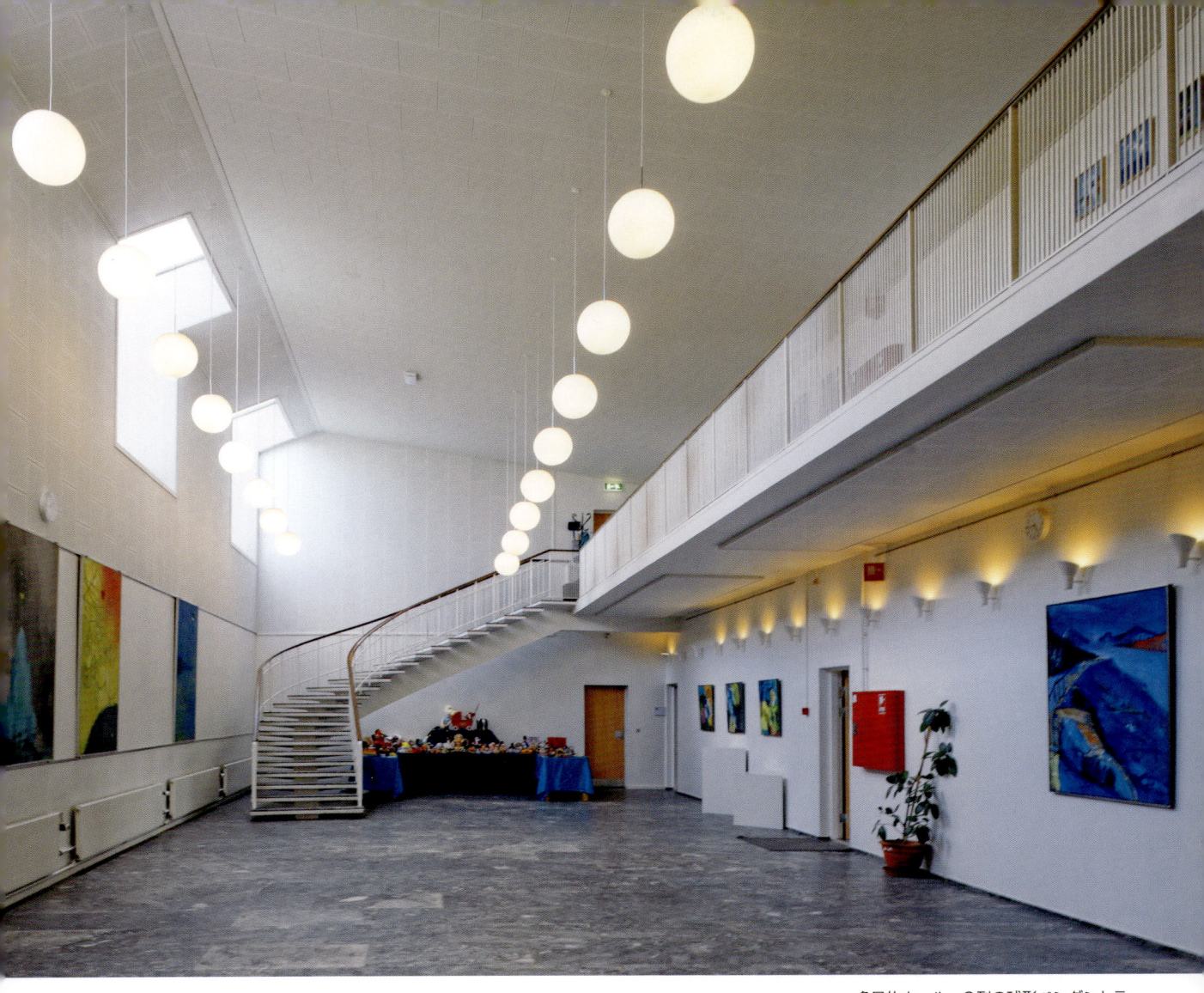

多目的ホール。2列の球形ペンダントライトが逆方向に傾斜して吊られ、空間に動きを与えている。

The multipurpose hall. Two lanes of pendant lights add movement to the space hanging low on one side and higher on the other.

階段側から見た多目的ホール。

The view from the stairway of the multipurpose hall.

Harby Central School

北側ファサードの水彩画。
A watercolor that depicts the north side facade of Harby Central School.

オリジナルの状態がよく残された更衣室。手前のベンチは座面を一部跳ね上げて内側に入ることができる。
A changing room preserved in its original condition. A part of the front side bench seat is a flip-up.

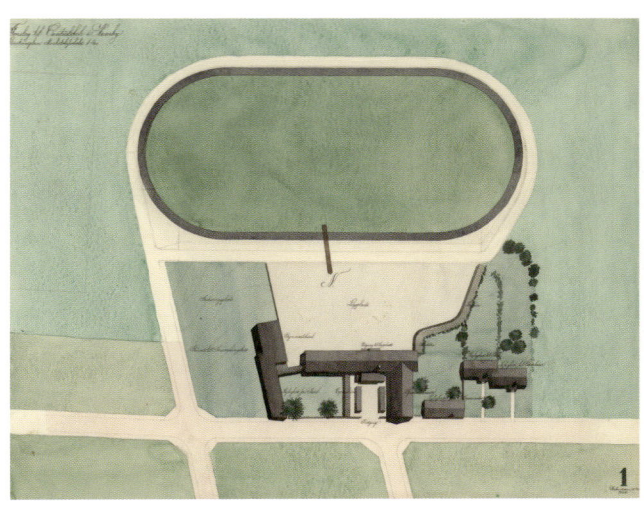

水彩画の配置図。
A watercolor for layout drawing.

教室のドアハンドル。
A school room door handle.

体育館内部。右奥の扉から校庭へとつながる。
Inside of the gymnasium. The door in the back on the right opens up to the schoolyard.

Harby Central School 139

シモニュー邸 1954年／ホルテ

The Simony House／Simony's Hus, 1954, Holte

南側外観。屋根勾配を敷地の傾斜に呼応させ、立体的な室内空間を生み出している。

External view of the southern facade. The slant of the roof matches the slope of the site to create a three-dimensional internal space.

「シモニュー邸」は、コペンハーゲン北部の閑静な住宅地にある。道路側から見ると、白く低い煉瓦積みの壁の上に箱状のボリュームが屋根勾配に沿って正面に飛び出したかのように見える。シモニュー氏は「ノヴォ治療ラボラトリウム」(p.64)のエンジニアで、ヤコブセンにノヴォ社の施設を設計する際の建設担当者であった関係から、自邸の設計を依頼した。

道路から少し奥まったところで下り斜面になる敷地形状を生かして、ヤコブセンは斜面に沿った勾配屋根を想定し、その下に居室を並べていった。玄関は正面右手を1mほど下ったレベルにある。斜面を下った先の一番下の庭のレベルにプレイルームとホビールーム、その上階にリビングと主寝室、半階上がるとダイニングとキッチン、そして最上階の屋根裏部分に3室の寝室とバスルームを配した。この最上階は道路面から半階上がったレベルにある。ふたつの屋外テラスがダイニングとリビングの南側のそれぞれのレベルに設けられた。

ダイニングから半階下がったリビングをとおして庭を望む伸びやかな空間構成は、「ヤコブセンの夏の家」、「スーホルムⅠ」(p.120)と共通する。床のレベル差を吹抜けの勾配天井で覆い、連続した空間に仕上げる手法をヤコブセンは得意としていた。最上階の3つの個室にも、屋根裏の狭いスペースを巧みに間仕切り、斜めの壁と天井をうまく生かした手腕がうかがえる。

"The Simony House" is located in a quiet residential area of northern Copenhagen. In looking at the house from the road side, a large, box-shaped roof appears to be bursting out from the low and white brick walls. Mr. Simony was an engineer at "Novo Terapeutisk Laboratorium" and the person in charge of the construction when Novo asked Jacobsen to design a facility for Novo. So he also asked to design his own house.

Jacobsen took advantages of the shape of the site, which sloped downward away from the house on the side furthest from the road. He designed a pitched roof that was inclined downwards along the original slope, and created a room beneath the roof. The house has an entrance on its right side at a level that is one meter lower than the road surface. Jacobsen created a play room and a hobby room on the lowest garden level. There is a living room and the main bedroom on the upper floor. There are a dining and a kitchen on the half upper floor. Three bed rooms and a bath room were created in the attic part of the top floor. This top floor is half a floor level higher than the road. An outdoor terrace was provided on each of the two levels on the south side of the living room and dining room.

The Spacious configuration of the dining room that enables one to see the garden through the living room that is half a level lower appears also in "Jacobsen's Summer House" and "Soholm I" (p.120). Jacobsen was good at creating continuous space in which the slanted roof covered different floor levels. The three private rooms on the top floor demonstrate his talent in dividing narrow attic space skillfully and making good use of diagonal walls and ceilings.

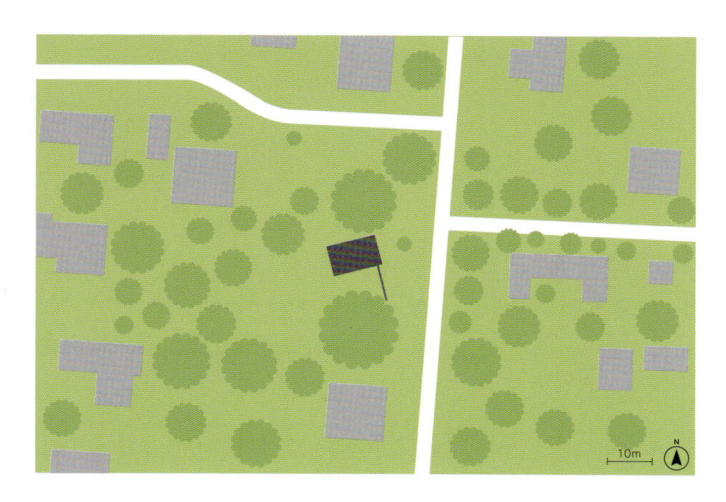

右頁上：大きなスレート屋根を見せる東面の道路側外観。

Right page top: External view from the road, showing the large slate roof on the eastern facade.

右頁下：北側妻面にある玄関。屋根勾配が直角であることが分かる。

Right page bottom: The entrance in the northern gable end. The angle of the slanting roof is clear.

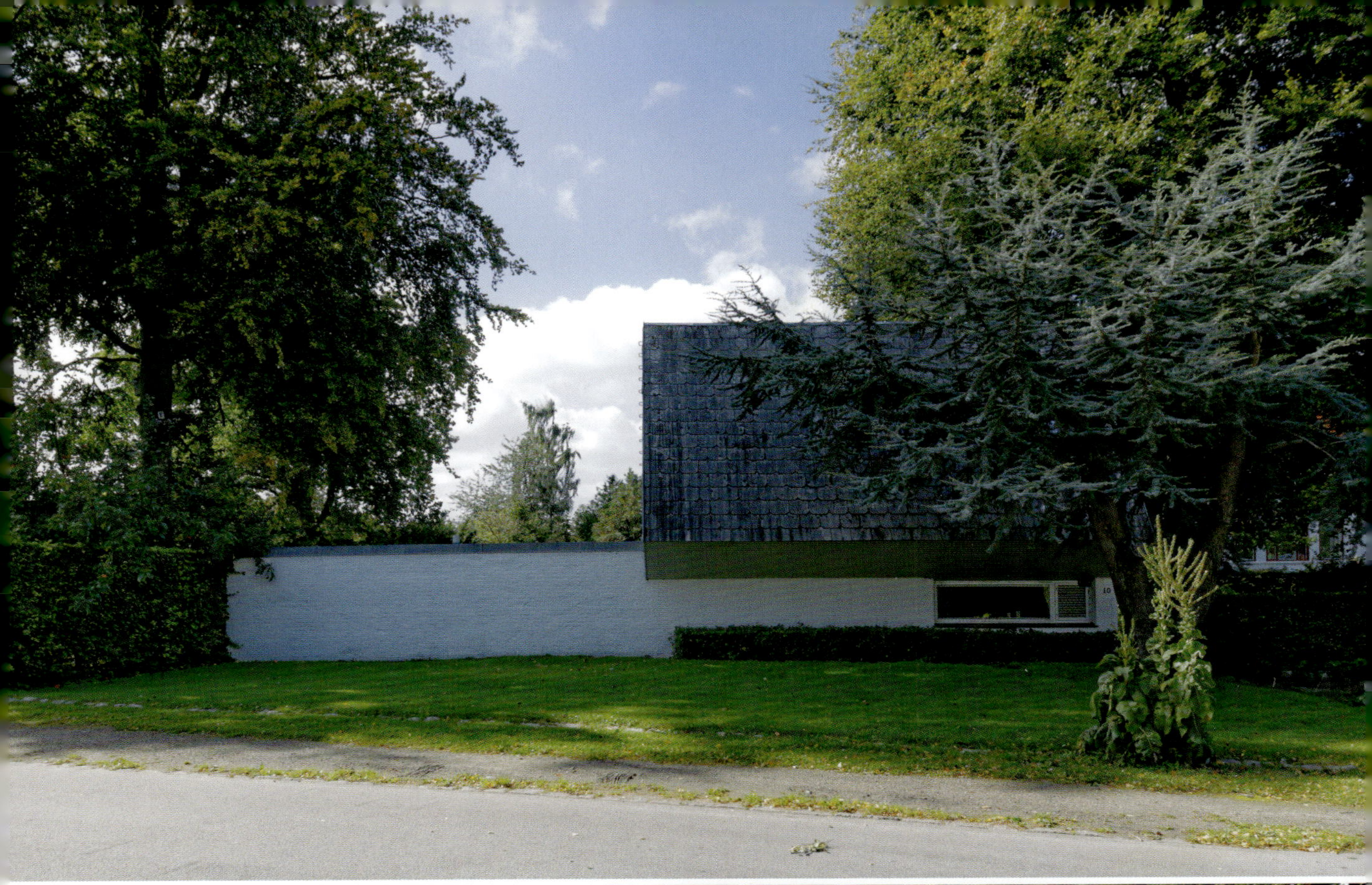

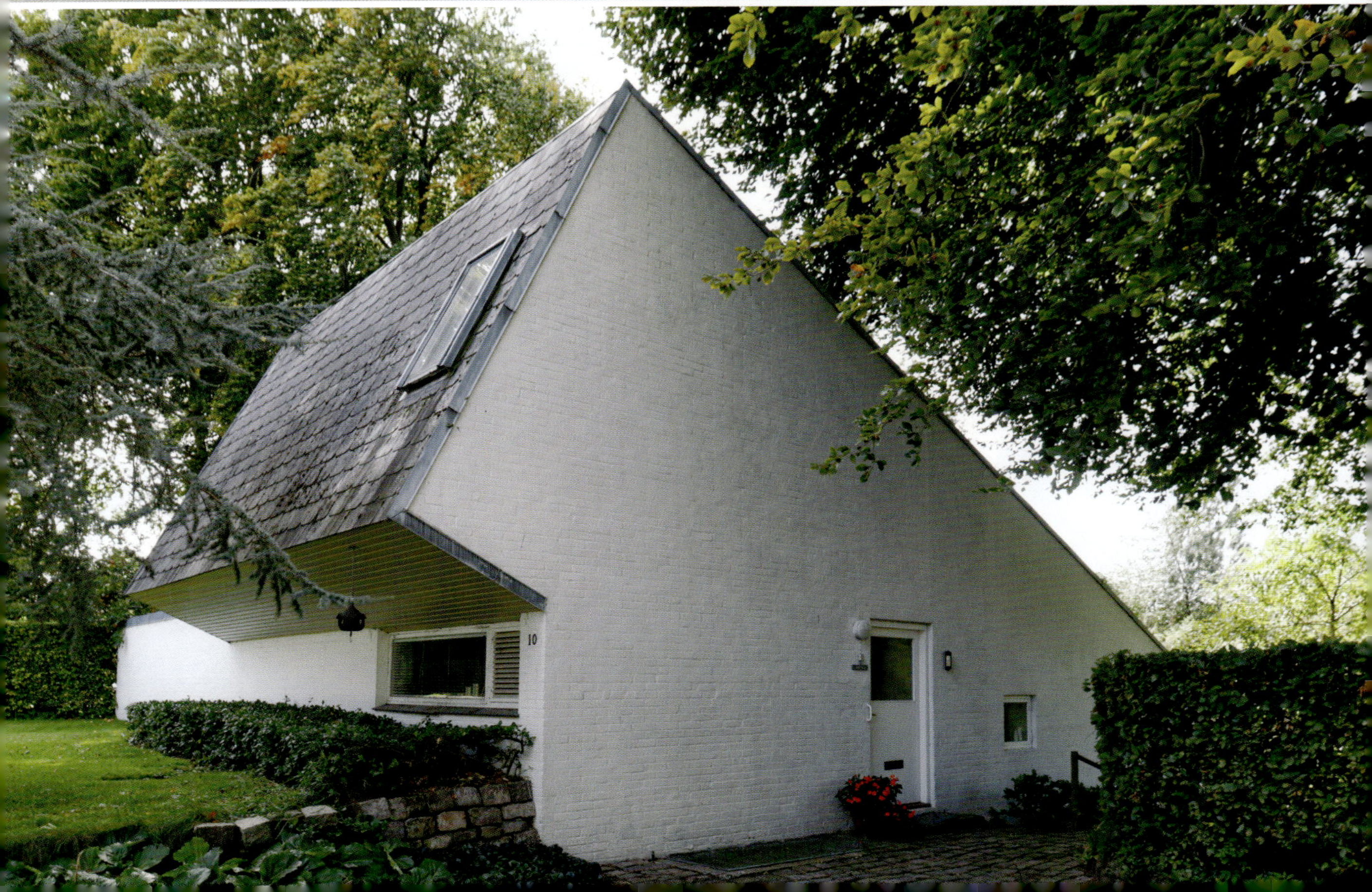

Elevations

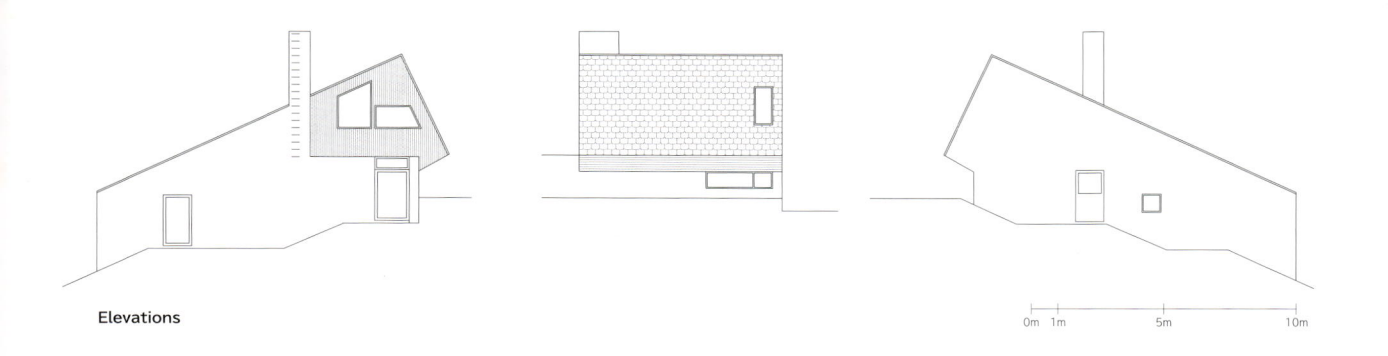

0m 1m   5m   10m

左：敷地の傾斜に合わせて2か所の屋外テラスが設けられている。それぞれダイニングルーム、リビングルームから直接出入りすることができる。

Left: There are two external terraces aligned with the slope of the site. They allow direct access to the dining room and living room.

右頁：西側に広がる庭からの全景。建物の奥と手前に階段が設けられている。傾斜地に建つ「庭付き戸建て核家族住宅」の好例。

Right page: Full view from the west garden. There are steps in the foreground and to the rear. It is a good example of a "nuclear family home with garden."

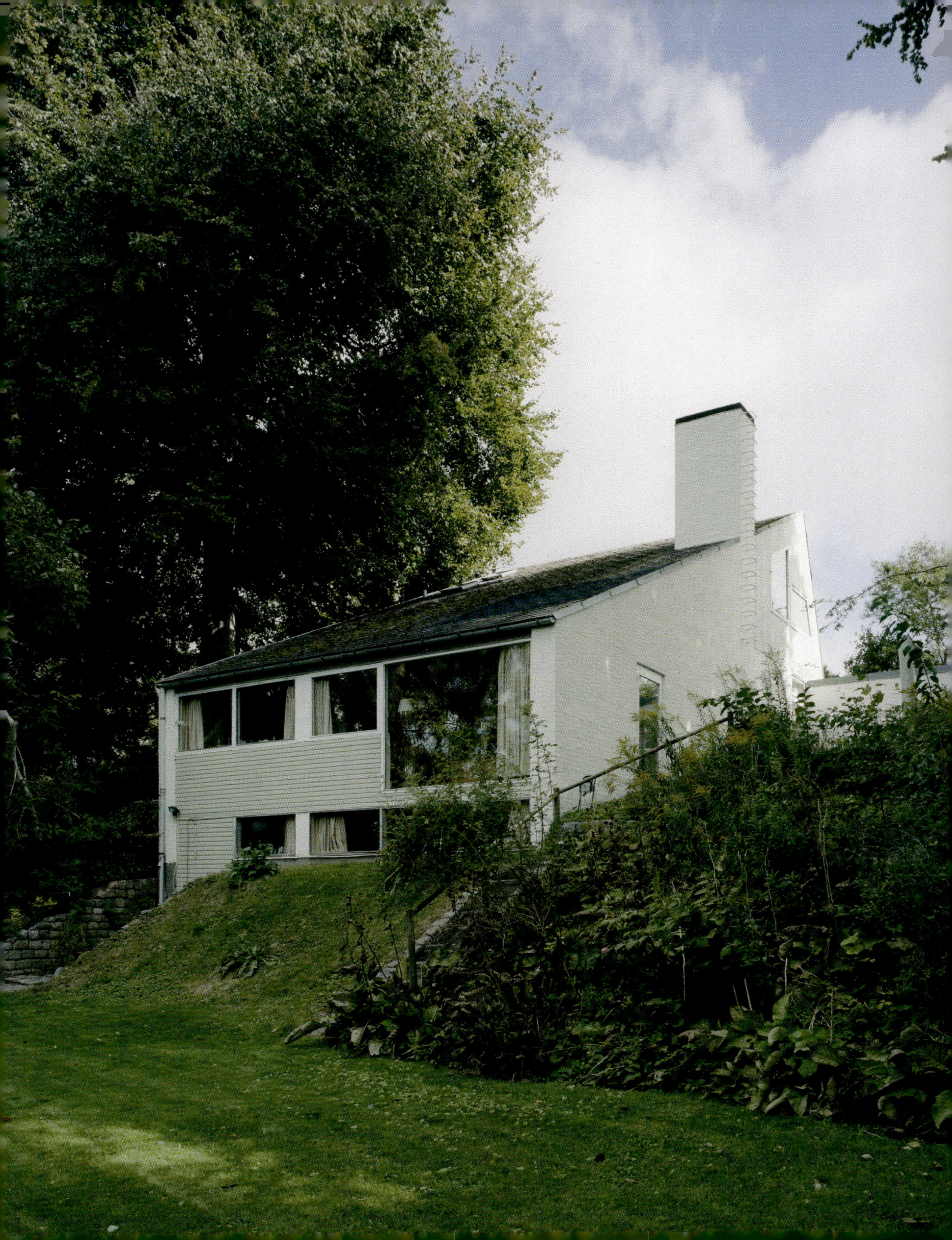

リビングルーム全景。階段を上がったところがダイニングルーム。左奥には主寝室が見える。壁と天井は微妙な色遣いで塗り分けられている。

Full view of the living room. The dining room is up the stairs. The master bedroom can be seen to the left. The walls and the ceiling were painted slightly different shades.

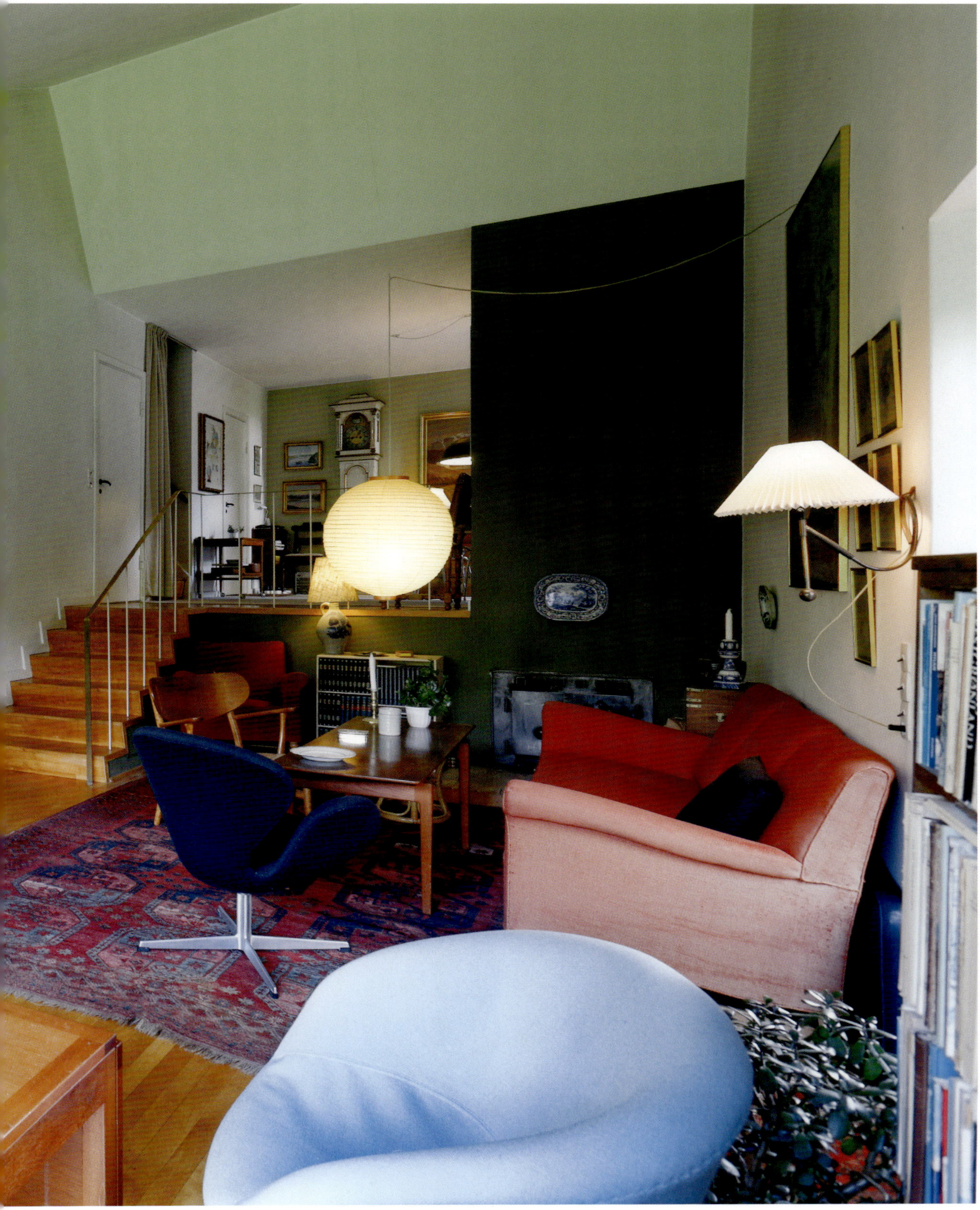

ダイニングルームより、1m下がったリビングルームを見下ろす。リビングルームの大きな開口部から、庭園の緑が見渡せる。左のドアはテラスに通じる。

The view from the dining room down to the living room, which is one meter below. The greenery of the garden can be seen through the large living room window. The door to the left opens onto the terrace.

辛子色に塗られた壁の寝室。三方枠に引き込まれている建具で仕切ることができる。

A bedroom with mustard colored walls. The space can be partitioned with sliding doors.

モスグリーンに塗られた壁がアクセントとなっているダイニングルーム。中央のドアから外部のテラスに出ることができる。

The moss green colored walls are a feature of the dining room. The door in the center leads to the terrace.

リビングルームの階段から1mのレベル差をもつダイニングルームを見る。濃いモスグリーンの壁は暖炉の煙突。

The view of the dining room as seen from the living room stairs one meter below. The dark moss green colored wall is the chimney of the fireplace.

The Simony House 149

2階に3室ある個室。それぞれ窓の形状と位置、壁と天井の傾斜、色遣いが異なり、ヤコブセンの洒落っ気を感じさせる。

The three bedrooms on the second floor. Jacobsen's sense of style can be felt in the various shapes and positions of the windows, the angles of the walls and ceilings, and the use of colors.

2階階段室。奥の踊り場はトップライトの採光で明るい。踊り場の左側はバスルーム。

The second floor stair hall. The far landing is brightly lit by a skylight. To the left of the landing is the bathroom.

狭い階段幅を広く使えるよう、踊り場の手摺壁を斜めにしている。

In order to allow wider use of the narrow staircase, the handrail wall on the landing is slanted.

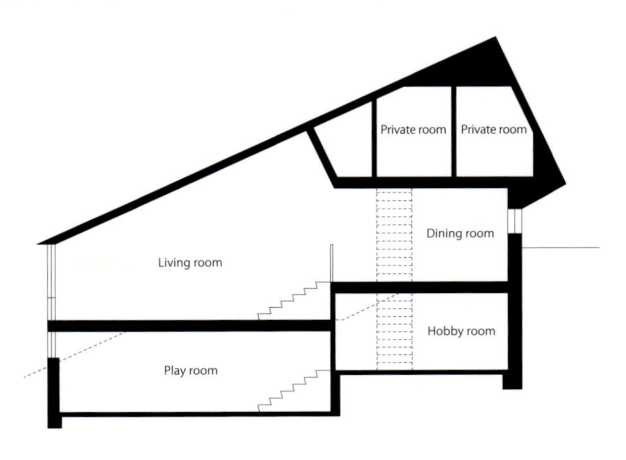

Section

Second floor plan

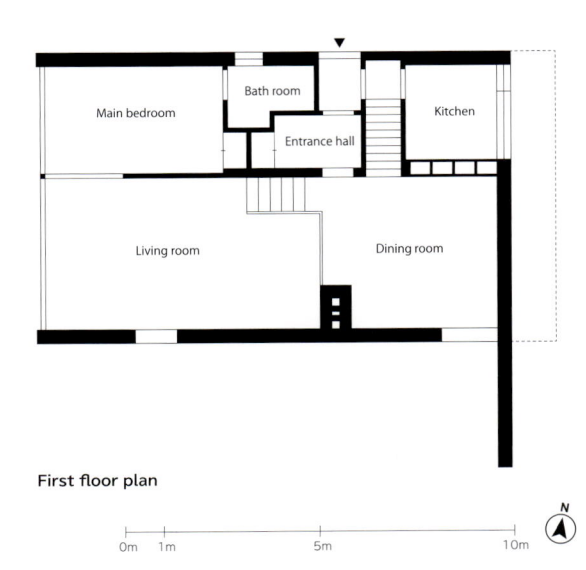

First floor plan

0m 1m 5m 10m N

階段の踊り場にある小さなバスルーム。
The small bathroom off the staircase landing.

The Simony House 151

ムンケゴー小学校 1957年／ソボー
Munkegard Elementary School ／ Munkegårdsskolen, 1957, Søborg

校庭より西側外観全景を望む。右端は体育館。
The view of the west facing side of the school from the schoolyard. On the far right is the gymnasium.

コペンハーゲンから北北西に7km、大きな団地の一画にこの小学校はある。周辺は一戸建ての住宅でびっしりと埋まった緑豊かな住宅地だ。

敷地の西半分には芝生のサッカーグラウンドと体育館のスポーツゾーンがあり、東半分には整然と教室が配置された校舎がある。東西に延びた平屋の教室棟が隣棟間隔を空けて南北に並ぶ。北側の4棟目は2階建てで特別教室が並ぶ。この教室棟を南北に延びた5列の廊下が垂直に貫通する。こうして生まれた格子状の構成の中に17の中庭を区画し、それぞれに異なる敷石パターン、植物、さまざまな彫刻をあしらった。

ヤコブセンが学校建築において最も重視したのは光である。いかに教室に自然光を取り入れるかを考え、隣棟間隔と断面構成を決定した。各教室の庭は隣棟間隔を十分に確保しており、教室の南側の窓から自然光が入る仕組みだ。断面構成を見ると、「スーホルムⅠ」(p.120) で試した光を取り入れる勾配屋根をベースに、教室内部に自然光を取り込み、隣接する補助室まで光を届ける工夫が見られる。

ヤコブセンは学生生活のためのトータルデザインを徹底した。学年に応じた3段階の大きさのデスクや椅子のみならず、スピーカー、照明器具、カーテンまでもデザインした。「タンチェア」や「ムンケゴーランプ」はこの時に生まれた。

"Munkegard Elementary School" is located seven kilometers north northwest of Copenhagen, in one section of a large housing complex. Vegetation and detached houses surround this school.

The western half of the site is used for sports and contains a soccer field and a gymnasium. The eastern half of the site contains a school building in which classrooms were arranged in an orderly manner. In addition, one-story classroom buildings extended east and west in three, parallel rows with spaces between the one-story buildings for the pitch of the building. The northernmost two-storied building contained special classrooms. Five corridors, which extended north and south, connected these buildings at right angles. 17 courtyards within lattice-shaped construction feature a different flagstone pattern, plants and various sculptures.

Jacobsen considered how to expose classrooms to natural light and decided to work with the pitch of the buildings and a cross-sectional configuration. Natural light enters each classroom through southward-facing windows. A cross section revealed his ingenuity; the pitched roof enabled light to enter the room, as it had in "Soholm I" (p.120), and further design brought the incident rays into adjacent auxiliary chambers.

Jacobsen thoroughly designed everything for student life; three different sizes of desks and chairs, speakers, lighting and even curtains. "The Tongue" and the "Munkegard Lamp" were made at this time.

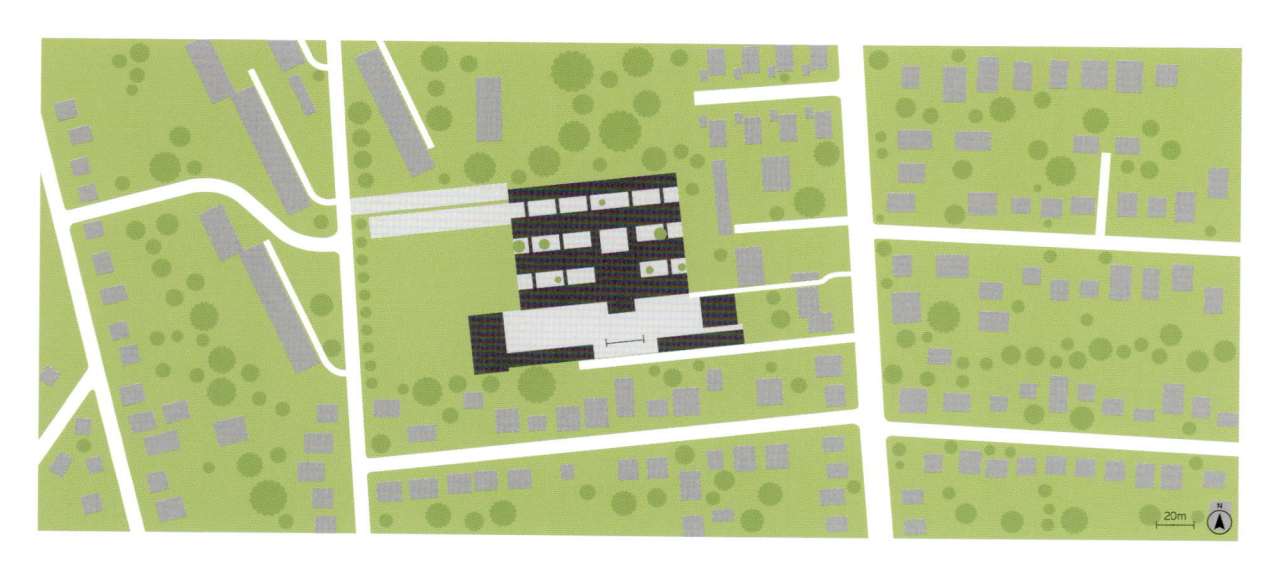

教室に囲まれた中庭への外部階段。教室のレベルより2.2m下がっている校庭。
Steps leading up to the courtyards backed on by classrooms. The schoolyard is at a level 2.2 meters below that of the classrooms.

校舎西側の体育館。
The gymnasium on the west side of the school.

教室入口へ続くガラス屋根の通路。

Covered glass walkway leading to the classroom entrance.

教室通路への入口。

Entrance to the classroom corridor.

南西側からの校舎外観。右手前の床開口部は、2009年に増築された地下教室のための光井戸（設計：Dorte Mandrup Architect）。

The school's exterior from the southwest. The open space in the ground front right is a light well for a basement level classroom additionally constructed in 2009 (designed by Dorte Mandrup Architect).

校舎西側の教室に囲まれた中庭。

The courtyards looked onto by a classroom on the west side.

左写真の中庭に上がる外部階段ディテール。

A detailed shot of the stairs leading to the courtyard pictured left.

Munkegard Elementary School

凹凸を繰り返しながら続く通路部分の屋根。右側にホールが見える。
The roof covering the corridor rises and falls into the distance. The school hall can be seen to the right.

1948年頃の原案における南西から見た鳥瞰図の水彩画。

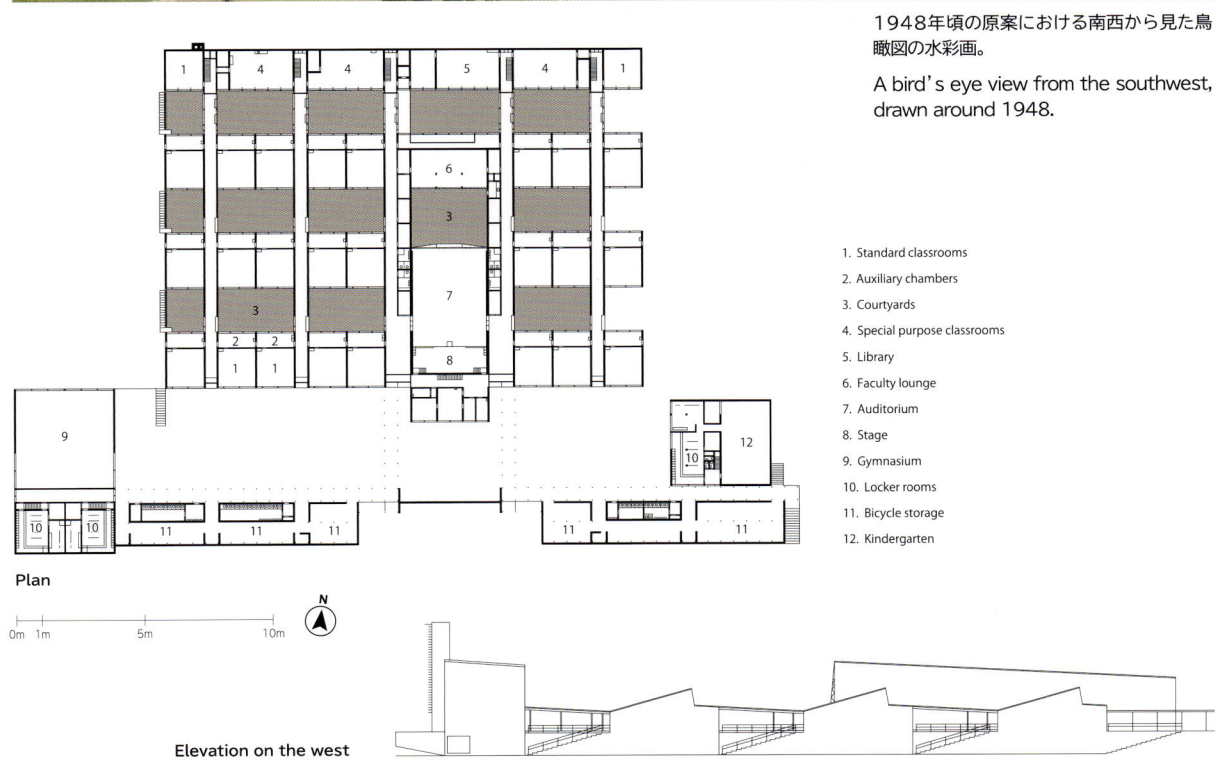

A bird's eye view from the southwest, drawn around 1948.

1. Standard classrooms
2. Auxiliary chambers
3. Courtyards
4. Special purpose classrooms
5. Library
6. Faculty lounge
7. Auditorium
8. Stage
9. Gymnasium
10. Locker rooms
11. Bicycle storage
12. Kindergarten

Plan

Elevation on the west

Munkegard Elementary School

中庭の水彩画。
A watercolor shows a courtyard.

教室に囲まれた17か所の中庭が設けられた。それぞれの中庭はさまざまな床仕上げと植生にデザインされ、多様な表情を生み出している。

There are 17 different courtyards looked upon by classrooms. Landscaped and tiled individually, each courtyard has its own varied characteristics.

北側にある中庭のひとつ。
One of the courtyards on the north side.

Munkegard Elementary School

２段採光で奥まで照度が確保される教室。
The classrooms get plenty of light thanks to the two level windows.

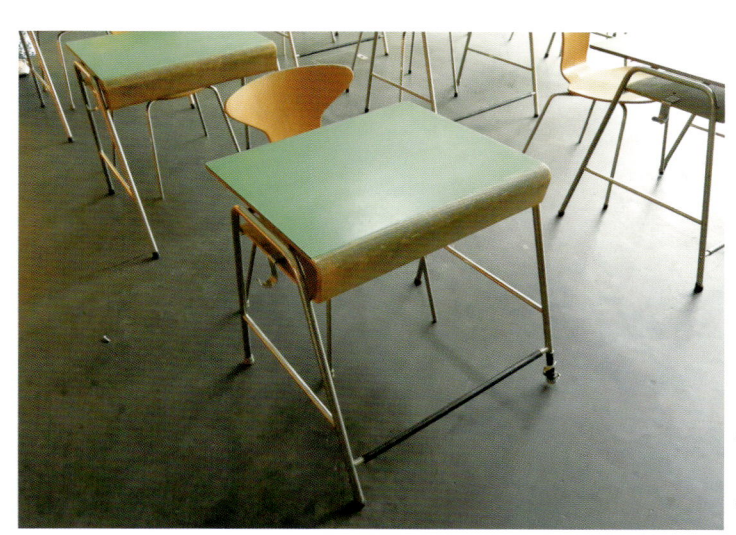

ヤコブセンがデザインしたムンケゴー小学校用の学童用机と椅子。
Desks and chairs designed by Jacobsen for the students at Munkegard Elementary School.

教室の補助室。家具や枠回りには彩度の高い色が使われている。天井にはヤコブセンがこの学校のためにデザインした「ムンケゴーランプ」と呼ばれる照明が各所に使われている。

In the auxiliary chamber, highly saturated colors are used for the furniture and framework and Jacobsen's light fittings, called "Munkegard Lamp" after the school itself, can be seen on the ceiling.

大きなベースプレート付きのレバーハンドル。
A lever type handle with a large base plate.

教師机の引出しとトレイ。
The teacher's desk with drawers and slide out tray.

Munkegard Elementary School

体育館内部。

Inside the gymnasium.

校舎中央にある多目的ホール。現在は改修され、図書館として使われている。

The multipurpose hall located at the center of the school was renovated and is now used as a library.

北側校舎の2階にある特別教室のひとつの家庭科教室。

The home economics classroom belonging to a number of special purpose classrooms on the second floor of the northern building.

通路の入口部分。

The interior of the corridor entrance.

教室棟をつなぐ通路の両側には、異なるデザインの中庭が配されている。天井の片側だけに照明器具が配置されている。

This corridor connects the classroom buildings with courtyards of differing design on either side. Light fittings are only found one side of the ceiling.

Munkegard Elementary School **165**

北側に建つ教室棟の階段室。壁が黄色に彩色されている。

The stairwell leading to classrooms in the northern building. The walls were painted in yellow.

東西に延びる教室棟を南北につなぐ5本の通路の天井は、勾配部分が青や黄緑などで彩色されている。

The classroom buildings that extended east and west are networked by corridors which extended north and south. The sloped ceilings of the corridors are colorful in blues and greenish yellows and such.

通路の階段回り。壁が赤、黄緑、黄で大胆に彩色された通路の階段部分。地下は増築部分につながる。

The walls surrounding the corridor stairwells were painted in bold reds, yellow greens, and yellows. The stairs leading down connect to the basement annex.

ニュエア小学校 1964年／ロドオア

Nyager Elementary School ／ Nyager Skole, 1964, Rødovre

校庭側からの全景。
The view of the school from the schoolyard.

コペンハーゲンの6km西にロドオア市がある。ヤコブセンは「ムンケゴー小学校」(p.152) の経験を生かし、一戸建てが整然と並ぶ緑豊かな郊外住宅地にこの「ニュエア小学校」をつくった。

　全体は、南側の芝生のグラウンドに面してふたつのアスレチックルームとプールが並ぶスポーツゾーンと、北側の格子状の教室ゾーンから成る。教室ゾーンでは、南北に中廊下式の教室棟が3列と西側に特別教室棟が並ぶ。この4列の教室棟を東西に廊下と校庭が貫く。

　1層の黄色い煉瓦の壁の上に、天井面が中央に傾斜した逆三角形の断面形状の屋根をハイサイドライトのガラスで持ち上げているような外観である。この構造は「ロドオア中央図書館」(p.200) の屋根にも見られる。

　南北に通る中廊下の両脇の教室は東西のハイサイドライトからの自然光を採り込めるが、その光は廊下にまでは届かない。その代わりに、廊下には天井から乳白のアクリルの円筒を並べて、トップライトの自然光を採り込み拡散する仕組みを考案した。同様に、特別教室の廊下には自然光が標本の展示品を照らし出すガラスのショーケースを並べた。このアイデアは、「SASロイヤルホテル」(p.212) の今はなき「ウィンターガーデン」や、「デンマーク国立銀行」(p.278) の「ガラスケース」の上部から光を採り込む仕組みにつながっていく。

Rodovre City is located six kilometers west of Copenhagen. Jacobsen built "Nyager Elementary School," based on experience gained from "Munkegard Elementary School" (p.152). The latter is located in the residential area of the city's verdant outskirts where detached houses have been constructed in an orderly fashion.

　A sports area contains two athletics rooms and a pool. Lattice-shaped classroom zone contains three buildings, each of which has a central corridor, and a special classroom building. The four buildings were built with the longest side of each paralleling those of the other three. A corridor that extends east and west joins these four buildings to each other and the schoolyard.

　The view of these building is one of brick walls that are one story in height and glass windows above that encircles the building and supports the concave roof. The same construction can be seen in the "Rodovre Library" (p.200).

　The classrooms that open to corridors that extend north and south are illuminated by natural right that enters from east-west high side lights. However it does not reach to the corridors. Therefore, Jacobsen inserted milky-white acrylic cylinders into the roof and enable natural light brighten the interior of the building. He also installed glass showcases in the corridors attached to the special class rooms to let the light in. Later he repeated this idea at "Winter Garden" in "SAS Royal Hotel" (p.212) and the "glass case" at "Danmarks Nationalbank" (p.278).

広場より教室棟を望む。
Looking on to the classrooms from the playground.

学校入口の壁にはヤコブセンの名前が記された銘板が取り付けられている。

The school plaque which bore the name of Jacobsen affixed to the wall at the main entrance.

学校の正面入口。

The main entrance.

Nyager Elementary School

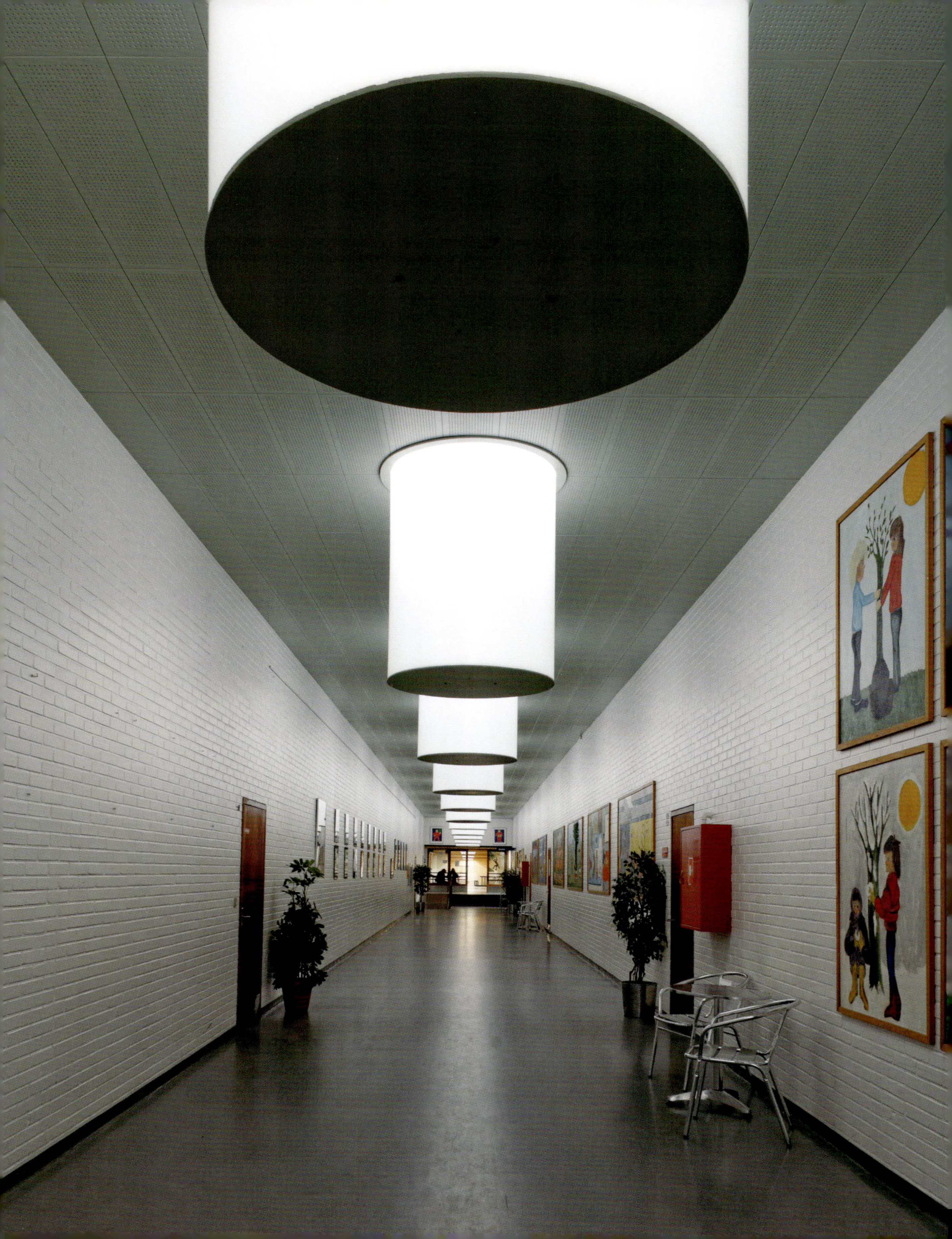

教室は2段採光で照度を確保している。左写真は校舎端部の低学年教室。2段採光に加え、妻面の高窓によって明るい空間。

With windows on two levels, the classrooms get plenty of light. The left picture shows the lower grade classroom at the far end of the building gets additional light from a clerestory of end panel.

Section of the corridor

左頁：事務棟通路。天井から光のシリンダーが下りる。曇天時には自然光に加えて、照明が加わる。

Left page: Large cylinders hang from the ceiling in the office building. In addition to letting in natural light, they also emit artificial light on overcast days.

Nyager Elementary School 173

図書室の入口受付。

The reception desk at the entrance to the library.

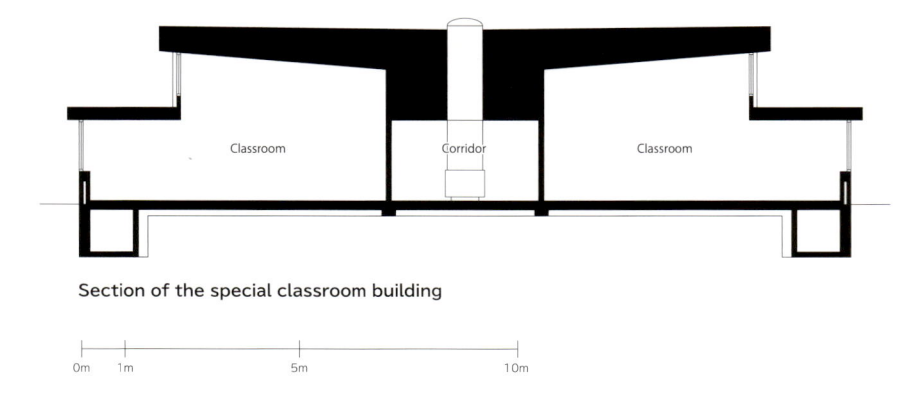

Section of the special classroom building

Classroom   Corridor   Classroom

0m 1m   5m   10m

インテリアがオリジナルで残されている図書室の一角。天井照明は「ムンケゴーランプ」。

A corner of the library where the original interior can be seen. The light fittings are "Munkegard Lamp."

教職員用の多目的スペース。

A free space for school staff.

頑丈なドアハンドル2種。上のドアハンドルは使用時に手前に起こす。

Two sturdy door handles. When occupied, the door handle above locks in a downward position.

教室内のシステム化された仕切り壁。必要な箇所にビルトインされた流し台などが取り付けられる。

Systemized dividing walls like the one in this classroom are used to attach built-in sinks and other fixtures.

教室棟通路。黄色のパネル部分に必要に応じて手洗いなどが取り付く。

The corridor outside the classrooms. Fittings like hand wash basins can be attached as necessary to the yellow walls.

保健室の待合室とその隣にある児童のための歯磨きコーナー。児童の虫歯予防が盛んな北欧では、校内に歯磨きコーナーが設けられている。2段採光で奥まで明るい。

The school infirmary waiting room and teeth brushing corner. Such corners are found in Scandinavian schools where an emphasis is placed on oral health. Windows on two levels light up the whole area.

Normalklasse - Perspektive 20-10.00

普通教室のスケッチパース。
A perspective drawing of a regular class.

Nyager Elementary School

事務棟の一角にはトップライトのあるプラントコーナーがある。
In the office building there is a plant corner lit up by a top light.

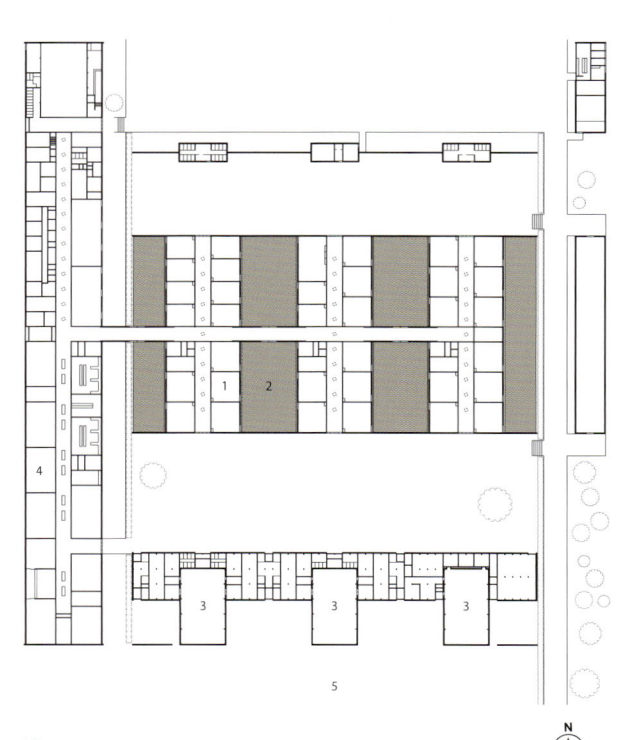

1. Standard classrooms
2. Courtyards
3. Sports area
4. Special classrooms
5. Playground

Plan

0m 10m 20m   50m

右頁：教室棟や事務棟の間には緑地が配置され、近くの植栽で目を休ませることができる。

Right page: Looking at the plants in the green spaces in between the classrooms and office building provides a moment of relaxation.

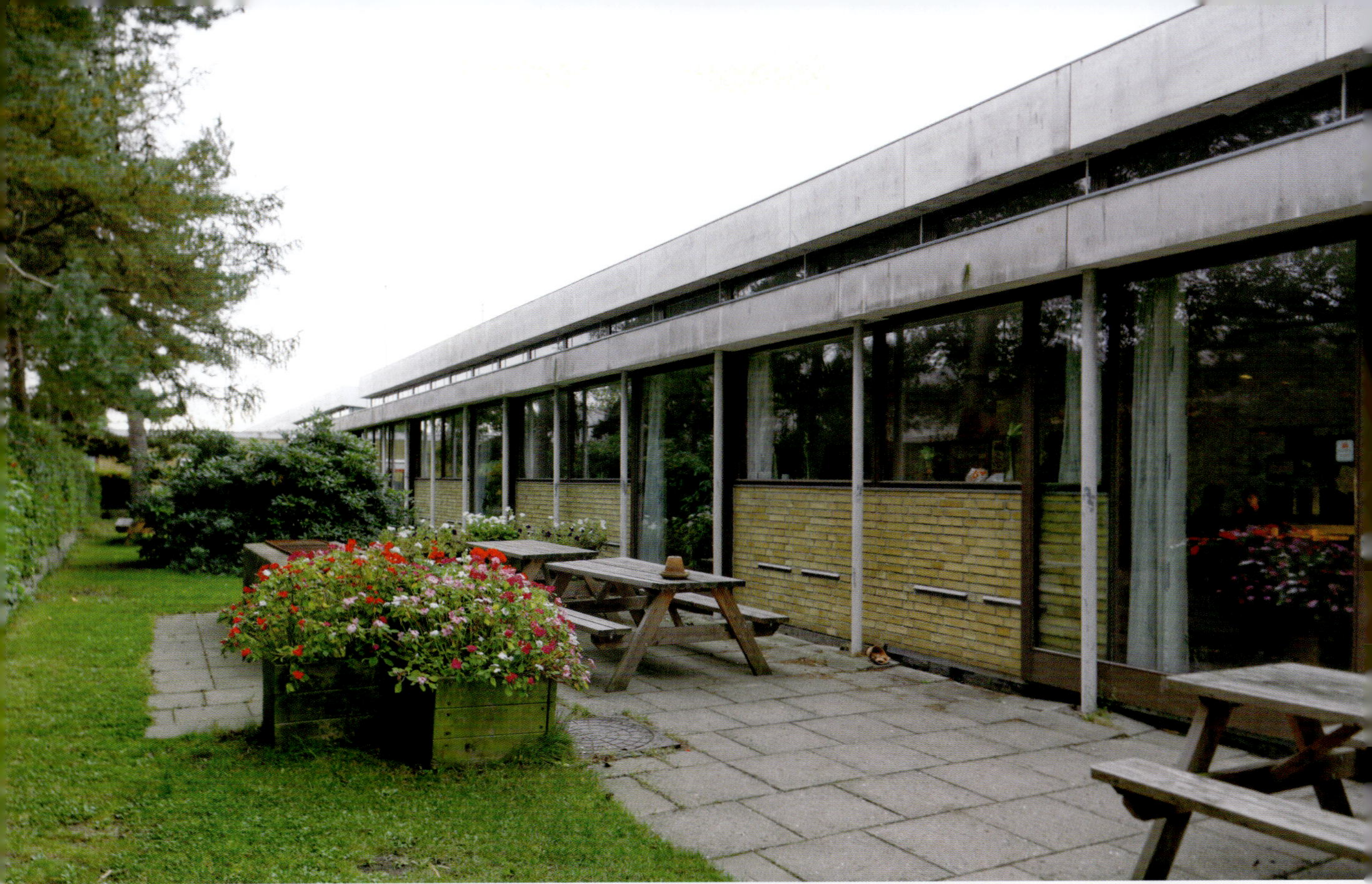

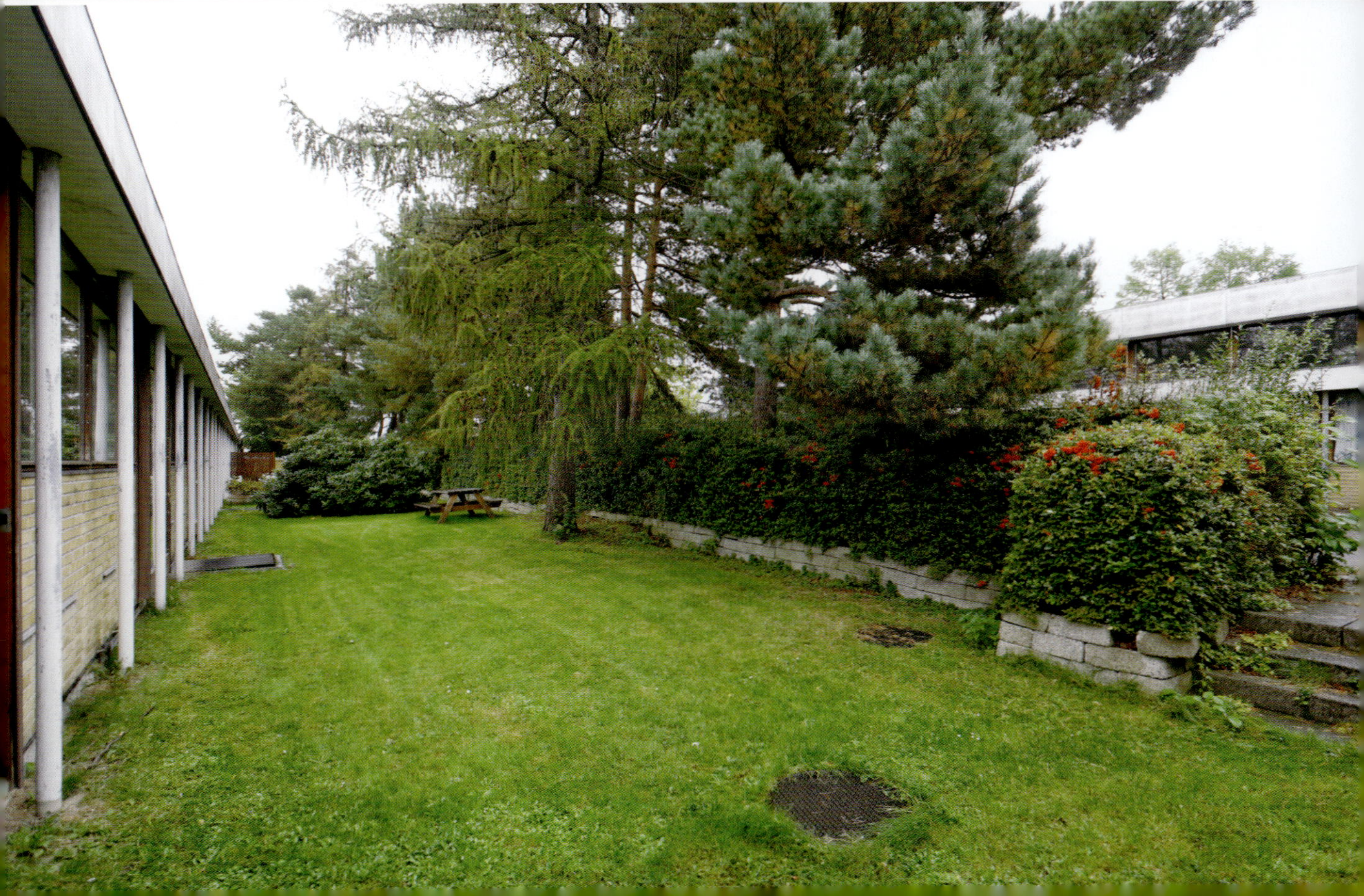

ラウンド・ハウス 1956年／シェランズ・オッデ
Round House ／ Det Runde Hus, 1956, Sjællands Odde

スモーク・ハウス(p.116)に隣接して建てられたオーナー、レオ・ヘンリクセンの自邸。南側に広大な緑地が広がる。左手奥の赤い屋根は、スモーク・ハウスの冷蔵倉庫。

Leo Henriksen's own house, built adjacent to the Fish Smokehouse (p.116), with an extensive green space on the south side. The red rooftop on the left behind his house is the cold warehouse of Fish Smokehouse.

「スモーク・ハウス」(p.116) の敷地の一角に、工場のオーナーであるレオ・ヘンリクセン氏の住宅がある。ヤコブセンは「スモーク・ハウス」と同様、1943年にこの家を設計したが、竣工は13年後になった。しかしヤコブセンにとっては、1929年に設計した「未来の家」を27年後に実現した、と言った方がむしろ正しいだろう。それくらいこの家のプランは「未来の家」を連想させる。

「未来の家」は海と陸の境に位置していたが、「ラウンド・ハウス」は岬の崖の上にある。建設に選ばれた場所は、生垣がカーブを描く、少し窪んだ平地であった。ヤコブセンはこのカーブを海と陸の境界線と見立て、円形の住宅を敷地に置いた。

「未来の家」と同様に、中央にホールがあり、内円と外円の間に各部屋を時計回りに配置している。北側の12時から1時の方向に玄関があり、1時から6時までにベッドルームを4室並べ、6時から9時にかけてリビング、10時半までダイニング、そしてキッチンへと続いて一巡する。リビングは、ホールの4分の1を切り取るように広がっていて、ダイニングとの境の仕切り壁の室内と屋外に暖炉が埋め込まれている。

夏の間、「スモーク・ハウス」に燻製を求めて多くの人が集まるが、「ラウンド・ハウス」は、カーブを描く生垣に守られるように年中静かに佇んでいる。

In one corner of the site of "Fish Smokehouse" (p.116), there is the house of Leo Henriksen, who was the owner of the factory. When Jacobsen designed this house in 1943, he intended it to be the same as "Fish Smokehouse," but it was completed 13 years later. It is also accurate to say that Jacobsen completed "House of the Future" 27 years after he designed it in 1929. Much in the plan of this house reminds us of "House of the Future."

Although "House of the Future" is located on the coast

南側の庭より、リビングルーム面を見る。建物外周の庇は、のちに取り付けられたもの。
View of the living room of his house from the garden on the south side. The canopy was added later.

between land and sea, "Round House" is located at the edge of a cape. The original site was slightly recessed land where the hedge formed a curve. Jacobsen used these plants like the border of land and sea and built "Round House" in a circular form.

As in "House of the Future," there is a hall in the center circle. Each room is located between the inner circle and the outer circle. An entrance is at positions numbers twelve and one of the clock. Four bedrooms occupy positions one to six in a clockwise direction. The living room and dining rooms are at positions six to nine and nine to ten thirty, respectively. The kitchen accounts for the remaining positions. The central living room is occupied one fourth. Fireplaces are installed on outside and inside of the partition between the living room and dining room.

In the summer, many people gathered at "Fish Smoke house" to purchase smoking fish, "Round House" stands quietly throughout the year protected behind the curved hedge.

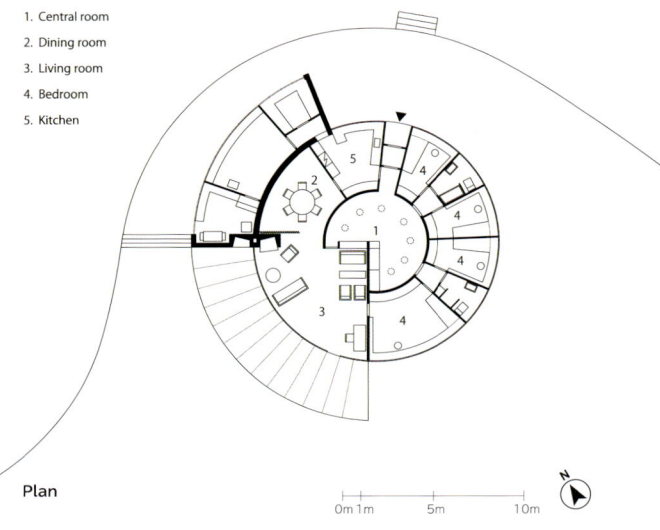

1. Central room
2. Dining room
3. Living room
4. Bedroom
5. Kitchen

Plan

0m 1m   5m   10m

伸びやかに広がる軽快な庇のテラス回りは円形住宅ならではのもの。
The circular deck with the large canopy has an air of openness.

テラスの一角には食卓コーナーが設けられている。
A corner of the deck has a dining space.

西側に付属するサービス諸室。
Service rooms on the west side of the house.

テラスの一角には、外部用の暖炉が設けられている。
Outdoor fireplace can be found on the deck.

北側のエントランス回り。
Entrance of the house on the north side.

Round House

テラスからリビングルームを見る。左端は屋外用暖炉。室内からは、眼前に庭園がパノラミックに広がる。
View of the living room from the deck, with the outdoor fireplace on the left corner. One can enjoy the panoramic view of the garden from the living room.

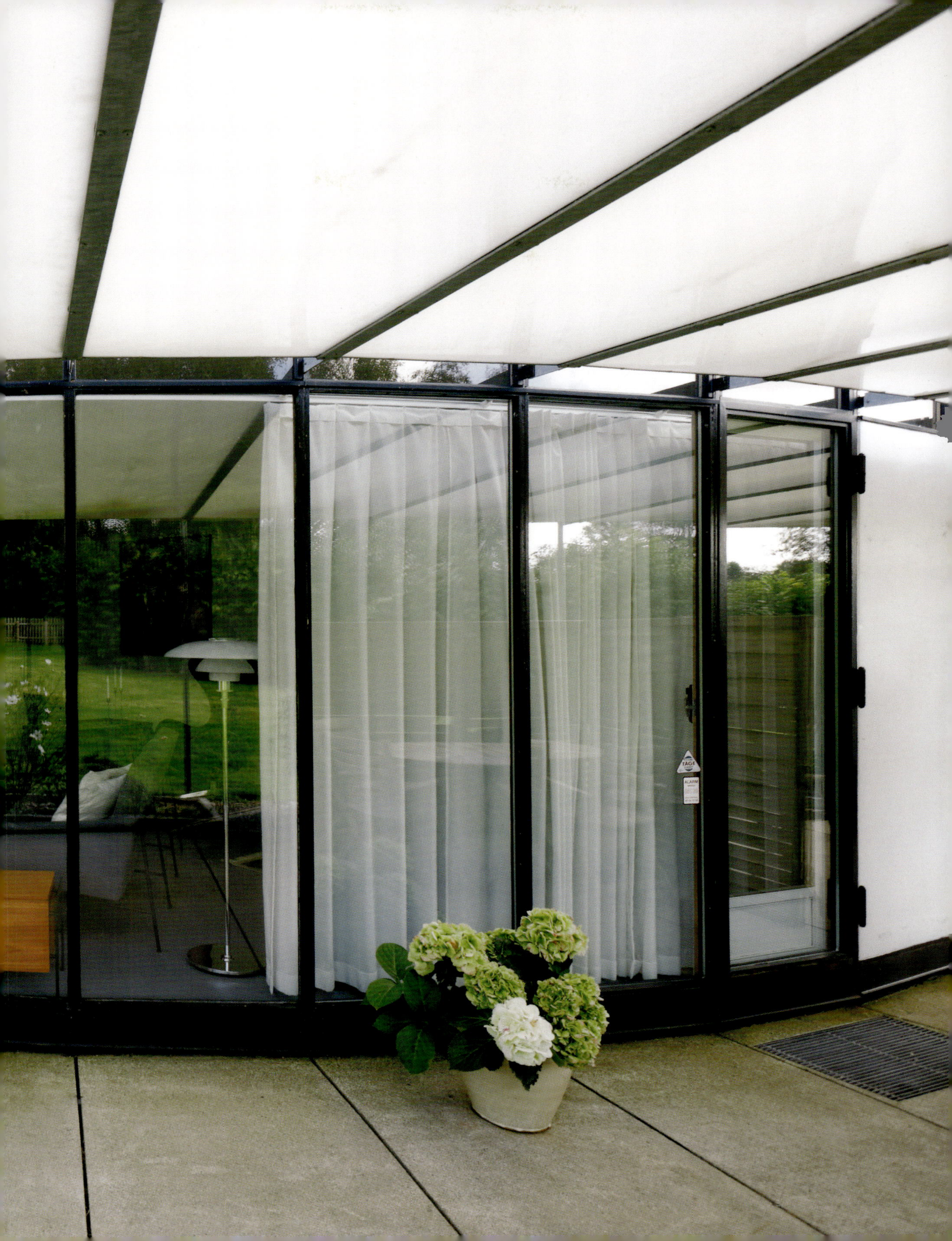

ロドオア市庁舎 1956年／ロドオア

Rodovre City Hall ／ Rødovre Rådhus, 1956, Rødovre

東側プラザからの全景。カーテンウォールによる簡潔なファサード。カーテンウォールの形状は SAS ロイヤルホテル(p.212)でリファインされる。

Panoramic view from the plaza on the east side. The curtain wall creates a simple facade. The curtain wall design would later be refined on SAS Royal Hotel (p.212).

「オーフス市庁舎」(p.78)と「スレロド市庁舎」(p.102)に続く、第2次世界大戦後に、最初にヤコブセンが手掛けた市庁舎である。コペンハーゲンの「SASロイヤルホテル」(p.212)から西に6km、ロドオア市の「ニュエア小学校」(p.168)からは1kmほど南に位置する。

敷地の中央に「ロドオア市庁舎」、西側に広大な芝生の広場、東側にプラザを介して「ロドオア中央図書館」(p.200)が建つ。14m×91mという細長い平面形状で地上3層の本館の事務棟は長辺全面をガラスカーテンウォールとし、短辺はどっしりとした窓のない石の壁で囲んだ。一方、13m×22mの平面形状で地上2層分の高さのある市議会の議場棟は短辺をガラス、長辺を石の壁とした。ヤコブセン自身がマッチ箱と比喩したふたつの異なるプロポーションの直方体は長さ13mのガラスの廊下でつながっている。

エントランスホールでは、天井から吊られた軽やかなスチール階段が強烈なアクセントとなっている。2層吹抜けの市議会議場には、121灯のレフランプが上向きに天井面を照らし出し、有孔ボードの壁面には「シティホールクロック」がデザインされた。このカーテンウォールの繊細なディテールは、やがて「SASロイヤルホテル」の高層ビルのカーテンウォールに、そしてエントランスの吊階段とレフランプの間接照明は「デンマーク国立銀行」(p.278)に受け継がれていく。

So far, Jacobsen had built "Aarhus City Hall" (p.78) and "Sollerod City Hall" (p.102). He undertook "Rodovre City Hall" (p.78) after World War II. It is located in the west at a distance of six kilometers from "SAS Royal Hotel" (p.212) and in the south one kilometer from "Nyager Elementary School" (p.168).

"Rodovre City Hall" is in the center of its site. A large square lawn is to its west, and an open space and "Rodovre Library" (p.200) to its east. The three-story main building, which contains offices, is rectangular in shape. It is 91 meters by 14 meters. The long sides are covered by a glass curtain wall. The ends are covered by a windowless, stone wall. In contrast, the smaller building is 22 meters by 13 meters, two-stories in height and contains the City Council Chamber. The finishing is the opposite of that used for the main building. These two buildings differ in proportion Jacobsen spoke of them as matchboxes that were connected by a 13-meter glass corridor.

In the entrance hall, a light steel staircase that is suspended from the ceiling makes a strong impression on visitors. In the City Hall with its atrium, which is two-stories in height, 121 ref-lamps light the ceiling. Jacobsen designed a "City Hall Clock," which now hangs on the perforated wall. The fine details of the curtain wall were used later in the curtain wall of "SAS Royal Hotel," whereas the suspended staircase and the indirect lighting using ref-lamps were also used in "Danmarks Nationalbank" (p.278).

西側緑地広場からの全景。事務棟と議場棟が渡り廊下でつながる。

Panoramic view from the green open space to the west. The office building and the City Council Chamber building are connected by a corridor.

東側エントランスの2段になった庇。軒裏は薄いモスグリーンと赤に塗り分けられている。ここでも天井照明は「ムンケゴーランプ」が用いられている。

The double canopy of the east entrance. The undersides were painted in different colors, light moss green and red. "Munkegard Lamp" are used for the ceiling lighting.

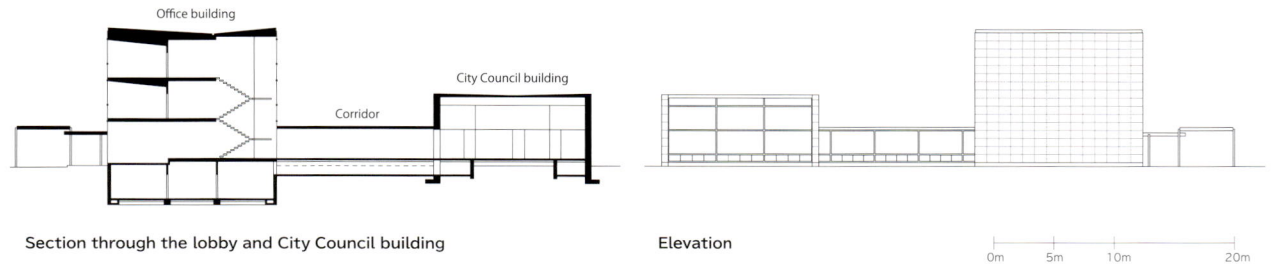

Section through the lobby and City Council building

Elevation

0m 5m 10m 20m

エントランスホールの吹抜けにあるスチールの吊階段。ガラスカーテンウォールの先には議場への渡り廊下が見える。

The suspended steel staircase in the entrance hall atrium. The corridor to the City Council Chamber is visible through the glass curtain wall.

スチールのササラ桁が軽快な印象の吊階段。ヤコブセンの他の階段同様、吊材は赤く塗られている。

The steel stringers give the suspended staircase an airy feel. As in Jacobsen's other staircases, the suspending rods are painted red.

この階段のディテールは、のちのデンマーク国立銀行(p. 278)でリファインされる。

These stair details were later refined in Danmarks Nationalbank (p.278).

Rodovre City Hall

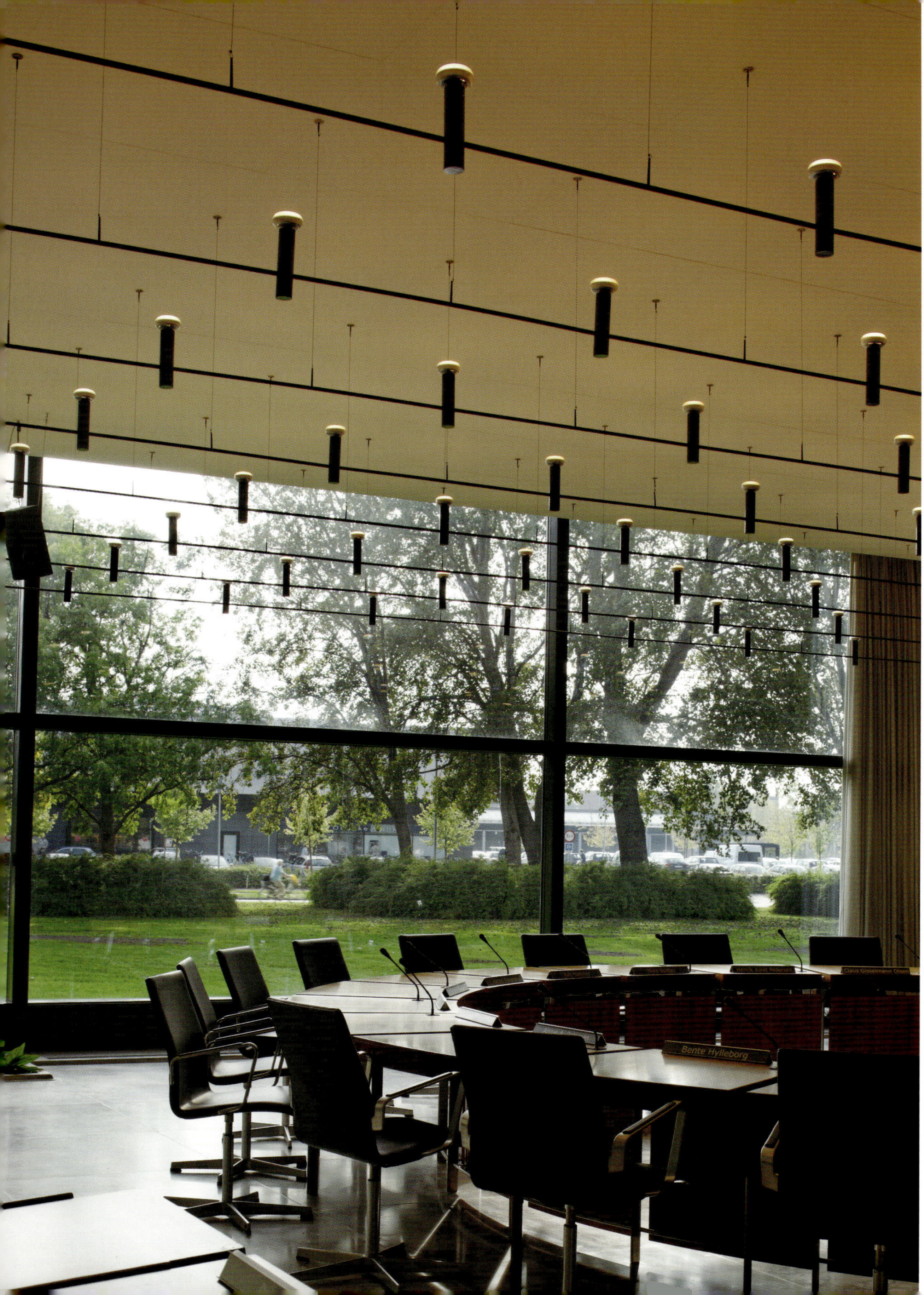
Bente Hylleborg

議場全景。レフランプを天井に向けただけのシンプルな照明は、のちにデンマーク国立銀行でさらに大規模に展開される。

Full view of the City Council Chamber. The simple system of ref-lamps facing the ceiling was later developed on a larger scale in Danmarks Nationalbank.

市議会議場の内観パース。

A perspective of the interior of the City Council Chamber.

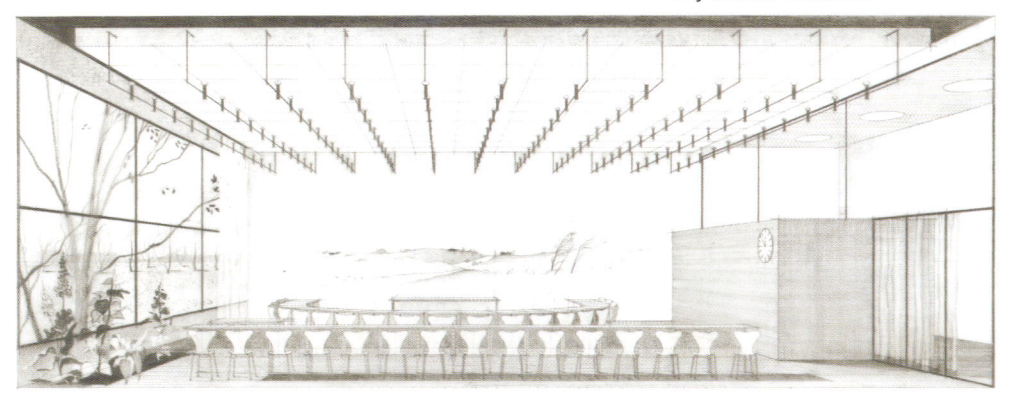

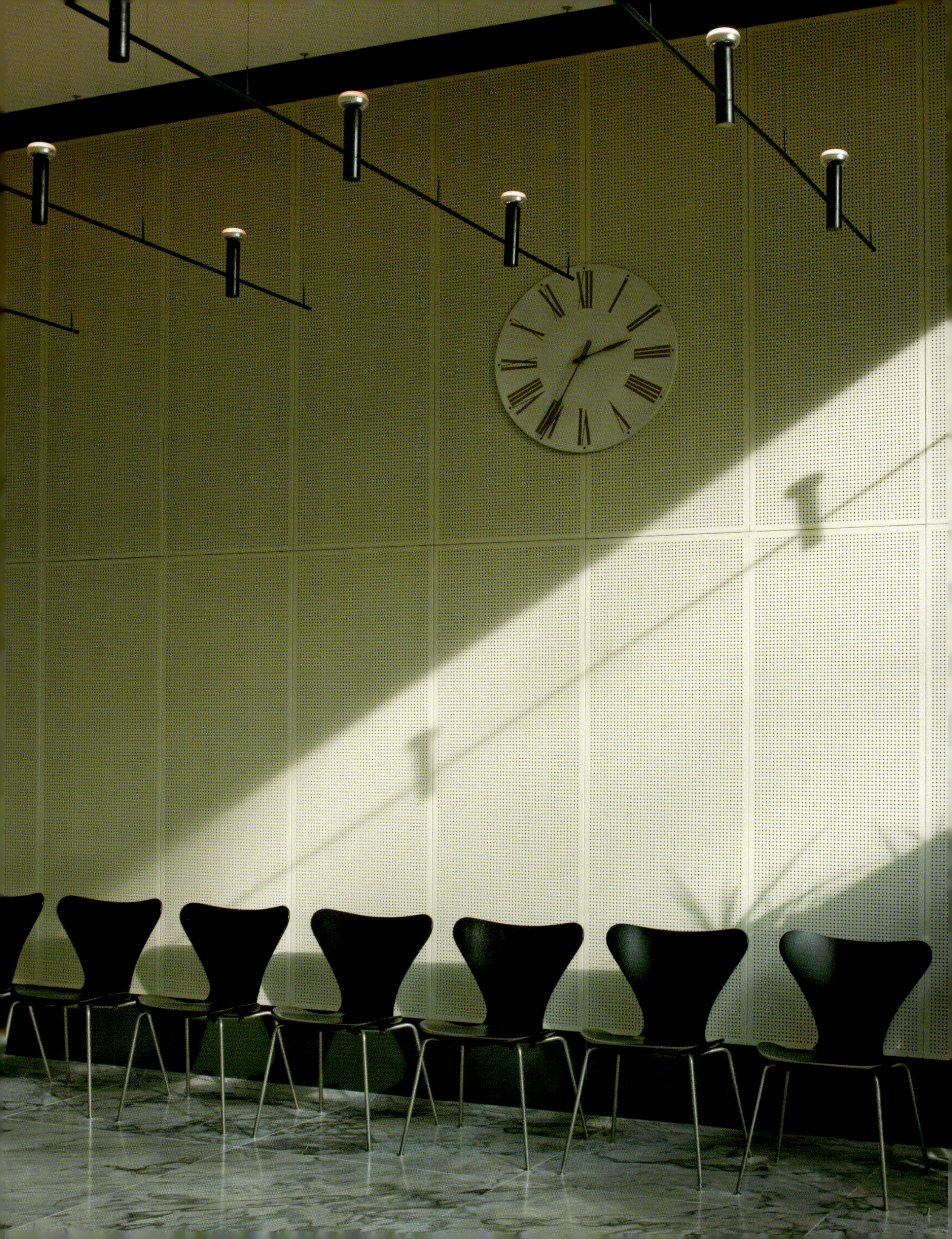

左頁：議場の側面壁ディテール。明るいモスグリーンの有孔ボードに、ヤコブセンデザインの「シティホールクロック」が取り付けられている。

Left page: Detail of the City Council Chamber side wall. Attached to the perforated board painted bright moss green is the Jacobsen-designed "City Hall Clock."

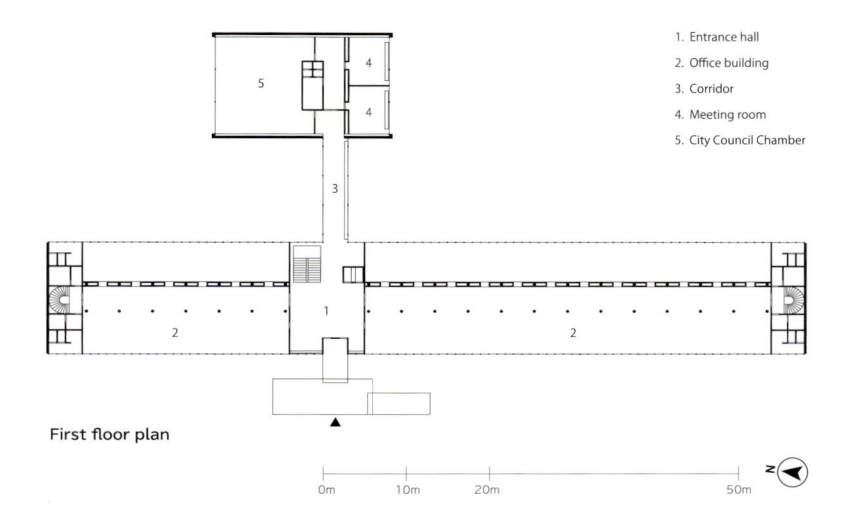

1. Entrance hall
2. Office building
3. Corridor
4. Meeting room
5. City Council Chamber

Section

First floor plan

0m 10m 20m 50m

1階の通路。間仕切り壁の前に並ぶスツールと背もたれ。通路の先は建物端部の螺旋階段。

First floor corridor. Arranged along the partition wall are stools and back supports. Beyond the corridor is the spiral staircase at the end of the building.

Rodovre City Hall

通路両端の半円の螺旋階段見上げ。段裏とササラを赤く塗っている。

The view up through the spiral staircase that is at both ends of the corridor. The underside of the stairs and the stringers were painted red.

通常の螺旋階段にはない段裏の赤い曲面が美しい。

The beautiful red curved surface under the stairs, something not usually seen on spiral staircases.

2階から見た螺旋階段。手摺の下端が階段のササラを隠す位置まで下げられ、段裏の曲面を薄く繊細に見せている。

The spiral staircase as seen from the second floor. The base of the handrails hide the stringers and make the curved surface of the staircase seem slim and delicate.

ロドオア中央図書館　1969年／ロドオア
Rodovre Library／Rødovre Bibliotek, 1969, Rødovre

ロドオア市庁舎(p.188)の入口からプラザを挟んで、市庁舎と軸線を通して建つ中央図書館の入口。

The view from the Rodovre City Hall (p.188) entrance to the plaza and the entrance to the Library, which are directly aligned.

「ロドオア中央図書館」は正面玄関を「ロドオア市庁舎」(p.188)と広場を介して向かい合うように配置された。図書館の東側にある長さ183mの「ロングアパートメントハウス」(1960)も同じくヤコブセンの設計による。

ガラスのカーテンウォールの市庁舎や細長いアパートとは対照的に、76m×46mの平面形状で平屋の中央図書館は、平面的に市庁舎の3倍以上の奥行きがあり、入口以外には開口部がない高さ4mの石の壁で四方を囲んだ。公園内の公共施設としての一体感は、壁の仕上げが市庁舎と同じノルウェー産の大理石であることによって保たれている。

全体は、中央のレクチャー・ホール、北側の子供のための図書館、南側の一般利用の図書館という3つのゾーンから成る。中央の正方形のレクチャー・ホールの屋根が「ニュエア小学校」(p.168)のように一段高く浮いているのは、ハイサイドライトの大きなガラス面からホール内部に自然光を採り込むためである。ふたつの図書館のゾーンを東西に3つに分割するように中庭を配置し、自然の光と風と緑を閲覧室にも採り込んだ。閲覧室の天井には「ムンケゴーランプ」が規則的に並び、その中に散見される円形の大きな照明は、受付、ラウンジ、地下階へ続く螺旋階段などの要所を照らし出すトップライトである。壁には「AJブラケットランプ」が並び、ラウンジには「スワンチェア」や「3300シリーズ」のソファなどヤコブセンのプロダクトが集結した。

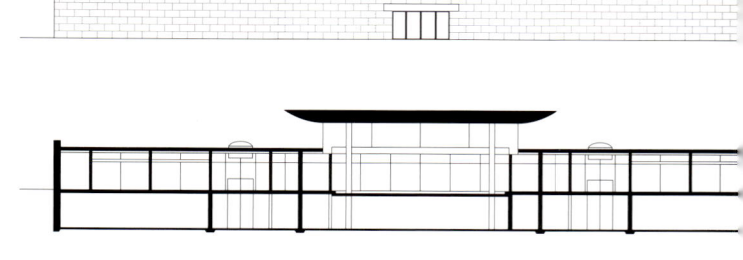

プラザの緑道に沿って建つ中央図書館。暗褐色の自然石で囲まれた外観。中央の高くなった部分はレクチャーホール。

The City Library, built alongside the pedestrian path of the plaza. The exterior is encased by dark brown fieldstone. The central tall structure is the lecture hall.

Elevation

Longitudinal section
0m 5m 10m 20m

The main entrance of "Rodovre Library" is facing to the plaza and "Rodovre City Hall" (p.188). Jacobsen also designed the "Long Apartment House" (1960), which is 183 meters in length and located on the eastern side of the library.

In contrast to the city hall with its glass curtain walls and narrow offices apartments, the library is a flat, one-story building that is 76 meters by 46 meters and with a depth that is more than triple that of the city hall. The library is encased by Norwegian marble stone wall that is four meters in height and with an opening only as the entrance. It provides a sense of unity with the public facilities in the park, because the wall of the library is finished in as is the city hall.

The site comprises three zones: a lecture hall in the center, a library for children on the north side and a library for the public on the south side. The square roof of the lecture hall is higher than that of the surrounding roof to admit natural light through the large glass panels of the clerestory, like that at "Nyager Elementary School" (p.168). Jacobsen divided a zone, which includes two libraries, into three parts, and created courtyards that receive natural light and wind and make it possible to have plants in the reading room. "Munkegard Lamp" line the ceiling of the reading room. The larger circular lamps are top lighted to illuminate the reception area, lounge and spiral staircases leading to the basement. In addition, "AJ Bracket Lamp" lines the wall and Jacobsen's products, such as "The Swan" and the "3300 Series" of sofas, have been assembled in the lounge.

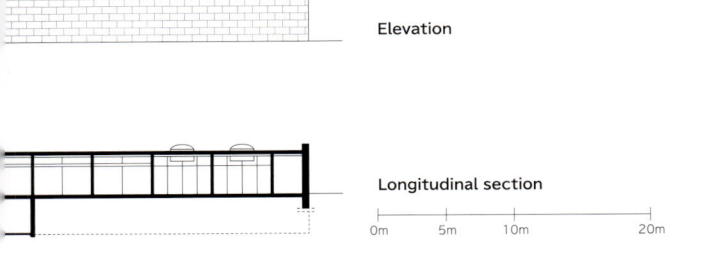

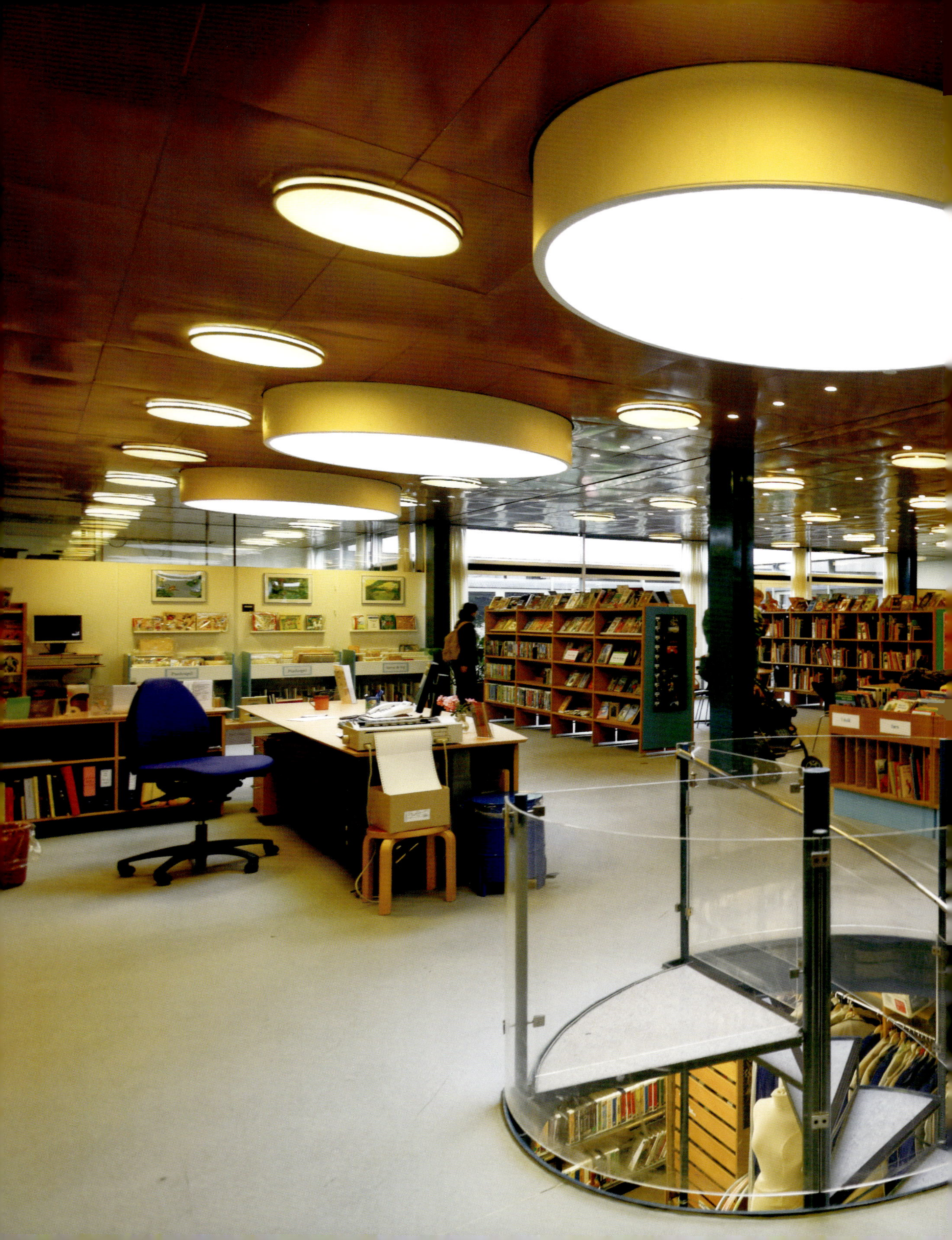

広々とした児童図書館。乗り物などの遊具とともに、ヤコブセンデザインの水色の子供用椅子が置かれている。天井には大小さまざまな照明器具が並ぶ。螺旋階段上部の大きな照明はトップライト兼用。

The spacious children's library. It contains toys and the Jacobsen-designed light blue chairs for children. The ceiling has a variety of lighting fixtures, large and small. The large light above the spiral staircase doubles as a top light.

入口脇ラウンジコーナーのスワンチェア。
The Swan in the lounge adjacent to the entrance.

館内に３か所ある地下への螺旋階段。透明な手摺壁で存在感をなくしている。

One of three internal spiral staircases leading to the basement. The transparent handrail wall is inconspicuous.

コーナーのラウンジスペース。正面奥に中庭が見える。
A corner lounge space. The courtyard can be seen in the background.

秋の紅葉した中庭。5か所ある中庭はすべて植栽が異なり、利用者の目をしばし休ませてくれる。

Autumn leaves in one of the courtyard. Each of the five courtyards has different plants that give visitor's eyes a break.

通路より中庭を見る。

A courtyard seen from the corridor.

中央のレクチャーホール。四周の高窓から自然光が差し込む。

The lecture hall, centrally located in the building. Natural light enters through the clerestories on four sides.

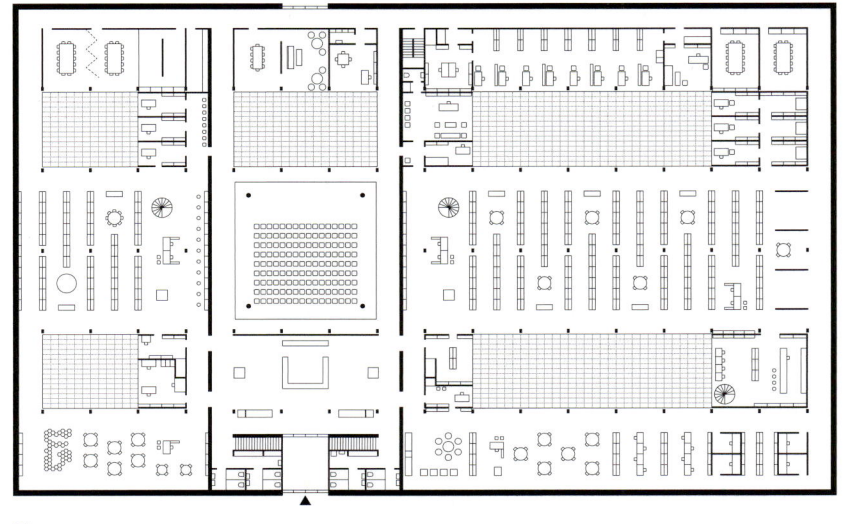

Plan

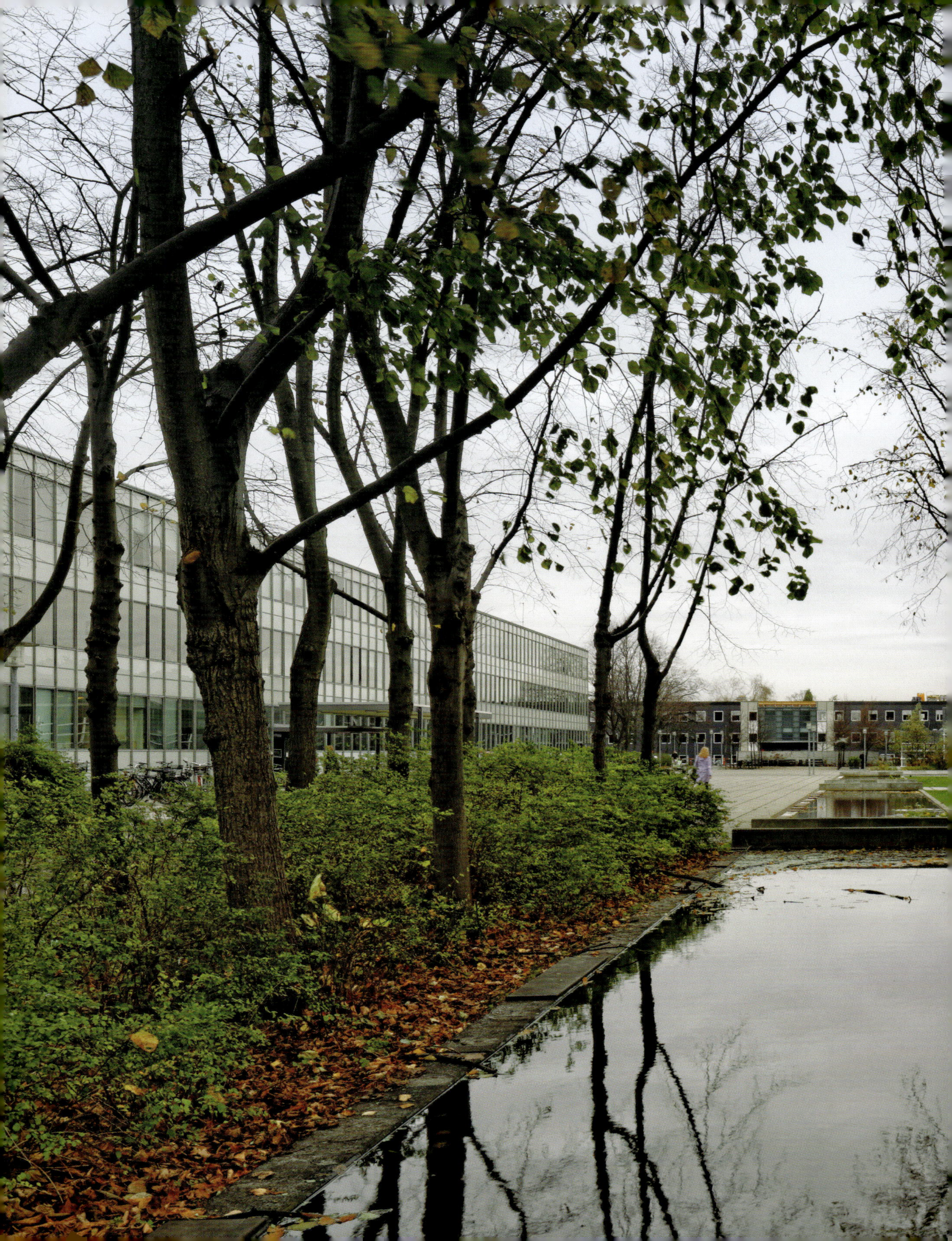

プラザを挟んで市庁舎(左)、中央図書館(右)が向かい合う。

The plaza is sandwiched between the City Hall (left) and the Library (right).

SASロイヤルホテル　1960年／コペンハーゲン

SAS Royal Hotel, Now: Radisson Blu Royal Hotel, 1960, København

ヤコブセンが5年の歳月を掛けて完成させた、デンマーク初の高層ビルである。コペンハーゲン中央駅とチボリ公園を眼下に一望する位置にある。当時最先端の全面ガラスのカーテンウォールを用いた。未来のホテル環境を創出するというコンセプトに基づき、内部もすべてヤコブセンがデザインした。家具、照明器具、カーテン、カーペット、テーブルウェア、ドアノブ、水栓まで建築家が手掛けた例は他に類を見ない。まさにトータルデザインの殿堂である。

　2001年に当初のコンセプトを継承しつつ全面改装を済ませ、各部屋には新しい「セブンチェア」や「スワンチェア」が置かれた。唯一、606号室は「アルネ・ヤコブセン・スイートと名付けられ、建築当時のままの色合いと内装が保たれている。月に何件か宿泊予約が入るほか、ヤコブセンのトータルデザインを見たいという見学客がひきもきらない。主室の右手には灰色がかったブルーグリーンのソファ、「エッグチェア」、テーブル、「ドロップチェア」が置かれている。左手には同色の2台のベッドがあり、カーテンで居間と仕切る仕組みだ。水平連続窓と淡い緑色の壁面の下部をぐるりと木の腰壁が覆う。この中にキャンチレバーの化粧台とベッドサイドテーブル、空調設備、可動式の照明が納められている。

Jacobsen completed the first high-rise building in Denmark in five years. From the top floor, you can see Copenhagen Central Station and The Tivoli Gardens below. He used only glass curtain walls, which ware the state-of-the-art at that time. Based on the concept of creating the hotel environment of the future, he designed all interior furniture. This included lighting, curtains, carpets, tableware, doorknobs and water faucets. This is just like the Hall of Fame for which the architects designed all elements. It is the total design unlike any other.

　In 2001, the hotel was renovated entirely in keeping with a new and original concept. Each room has equipped with "The Seven" and "The Swan." Room 606, which is named the "Arne Jacobsen Suite," is the only room remaining in its original colors and interior that was developed when the building has originally constructed. Some customers stay in this room several times per month and other visitors often drop into this room to see Jacobsen's total design. There are a sofa, a table, "The Egg" and "The Drop" that were colored in grayish-blue-green on the right side of the main room. On the left side, there are two beds in the same colors. The bedroom and living room can be divided by curtains. A wooden knee wall extends across the entire whole room below the large horizontal window and bright green walls. A dressing table and cantilever bedside tables, air conditioner and movable lighting are attached to the knee wall.

左頁：南東側外観。モスグリーンの低層部にガラスカーテンウォールの高層部が載る。

Left page: A View from the southeast side. The high-rise building with glass curtain wall sits atop the moss green low-rise building.

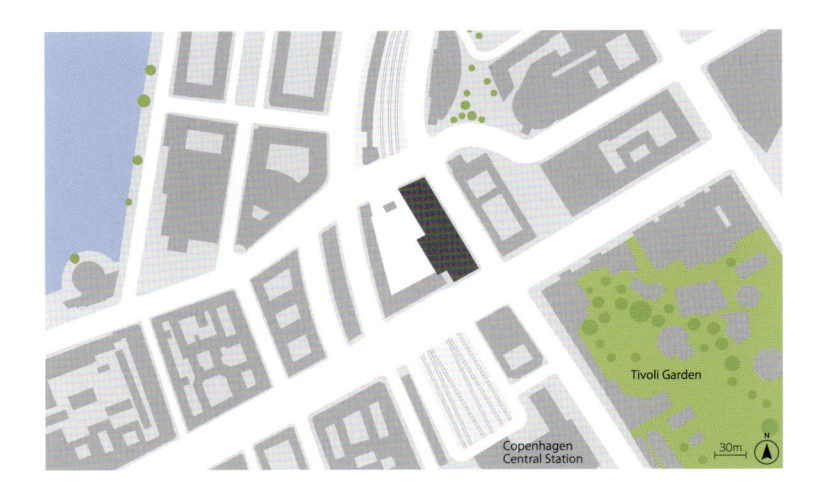

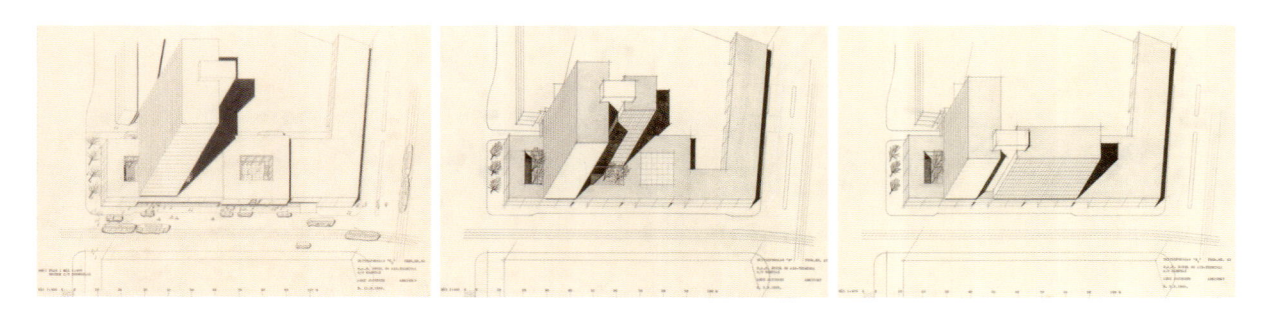

上：1955年8月付の低層棟および高層棟ブロックのボリュームスタディ。

Top: Drawings bearing the date August 1955. Volume studies of low-rise and high-rise building.

中：606号室アルネ・ヤコブセン・スイートに飾られている1957年付の完成予想透視図。この時点では、高層棟の側面はロドオア市庁舎と同じように石張りの仕上げであった。

Middle: A perspective drawing bearing a date of 1957 is hanging in the Arne Jacobsen Suite. It was planned that the side of the high-rise building would be finished with stones, like Rodovre City Hall.

下：ヤコブセンは高層棟のファサードを念入りにスタディした。

Bottom: Jacobsen frequently studied the facade of the high-rise building.

214 Arne Jacobsen

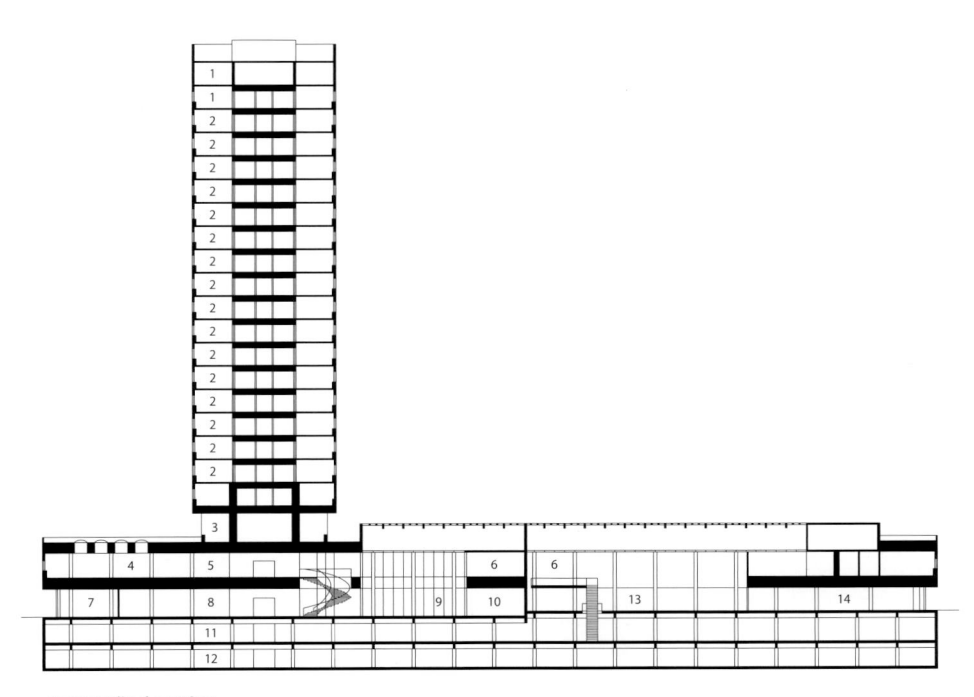

Longitudinal section

1. Suites
2. Guest rooms
3. Administration
4. Restaurant
5. Vestibule
6. Bar
7. Shops
8. Hotel lobby
9. Winter garden
10. Snack bar seating area
11. Service basement
12. Parking basement
13. Passenger hall
14. Travel agency

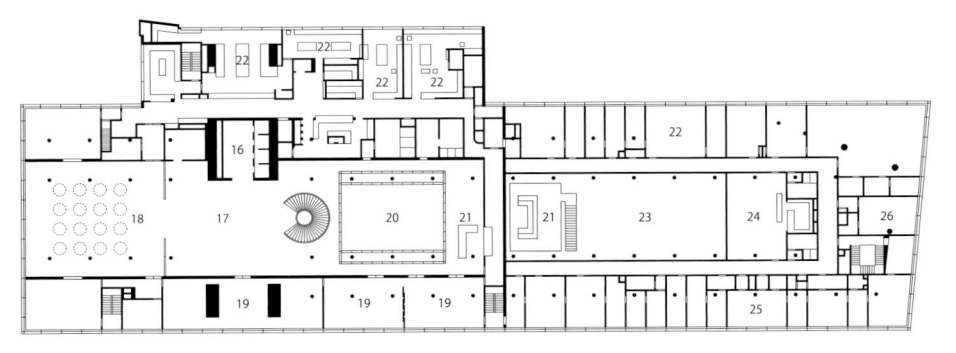

Second floor plan

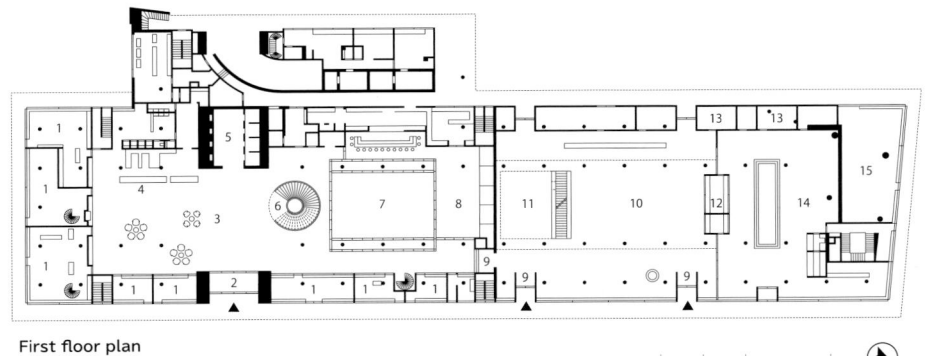

First floor plan

1. Shops
2. Entrance to hotel
3. Hotel lobby
4. Reception
5. Elevators
6. Stair
7. Winter garden
8. Snack bar seating area
9. Entrances to air terminal
10. Passenger hall
11. Stair to bar and basement
12. Bank
13. Offices
14. Travel agency
15. Car rental
16. Elevators
17. Vestibule
18. Main dining room
19. Sitting rooms
20. Opening to winter garden
21. Bar
22. Kitchen
23. Open to passenger hall
24. Staff dining room
25. Airline offices
26. Conference room

0m 5m 10m 20m

SAS Royal Hotel

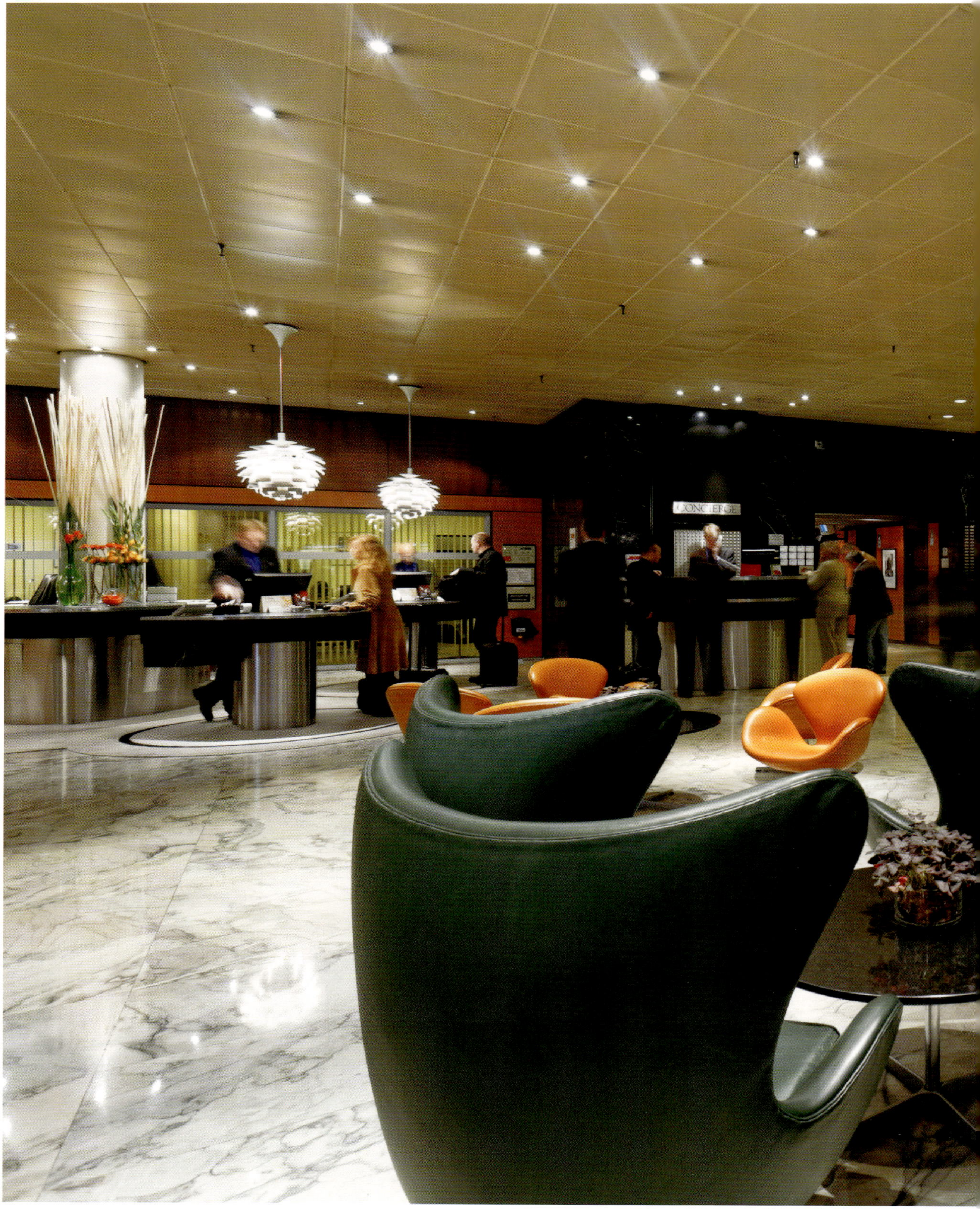
CONCIERGE

ホテルのロビー回り。広いロビー空間の中で、エッグチェアがセミプライベートな場をつくり出す。

The lobby of the hotel. The Eggs create semi-private space within the large lobby.

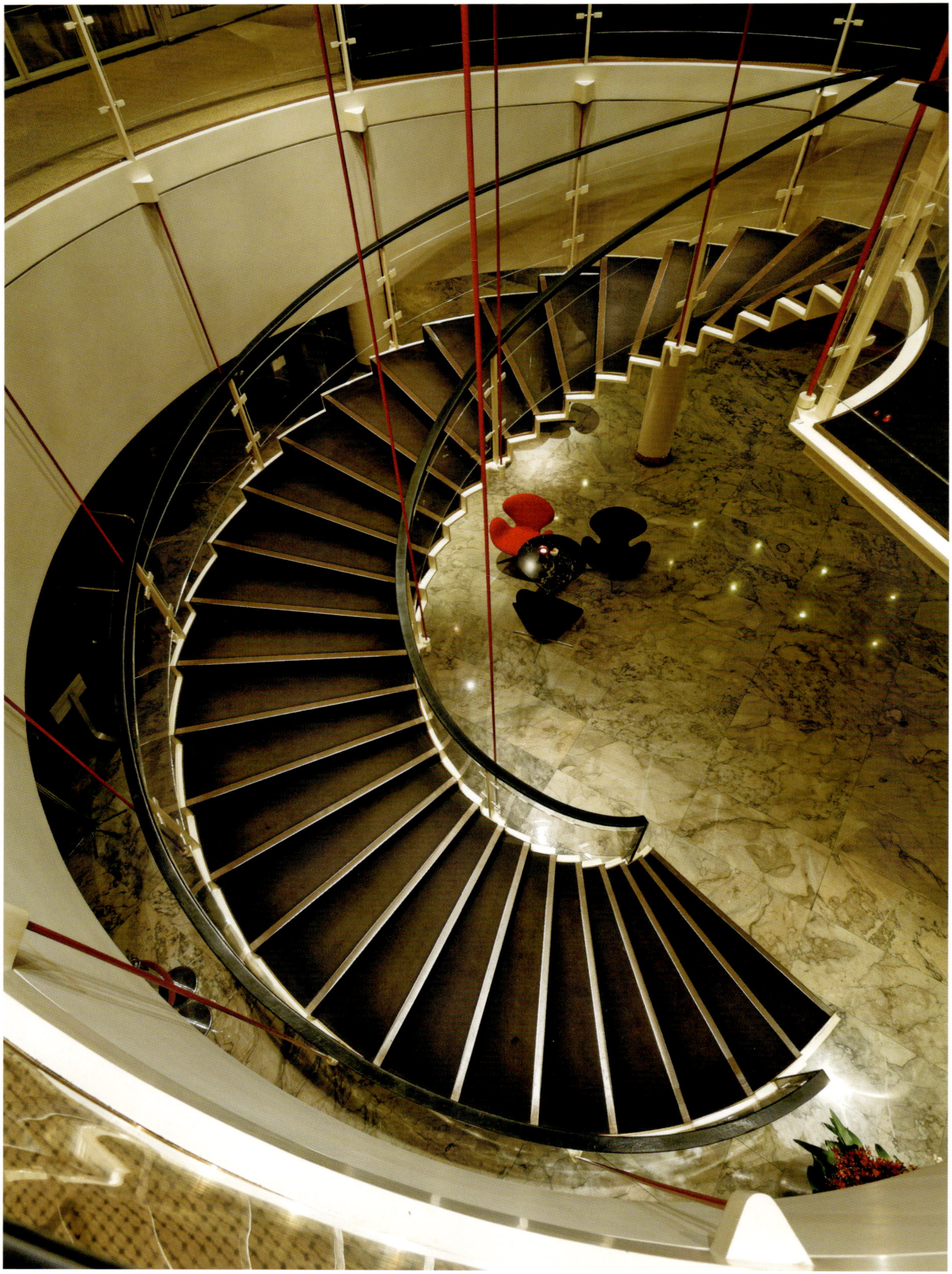

1階と2階をつなぐ螺旋階段。赤く塗られたスチール棒で天井から吊られ、軽快な浮遊感を演出している。

The sprial staircase between first and second floors. Suspended from the ceiling by red steel rods, this staircase has a sense of lightness and floating.

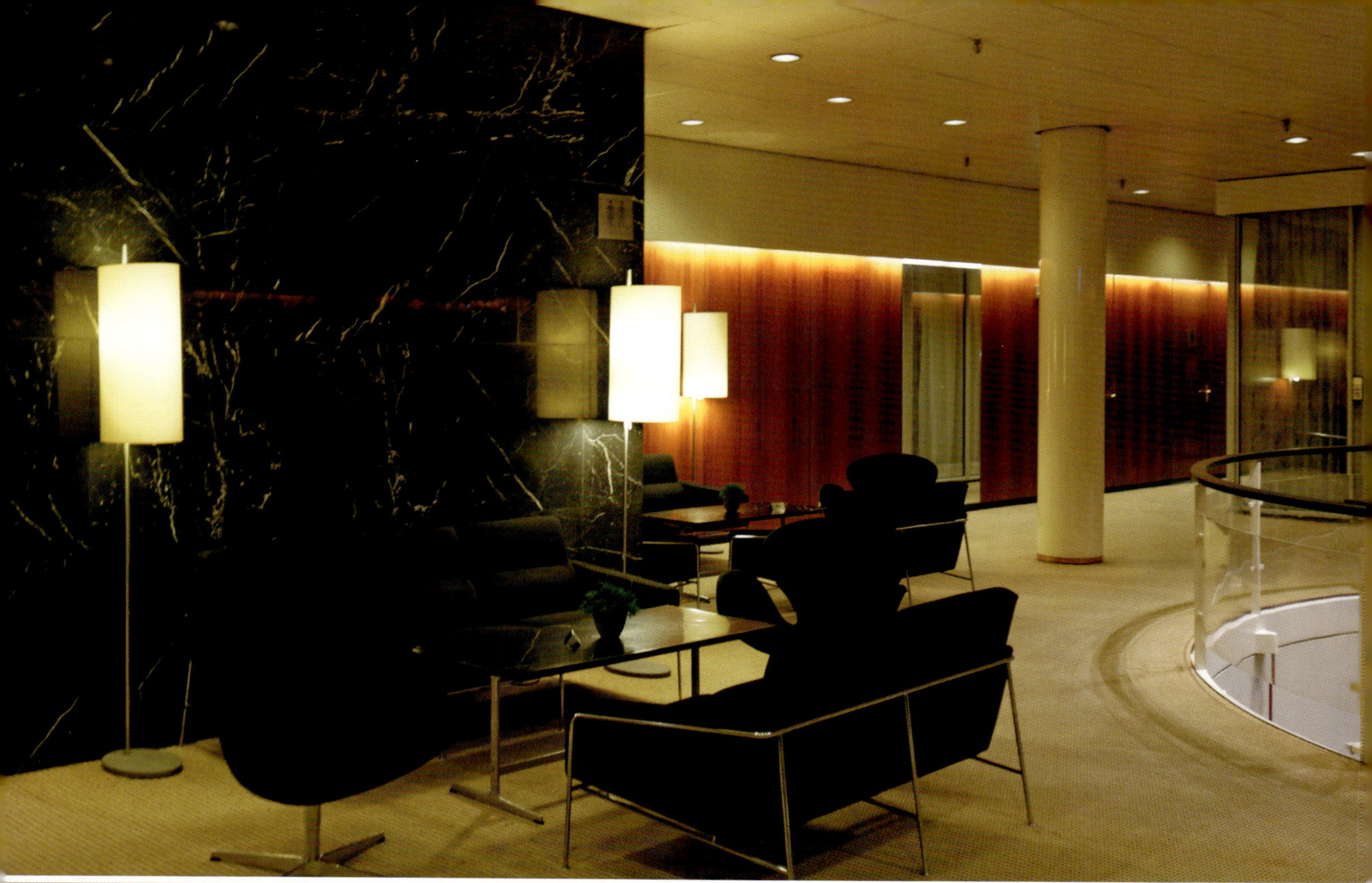

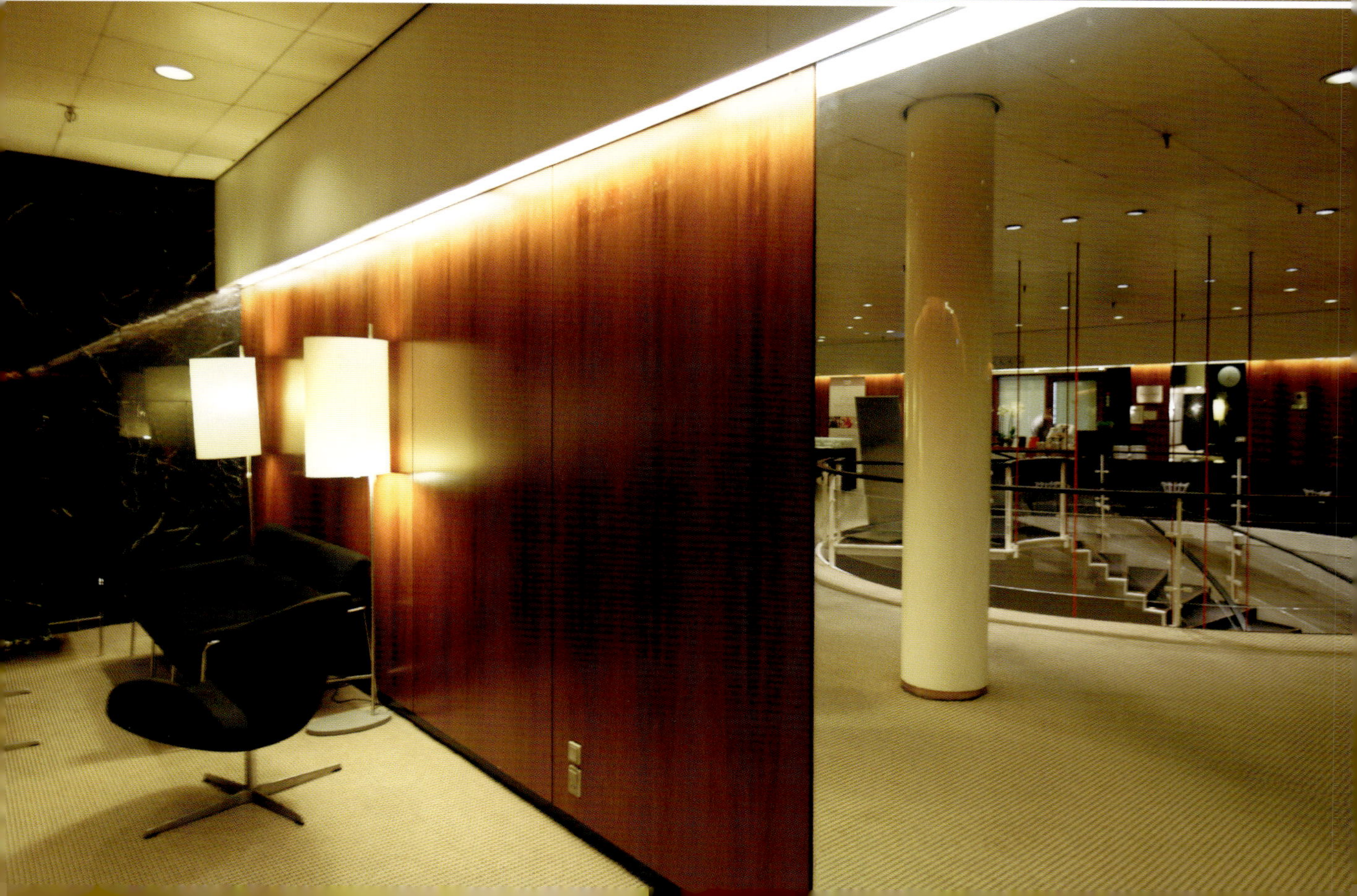

左頁上：2階ロビーのラウンジコーナー。家具、フロアスタンドともにヤコブセンのデザイン。

Left page top: Lounge corner of second floor lobby. Furniture and floor lamps also designed by Jacobsen.

左頁下：木製の間仕切壁の一部にミラーが取り付けられ、螺旋階段が映り込んでいる。

Left page bottom: Mirrors attached to wooden walls show the spiral staircase.

ロビーの螺旋階段越しにウィンターガーデンを臨む。

A view of the Winter Garden and the spiral staircase.

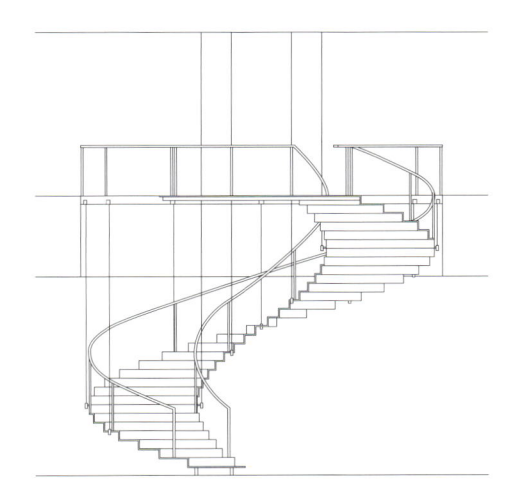

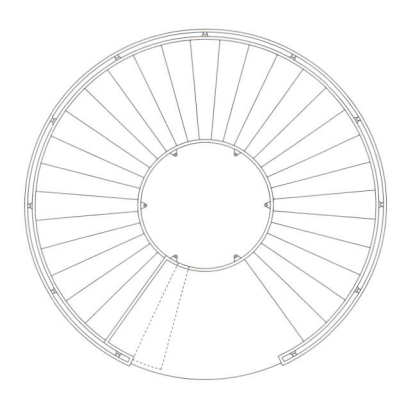

Plan and Section of the staircase in the lobby

0m   0.5m   1m   2m

客室階廊下。「アルネ・ヤコブセン・スイート」と呼ばれる606号室入口。

Guest room corridor. Entrance of room 606, known as the "Arne Jacobsen Suite."

SAS Royal Hotel

606号室「アルネ・ヤコブセン・スイート」。オープン当初のデザインを残したインテリアで、家具、照明器具から什器、カーテンまですべてヤコブセンのデザイン。

Room 606, the "Arne Jacobsen Suite." Retaining original interior design from the hotel's first days, everything from furniture and lighting to curtains was designed by Jacobsen.

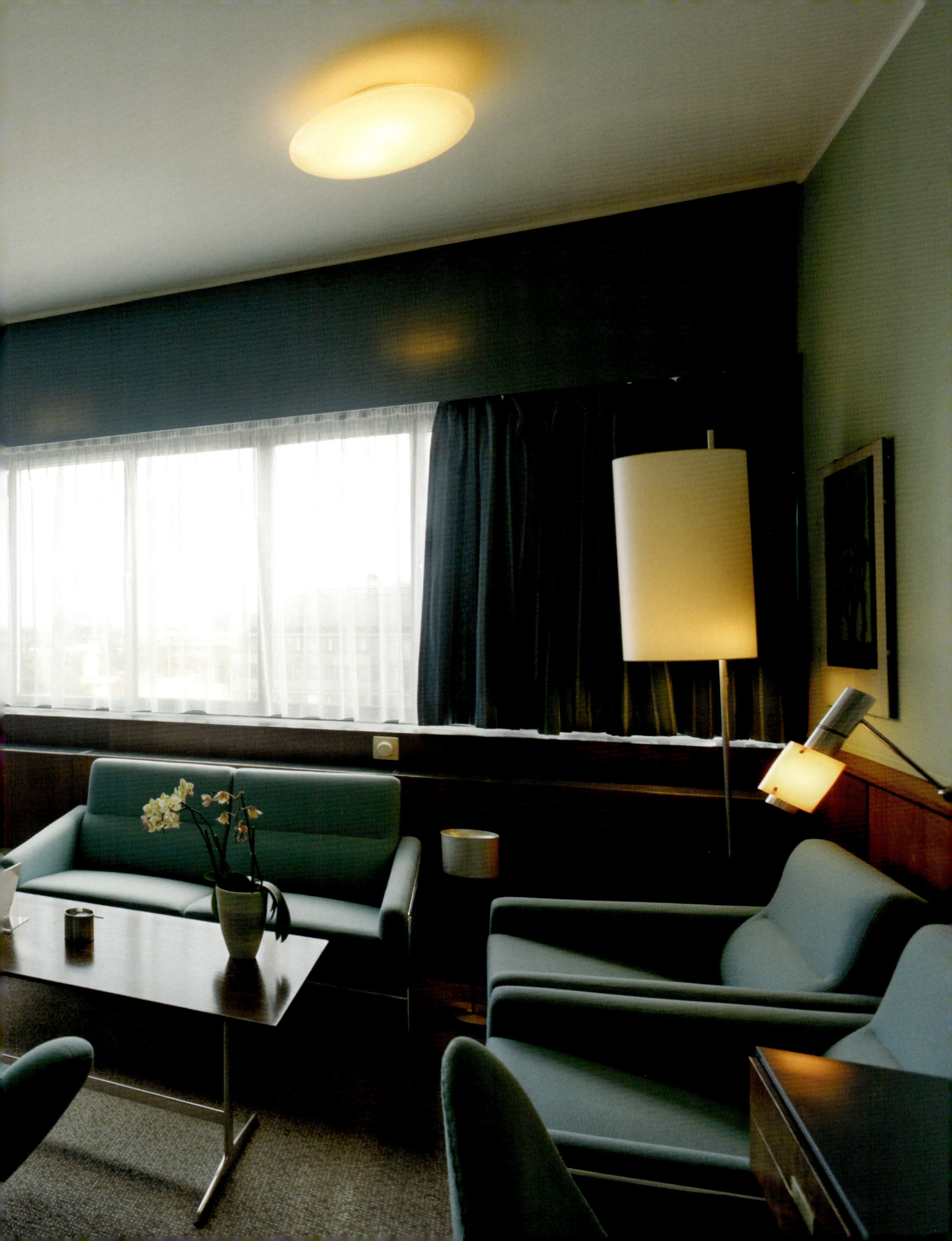

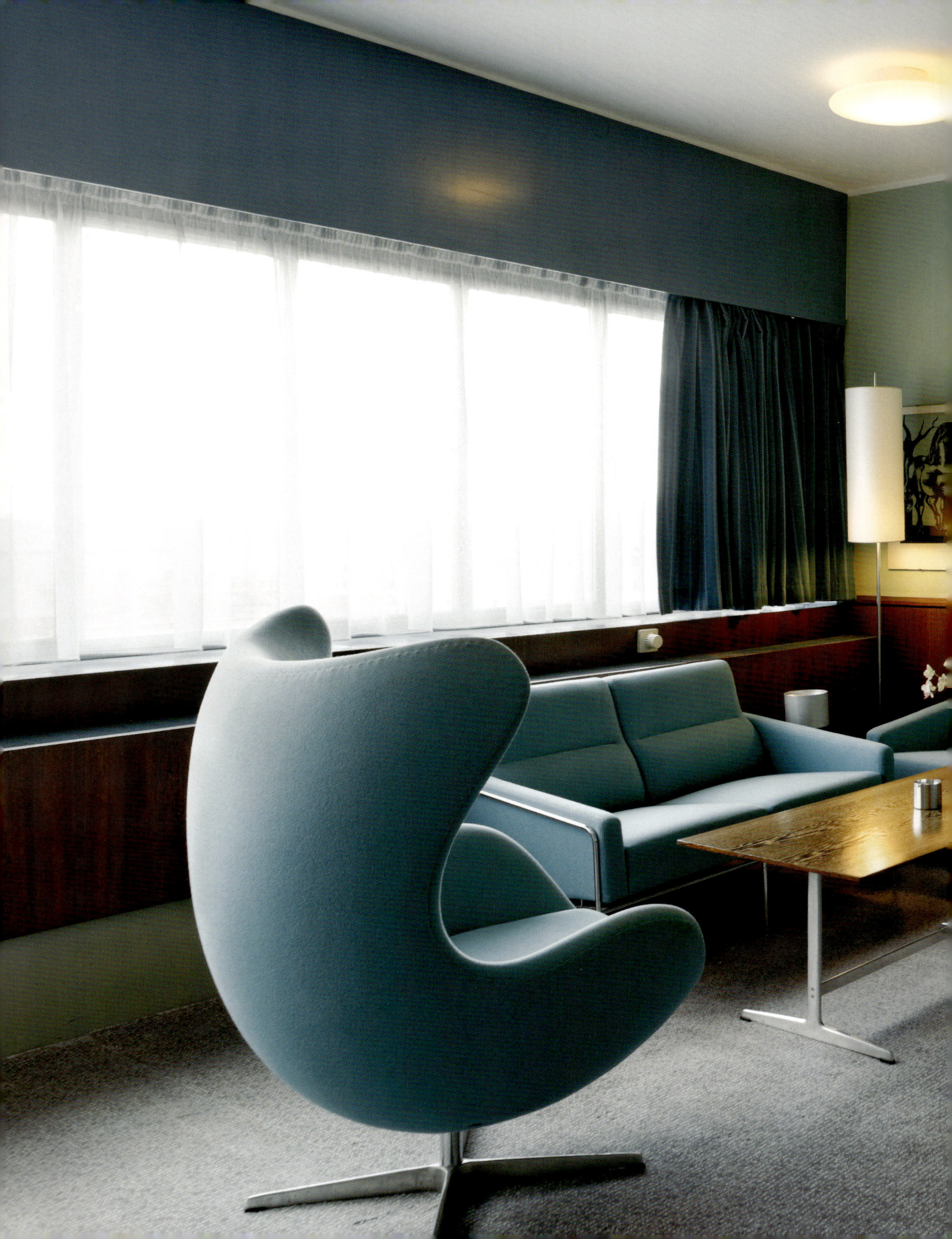

606号室「アルネ・ヤコブセン・スイート」。壁回りの造作家具はユニット式で自由に組み合わせを変更できる。椅子は左からエッグチェア、3300シリーズ、スワンチェア、ドロップチェア。テーブルは3515。

Room 606, the "Arne Jacobsen Suite." Furniture on the knee wall are in replaceable units, making it possible to change their combination. From the left: The Egg, 3300 Series, The Swan, The Drops. The table is 3515.

前室から客室を望む。
Guest rooms, seen from the front room.

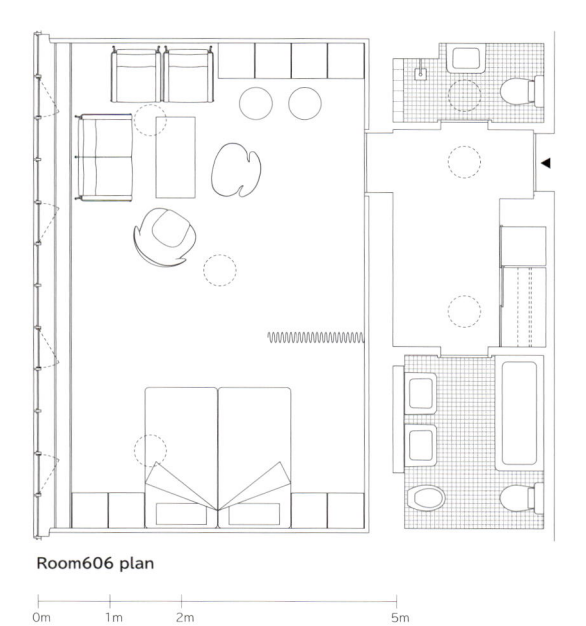

オリジナルの姿をとどめるバスルーム。
Bathroom in original state.

天板下部のレールにより、自由な位置に移動可能なブラケット照明。
SAS side lamp, adjustable along rails.

Room606 plan

0m 1m 2m 5m

226　Arne Jacobsen

ベッド回りのサイドテーブルも移動可能。
The bedside tables can also be moved.

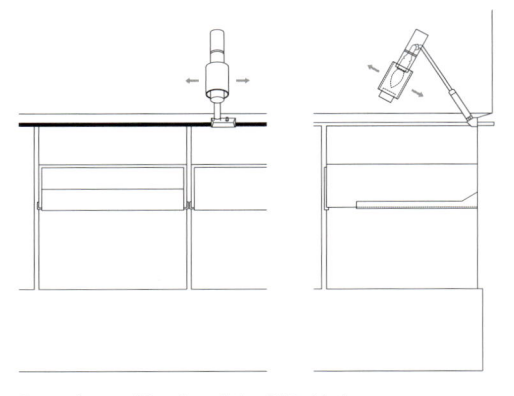

Front view and Section of the SAS side lamp

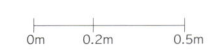

0m　0.2m　0.5m

化粧用のキャビネット。天板を開けると裏が鏡、内部に照明が仕込まれている。

The dressing table. The mirror on the bottom-side of the tabletop has lights in it.

SAS Royal Hotel

SASロイヤルホテルのためにデザインされたカトラリー、什器類。

Utensils and cutlery, designed for the SAS Royal Hotel.

右頁：南東側外観の見上げ。

Right page: Looking up at the building from the southeast.

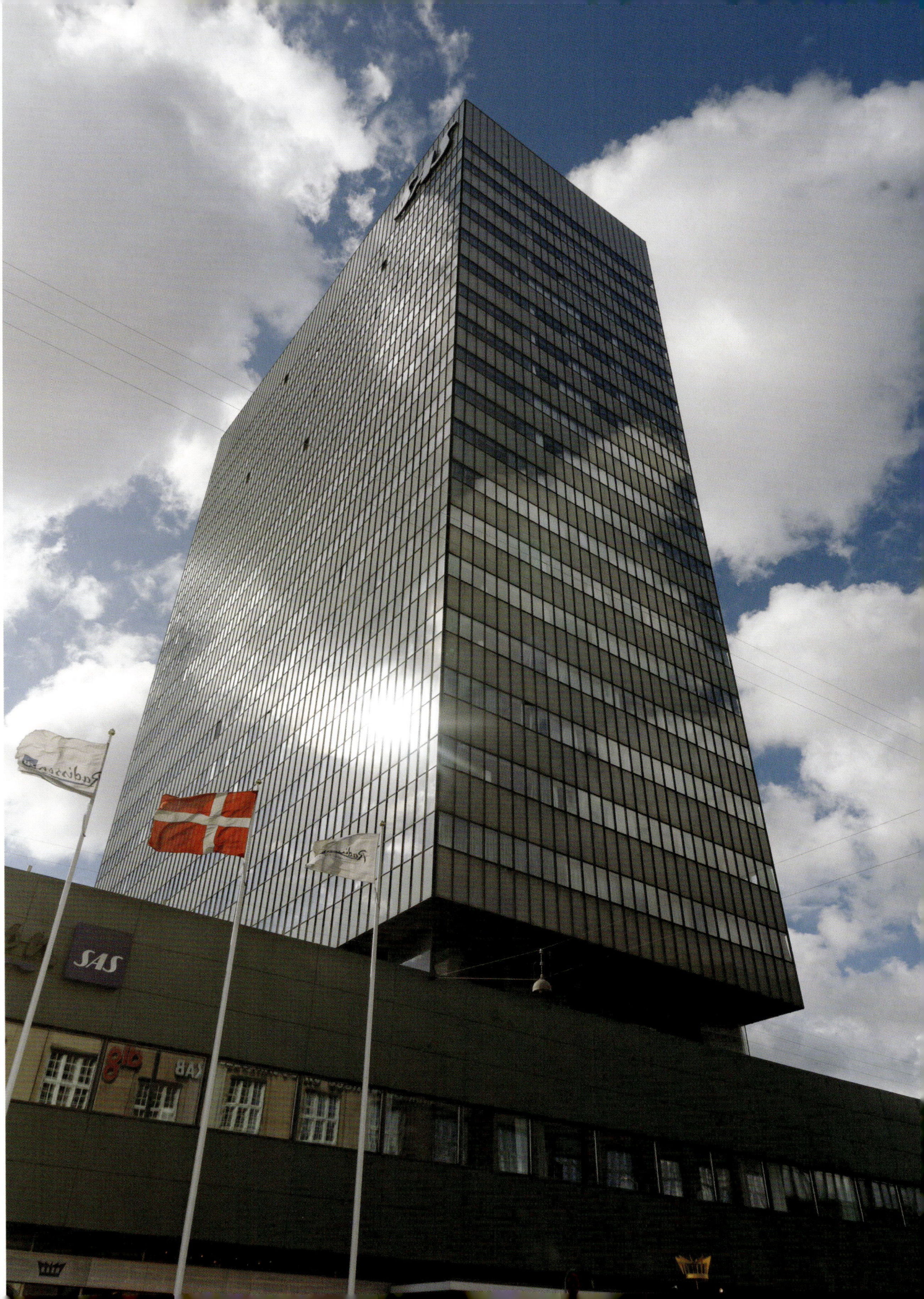
SAS

セント・キャサリンズ・カレッジ　1964年／オックスフォード
St Catherine's College, 1964, Oxford

アプローチからのカレッジ全景。すべての建物で黄土色の煉瓦が使われている。

View of college from approach. Ocher bricks are used in all buildings.

ロンドンから西に80km、オックスフォードの歴史的な街並みから少し外れたところに、この大学はある。ヤコブセンは全寮制のカレッジでの暮らしのすべてをデザインした。

全体は円形の芝生の広場を中心に、東側と西側に平行に南北に長く延びる3層の学生寮と、同心軸上に広場の北側に並ぶ事務棟と食堂棟、南側に並ぶ図書館棟と講堂棟から成る。

どの建物にも構造的な共通点がある。幾重にも東西軸方向に張り出す大きな梁だ。室内で梁を見上げると天井を横切り、壁やハイサイドライトを貫通し、リフレクターとなって光を導き入れているのが分かる。外構に目をやると、南北軸に自立する煉瓦積みの壁と生垣が外部空間を分節している。この建築の東西軸とランドスケープの南北軸が環境全体を秩序立てている。生活面では、「オックスフォードチェア」や「セーラーズハット・ランプ」などのプロダクトが、学生の暮らしをきめ細かく演出する。

イギリスの伝統あるオックスフォード大学のカレッジのひとつをデンマークの建築家に依頼した時、大きな議論が巻き起こった。しかし結果は明らかだ。このカレッジのためにデザインされたものは安易に他の物とは交換し得ない。現在でも職員や学生がヤコブセンの設計を誇りに思い、彼の思想を大事に守り続けている。

"St Catherine's College" is located in the suburbs of Oxford, a historical town that is 80 kilometers west of London. Jacobsen designed everything that is required in the life of the boarding collage.

There is a circular area of lawn in the center of the site. Two three-layer student accommodations that extend north and south are located on the eastern and western sides of the site. College offices and a dining hall are located north of the circular area of lawn. A library and a lecture theater are located at the opposite end of the site south of the lawn.

All of the buildings have structural aspects in common.

キャンパス中央の円形芝生広場を囲むように、正面に図書館棟、左右に寄宿舎棟が並ぶ。
Surrounding the central circular lawn are the library in the center and Student accommodation blocks on the left and right.

These include large beams to provide a layered ceiling and that overhangs it in on an east-west axis. When you stand inside the building and look up at the beams that cross the ceiling, pass through the walls and high side lights, you can see that the beams act as reflectors and permit the entry of natural sunlight. Walls of brickwork extend north and south on the exterior of the building. Hedges segment the external spaces. Working in tandem, the north-south axis of the buildings and the east-west axis of the landscape provide a sense of an orderly environment at the site. Product designs, such as "Oxford Chair" and the lighting "Sailor's Hat" complete the final preparations for student life.

When Jacobsen was asked to design one of the colleges of historical Oxford University, there was a considerable debate arose in England. However the result is clear. Everything that he designed for this collage remains today. There is nothing to change. The staffs and students are still proud of his designs and continue his spirit.

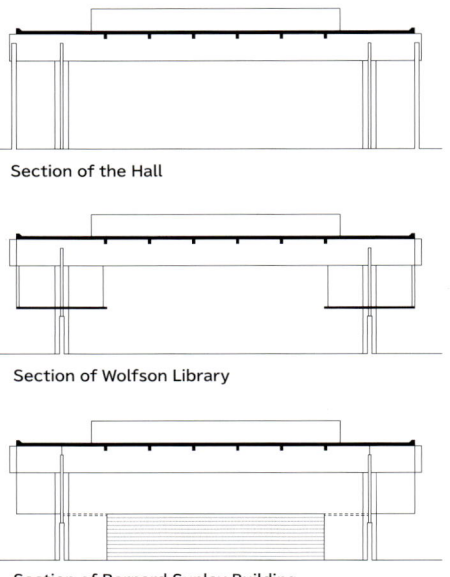

Section of the Hall

Section of Wolfson Library

Section of Bernard Sunley Building

西側の学生用入口。寄宿舎棟の下を通って中央広場の円形芝生に出る。

Student entrance in the west side. Passing under the accommodation block, students can enter the circular lawn.

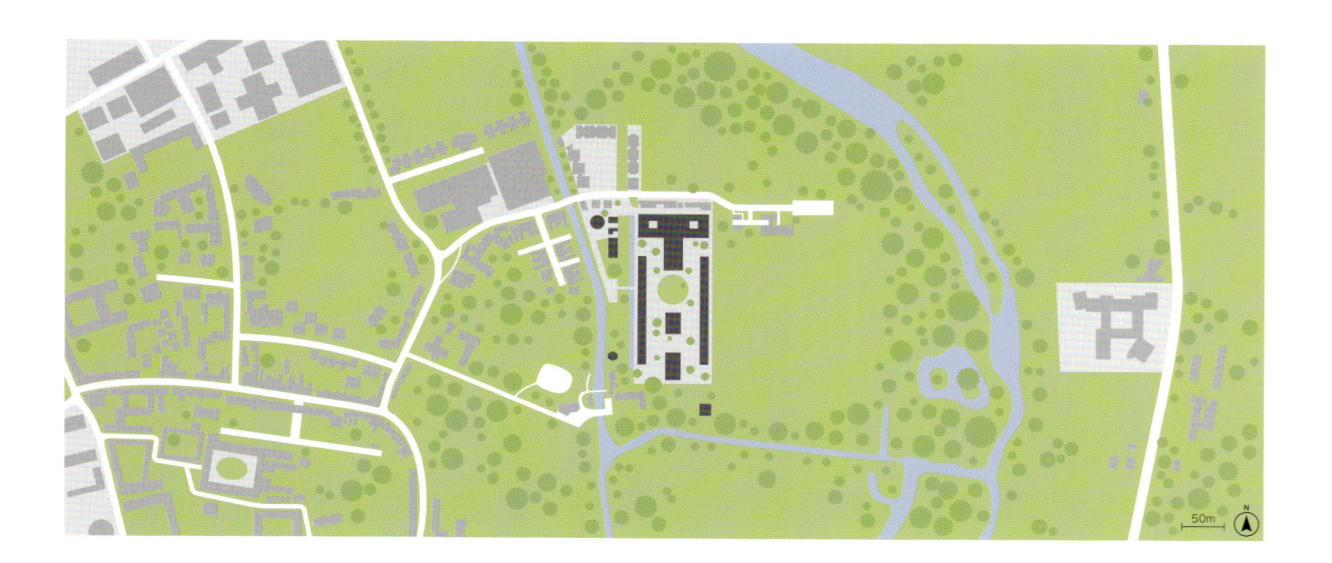

234　Arne Jacobsen

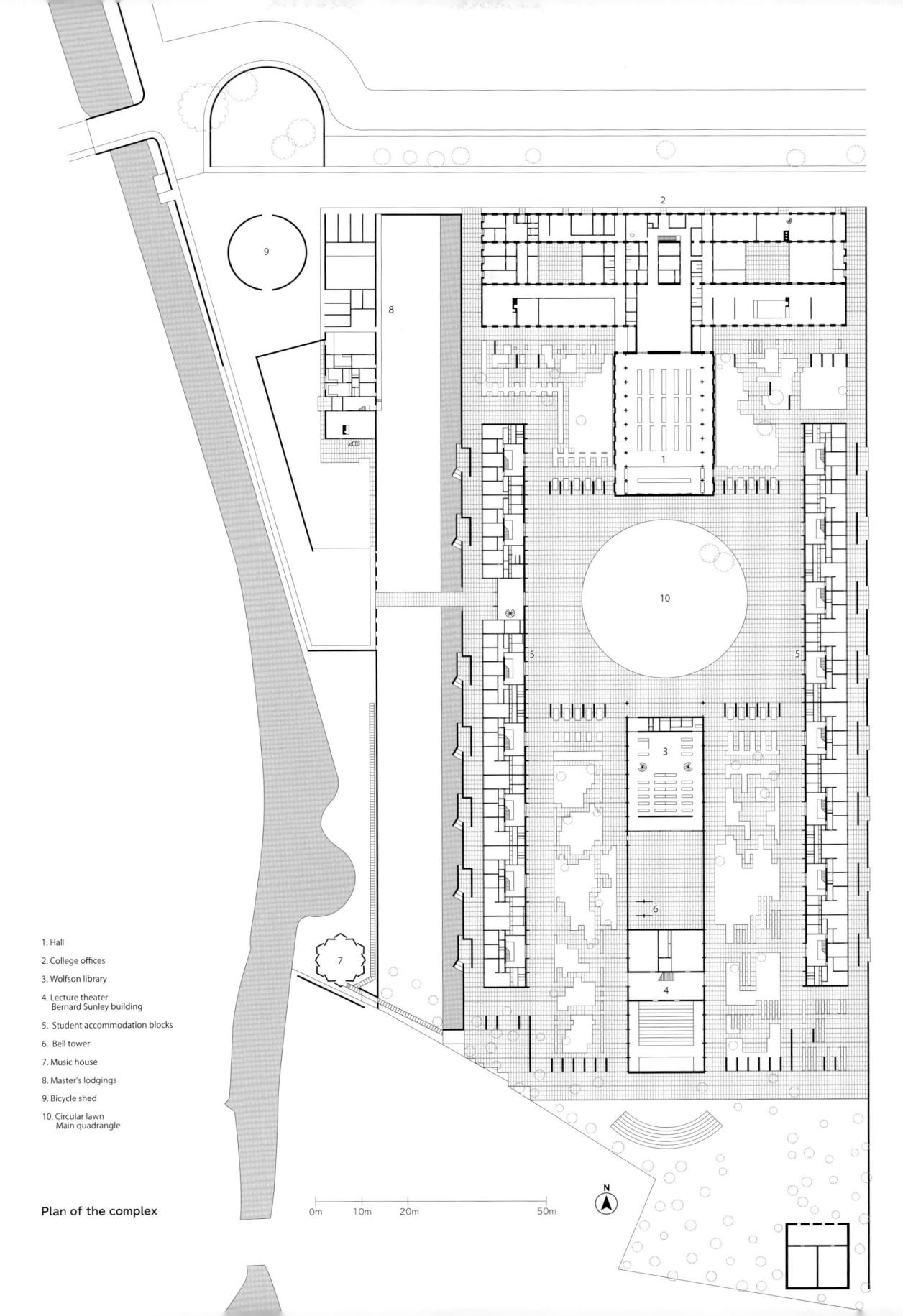

1. Hall
2. College offices
3. Wolfson library
4. Lecture theater
   Bernard Sunley building
5. Student accommodation blocks
6. Bell tower
7. Music house
8. Master's lodgings
9. Bicycle shed
10. Circular lawn
    Main quadrangle

Plan of the complex

図書館棟　The Wolfson Library

外壁の2階部分はブロンズパネル。
Bronze panels cover the outside of the second floor.

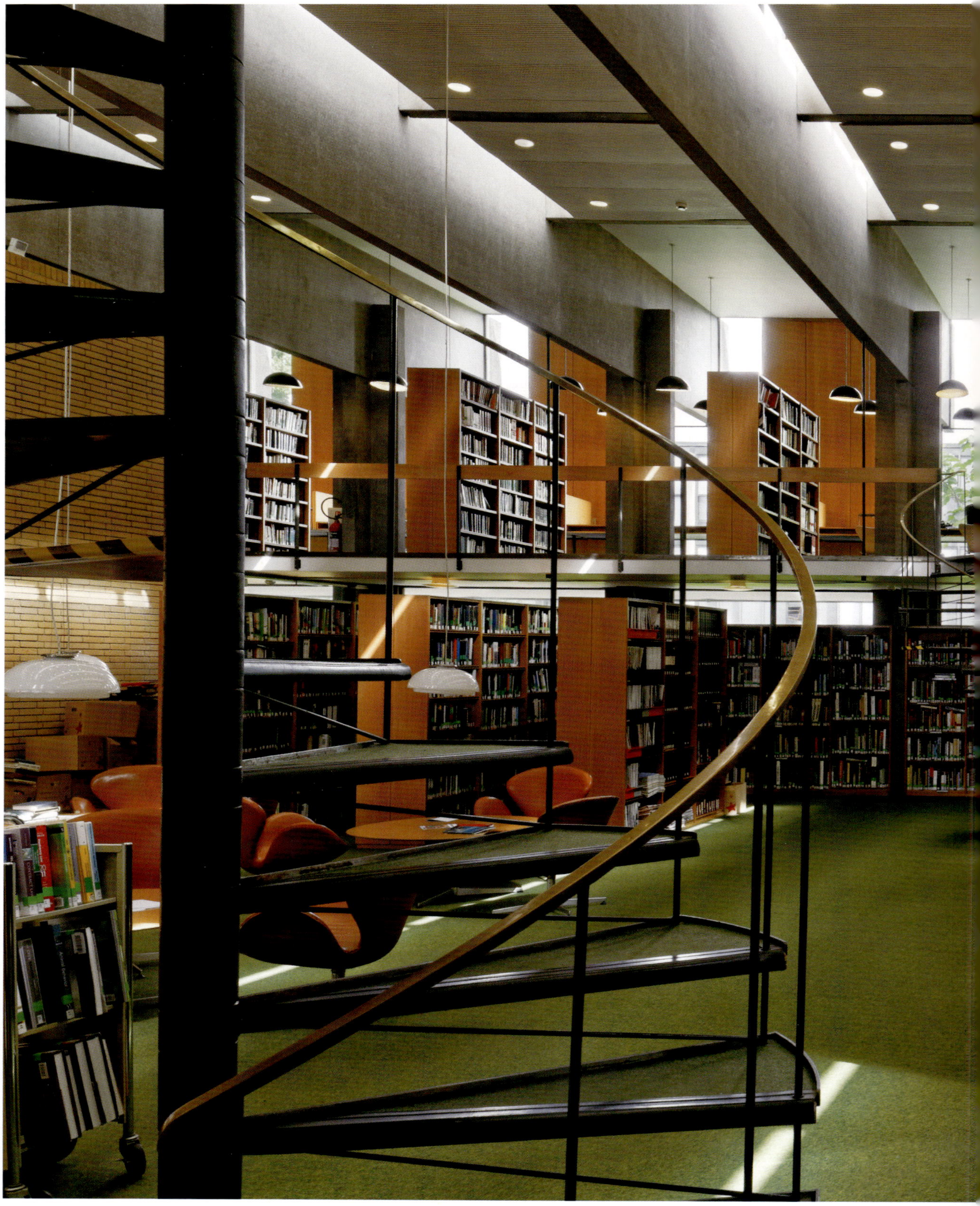

図書館棟内部。梁の上部にあるトップライトからの光は、梁の両側に反射し、拡散されて館内を照らす。1日に2回、限られた時間だけ直射光が、ダイレクトに入り込む。

Inside the library. Light from the top light reflects on the sides of the beams, illuminating the entire room. Just twice a day, direct sunlight enters the room.

2階閲覧コーナーへの螺旋階段。
A spiral staircase to reading corner on second floor.

2階より図書館棟内部を望む。1階コーナーにはスワンチェアが配されている。
View from second floor of the library. First floor lounge is furnished with The Swans.

東西方向に伸びた梁成の大きな梁が、十字形の柱で支えられる。
A cross-shaped pillar supports the large beam extend east-west.

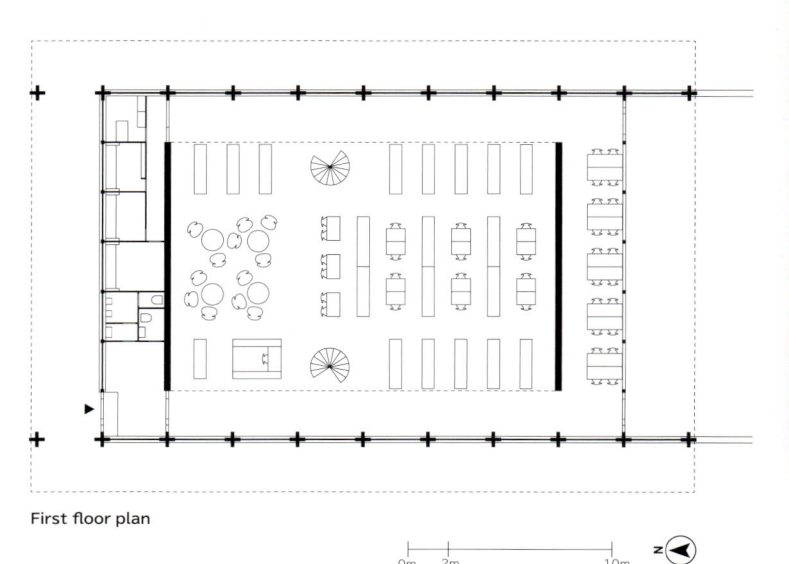

First floor plan

0m 2m 10m

2階窓回りの閲覧コーナー。梁が外部に飛び出している。
Reading corner near windows, second floor. Indoor beams protrude outside of the building.

St Catherine's College 241

図書館棟の外壁。キャノピーの先は講堂へとつながる。突き出した梁が外壁にリズムを与えている。

Outer wall of the library. A walk under the canopy leads to the lecture hall. Protruding beams give a rhythm to the wall.

中央広場に面した図書館棟。端部の十字柱が建物を支える。正面奥は夏の食堂棟。

The library faces central plaza. Cross-shaped pillars at the ends support the structure. Seen straight ahead is the dining hall in summertime.

講堂棟　The Bernard Sunley Building

低層棟が連なるキャンパスの中でアクセントとなる鐘楼とその奥の講堂棟。

The bell tower is a feature of the low-rise campus. Seen behind is the Bernard Sunley building.

講堂棟外部に取り付けられたルーバーが軒下まで延びる。
The louver on the outside of the building extends under the eaves.

St Catherine's College   245

多目的に利用される講堂。両側の開口部はロールスクリーンで遮光可能。
Multipurpose lecture theater. Rolling screens on side openings can be used to shield light.

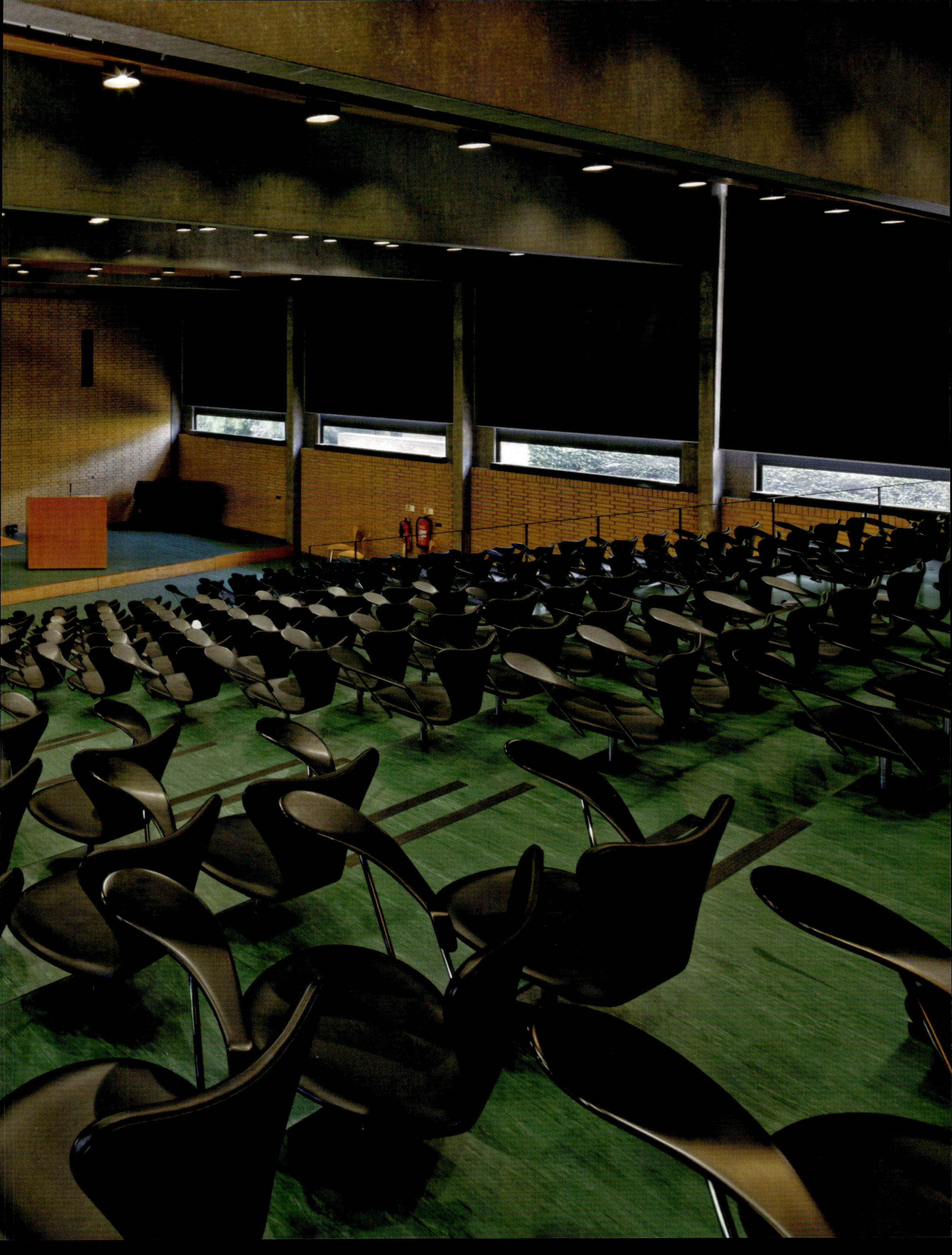

座席は講堂用にデザインされた片肘付きのセブンチェア。
The Seven with arm rest was designed for the lecture theater.

演壇からの講堂全景。
View of the lecture theater from the platform.

2階通路回り。左に談話室と会議室、右に講堂が配されている。トップライトからの光が梁とのわずかな隙間から差し込む。

Second floor landing. The Governing Body Room/Shaw Room and teaching room to the left, the lecture theater to the right. Light from the top light enters from the gap between the beam and the ceiling.

講堂棟2階会議室。窓の外に金属製のルーバーが取り付けられ、視界をコントロールしている。椅子はローバックタイプのオックスフォードチェア。

The Governing Body Room/Shaw Room on the second floor of the building. Metal louvers outside the window block the view. Chairs in this room are Oxford Low Back Chairs.

講堂棟2階談話室。ポットチェアが並ぶ。
Teaching room on the second floor of the building. The Pots line the room.

ルーバーのディテール。
Details of the louver.

St Catherine's College

講堂棟西側の庭園。
Garden, western side of the Bernard Sunley building.

講堂棟東側の通路。キャンパス各所には、煉瓦の壁が巧みに配置され、結界や空間の溜り場をつくっている。

Passageway east of the building. Cleverly placed brick walls in locations across campus create new spaces.

講堂棟と西側の庭園。キャンパス各所に点在する庭園が、さまざまな植生の組み合わせにより多様に変化しながら、全体としてのまとまりを見せている。

Westside garden and the building. Gardens placed around the campus are home to various combinations of plants. Diverse change creates entirety.

寄宿舎棟　Student Accommodation Blocks

中央広場の両側に建つ寄宿舎棟。左に食堂棟、右に図書館棟。
Student accommodation blocks stand on either side of the Quadrangle. To the left is the Hall and to the right is the Wolfson library.

エントランスホール正面にある寄宿舎棟階段室。

Stairwell in the entrance lobby.

右頁：機能的ながら美しいディテールの階段。

Right page: Details of the functional and beautiful staircase.

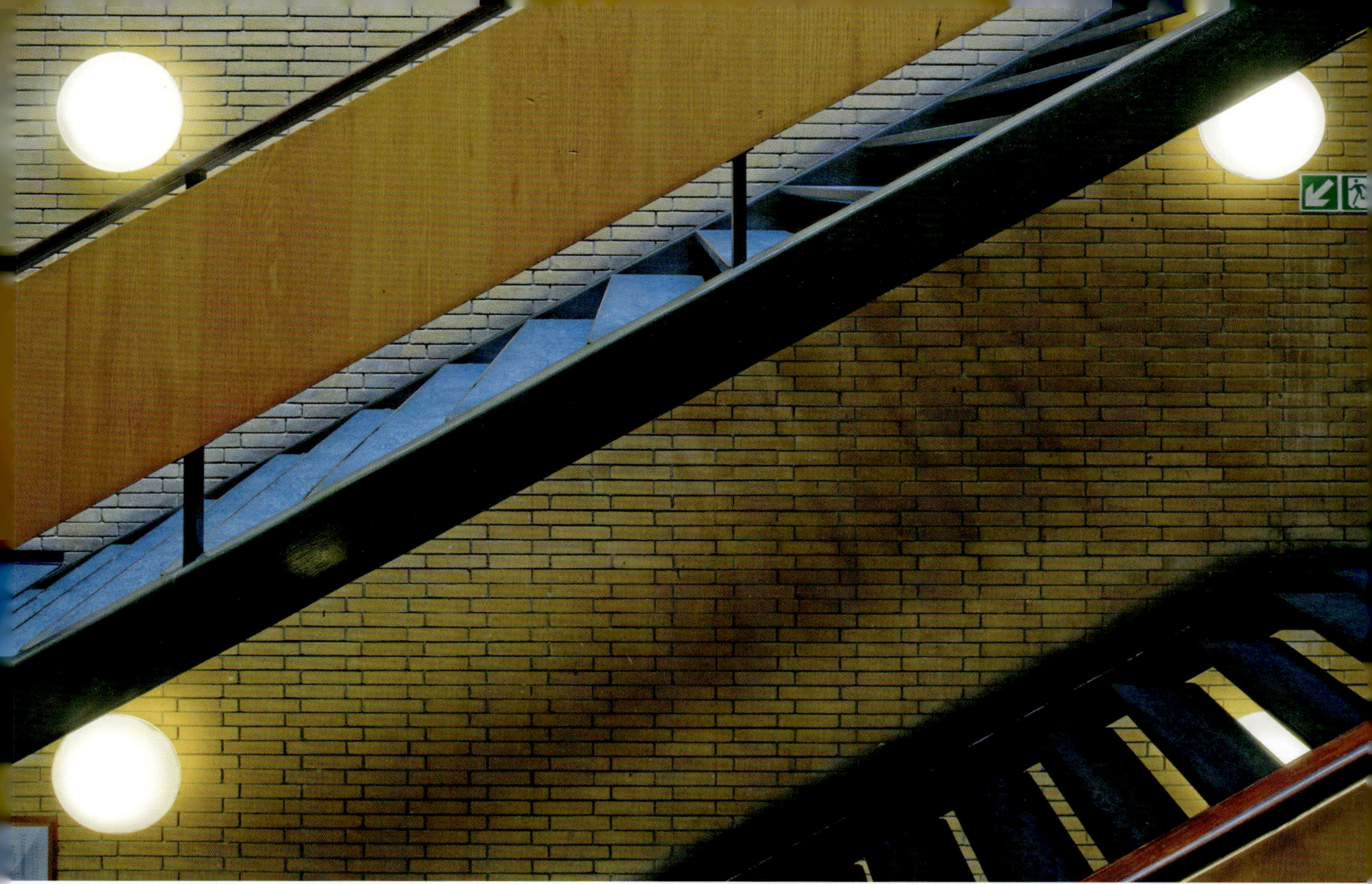

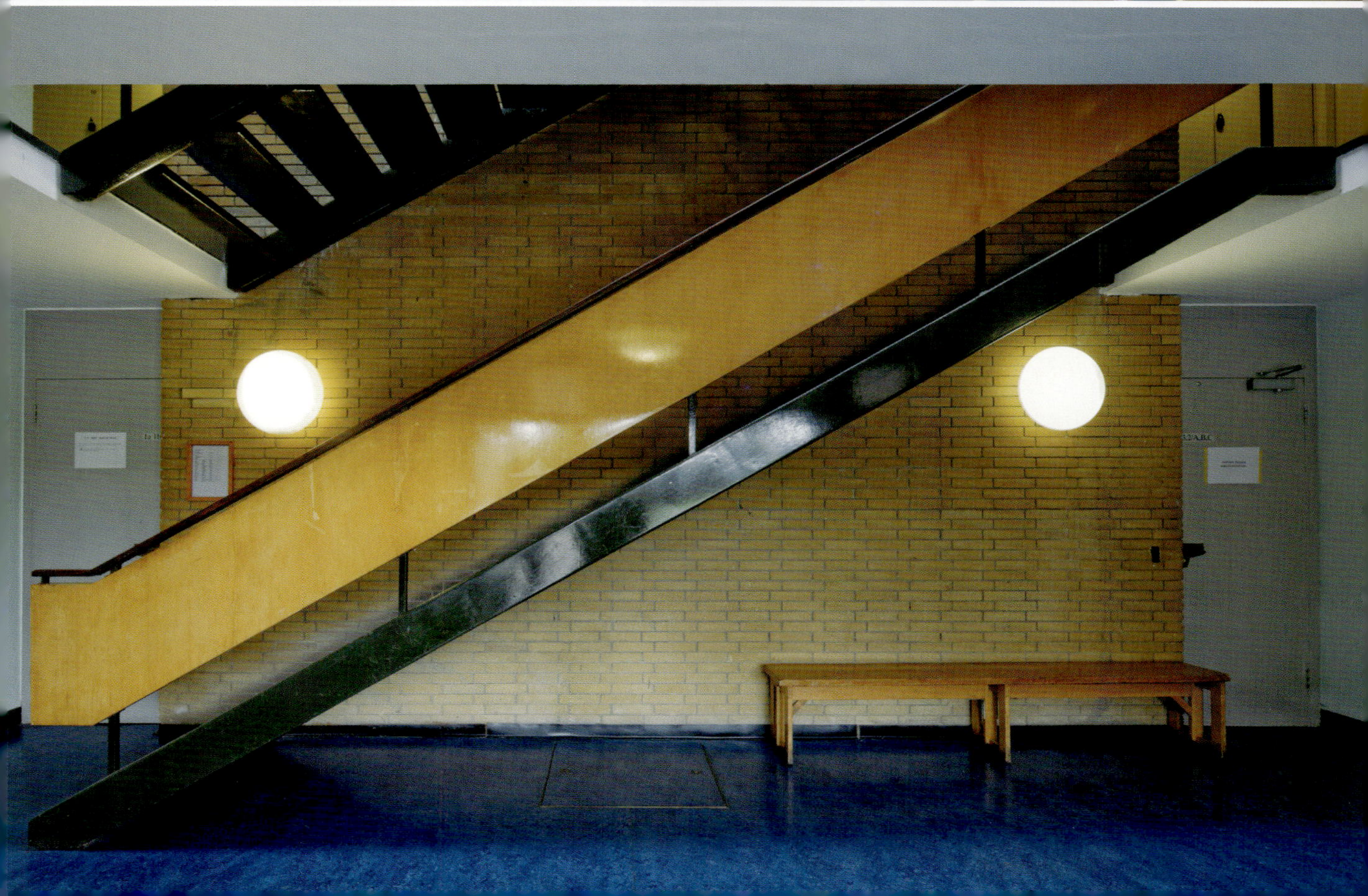

窓から中央広場が見える寮室。収納、ベッド、家具がコンパクトに納まるようにすべてデザインされた。

The Quadrangle can be seen from the window of the study bedroom. The storage and furniture have all been designed to be compact.

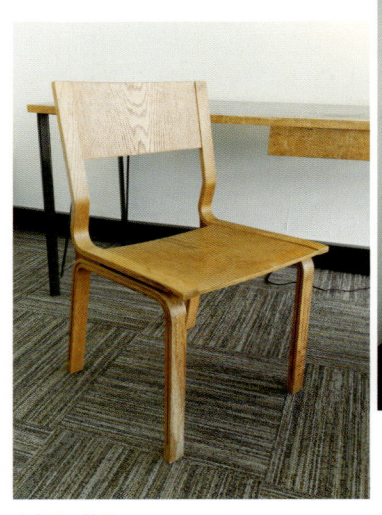

寮室用の椅子。
The chair in the room.

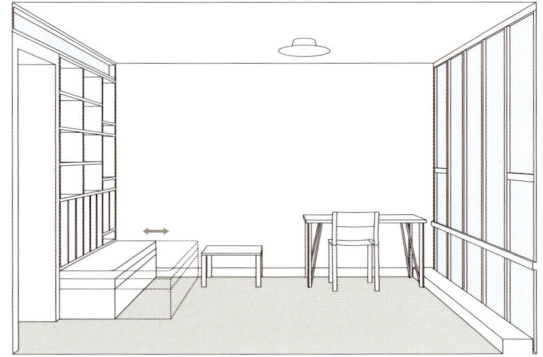

Perspective

学生寮棟に沿って長い池が続く西側外観。
A large water garden stretches along the western exterior of the accommodation blocks.

食堂棟・事務棟　The Hall and College Offices

事務棟側から北方向を見る。左に食堂棟、右に寄宿舎棟、正面奥に図書館棟と鐘楼が見える。

Looking north from the college offices, the Hall can be seen to the left and the student accommodation block to the right. The library and bell tower can be seen straight ahead in the background.

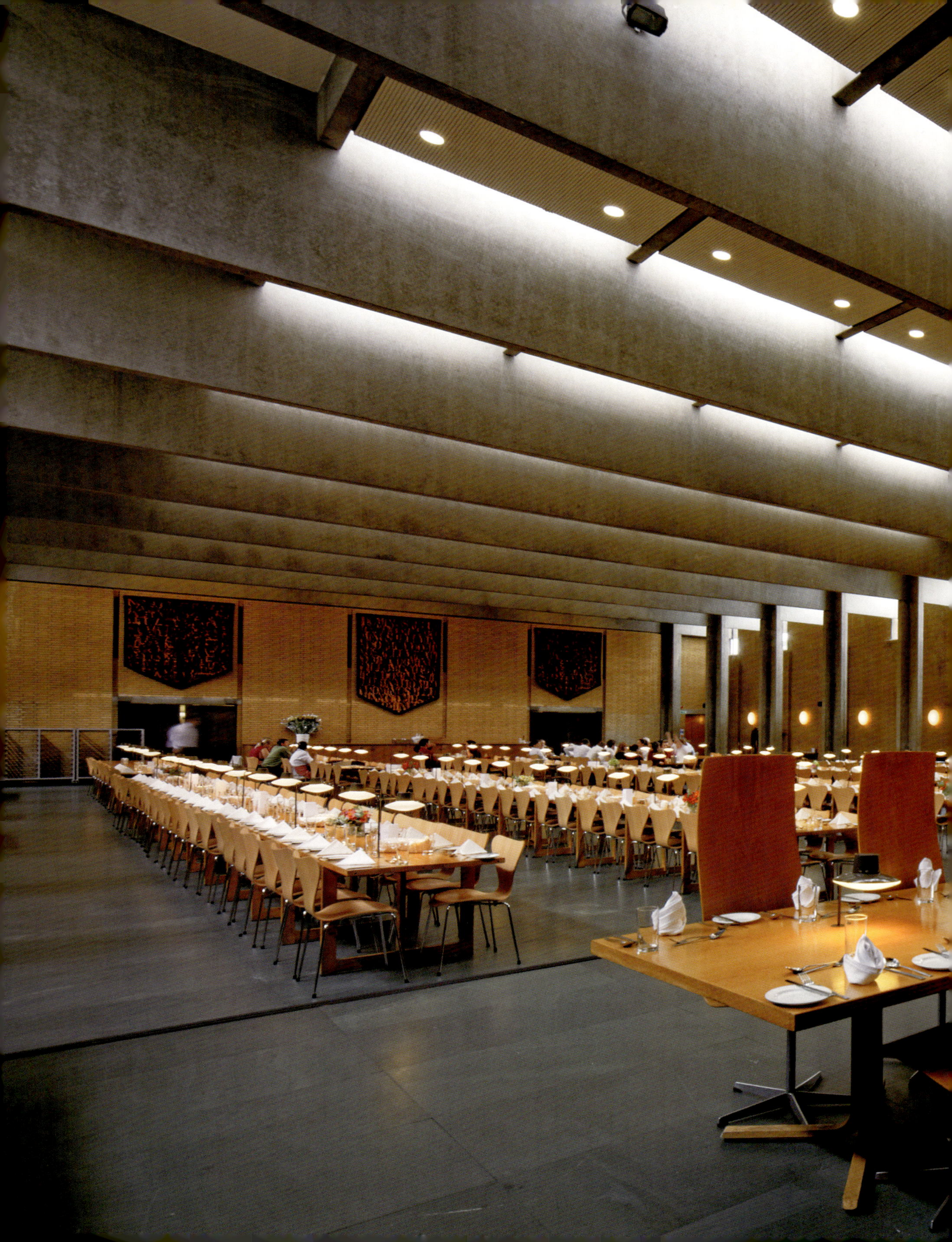

1段高い教授席より見る大食堂全景。教授席はハイバックのオックスフォードチェア。当初、学生席にはベンチが並べられていたが、現在はセブンチェアが使用されている。

The Hall as seen from the High table with its the Oxford High Back Chairs where the academic staff sit. Benches were originally used for student seating, but now The Sevens are used.

教授席のテーブルセッティング。テーブルランプは学生用と高さ、ガラスグローブの面が異なる。

The High table setting. Both the height and the glass globe of the lamps differ from those on the students' tables.

学生席側からの大食堂全景。正面奥が教授席。晴天時には1日に2回東西方向に走る梁と屋上トップライトとの隙間を通過した光がテーブルや床に光の帯を描く。

The Hall as seen from the student seating. The High table can be seen in the background. Bands of light decorate the floor and tables as they shine from the gaps between the top lights and beams which run from east to west. On a sunny day this can be seen at two times.

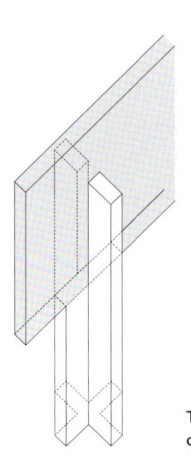

The relationship between the basic constructive elements: pillars and beams

柱・梁と外壁開口部の取り合い。

The configuration of the pillars, beams and outer wall apertures.

St Catherine's College   265

梁間方向から見る大食堂。構造方式や採光方法は図書館棟や講堂棟と同じであるが、外壁の位置や外装仕上げなどでバリエーションを生み出している。正面の煉瓦壁には乳白ガラスのAJエクリプタが並ぶ。

Beams as seen from the side of the Hall. The structure of the beams and lighting method are the same as seen in the library and the lecture hall, but variations are noticeable in things such as the position of the outer wall and the exterior finish. Milky white glass AJ Eklipta line the far brick wall.

学生席(上)、教授席(下)のテーブルランプ。高さとガラスグローブの発光面が異なる。

Table lamps in the student seating area (top) and those in the High table (bottom). Both the height and the luminescent area of the lamps differ.

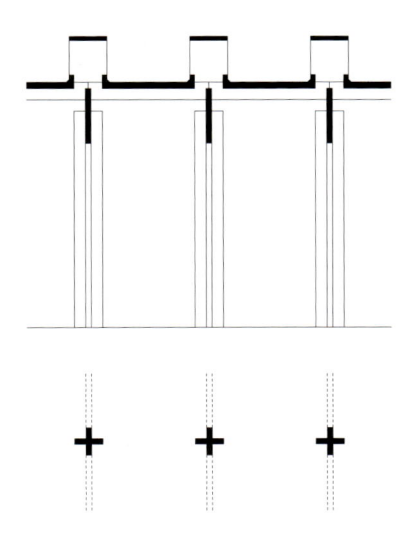

Part of the lengthwise section of the dining hall

St Catherine's College **267**

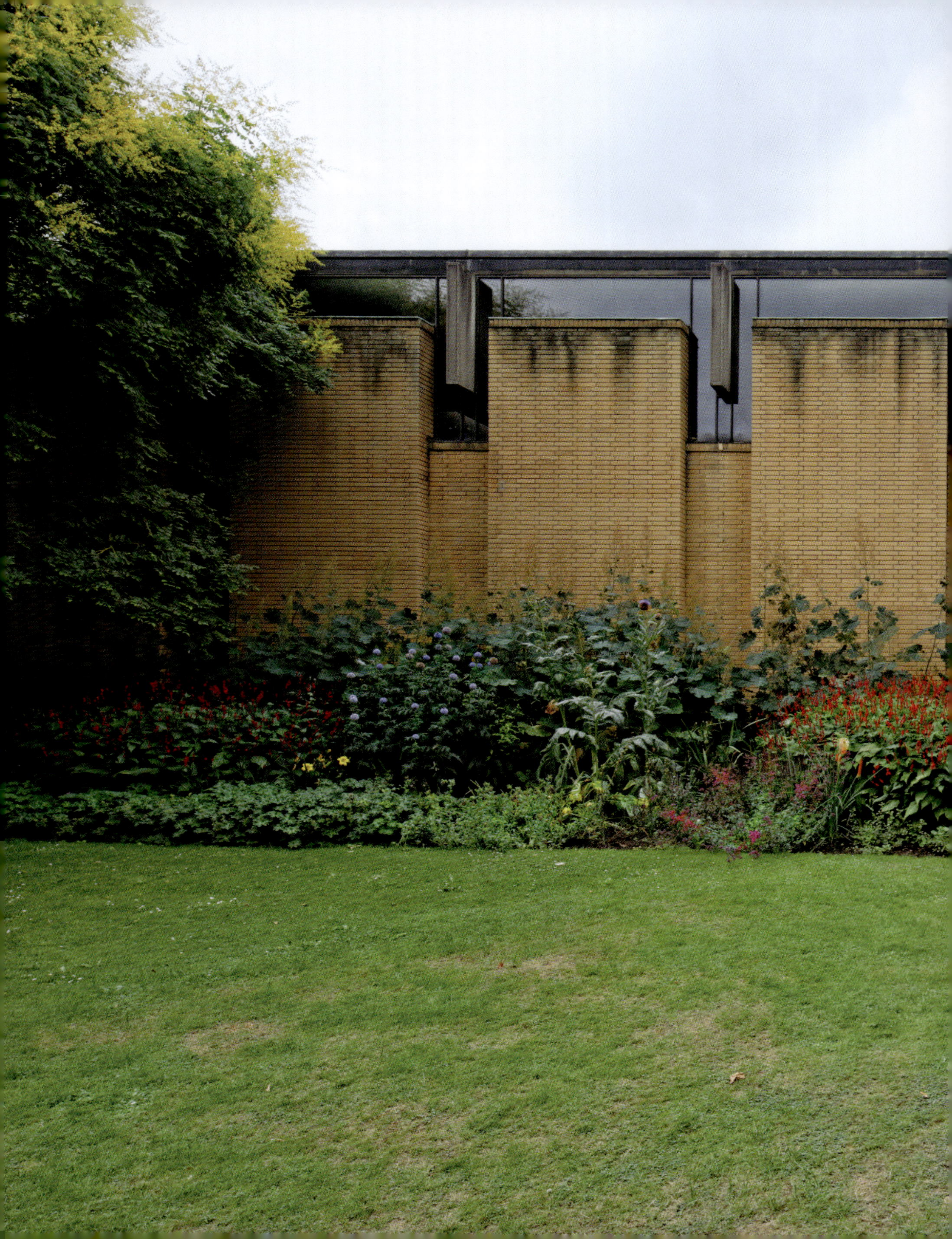

食堂棟西側の外壁回り。ヤコブセンの植栽デザインで季節の草花が彩りを添える。
The outer wall on the west side of the Hall. The plants and seasonal flowers Jacobsen incorporates into the design add color to life.

事務棟の前庭。煉瓦の自立壁が空間を巧みに仕切る。

The garden of the Senior Common Room, where self-standing brick walls skillfully divide up the space.

事務棟の教職員用ラウンジ。左手中央壁に暖炉が見える。

The faculty lounge in the college offices. A fireplace can be seen in the center of the left side wall.

事務棟会議室に面した中庭。
The Gaskin Garden courtyard facing the Small Dining Room in the Senior Common Room.

中庭に面したダイニングルーム。中庭とはサッシュレスのガラス引戸でつながる。
The small dining room facing the courtyard through sashless sliding windows.

事務棟通路。部分的にトップライトが設けられている。

The corridor in the Senior Common Room. Top lights are fixed in places along the ceiling.

事務棟内の特別食堂。

The long dining room located in the college offices.

ハイバックのオックスフォードチェアが並ぶ。
Oxford High Back Chairs line the table.

St Catherine's College

274 Arne Jacobsen

St Catherine's College

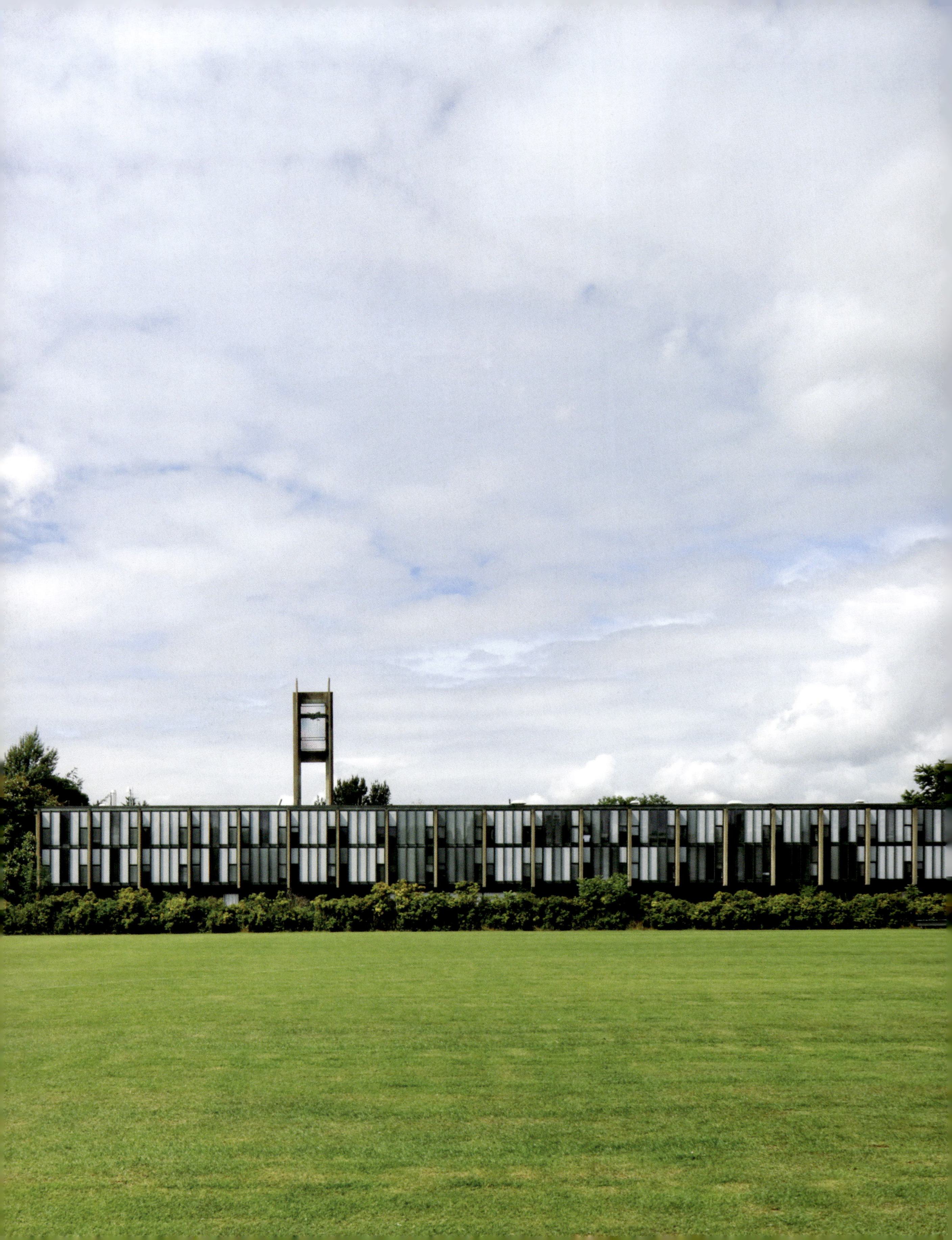

東側寄宿舎棟の全景。全長120mの寄宿舎棟の奥に鐘楼が見える。

A panoramic view of the eastern student accommodation block. Behind the block, which boast a length of 120 meters, stands the bell tower.

デンマーク国立銀行　1971年／コペンハーゲン

Danmarks Nationalbank, 1971, København,
Design of Second and Third Phases: Dissing + Weitling

ガラスカーテンウォールに反射する夕日が美しい南側運河からの全景。

View from the canal to the south, with the glass curtain wall reflecting the sunset.

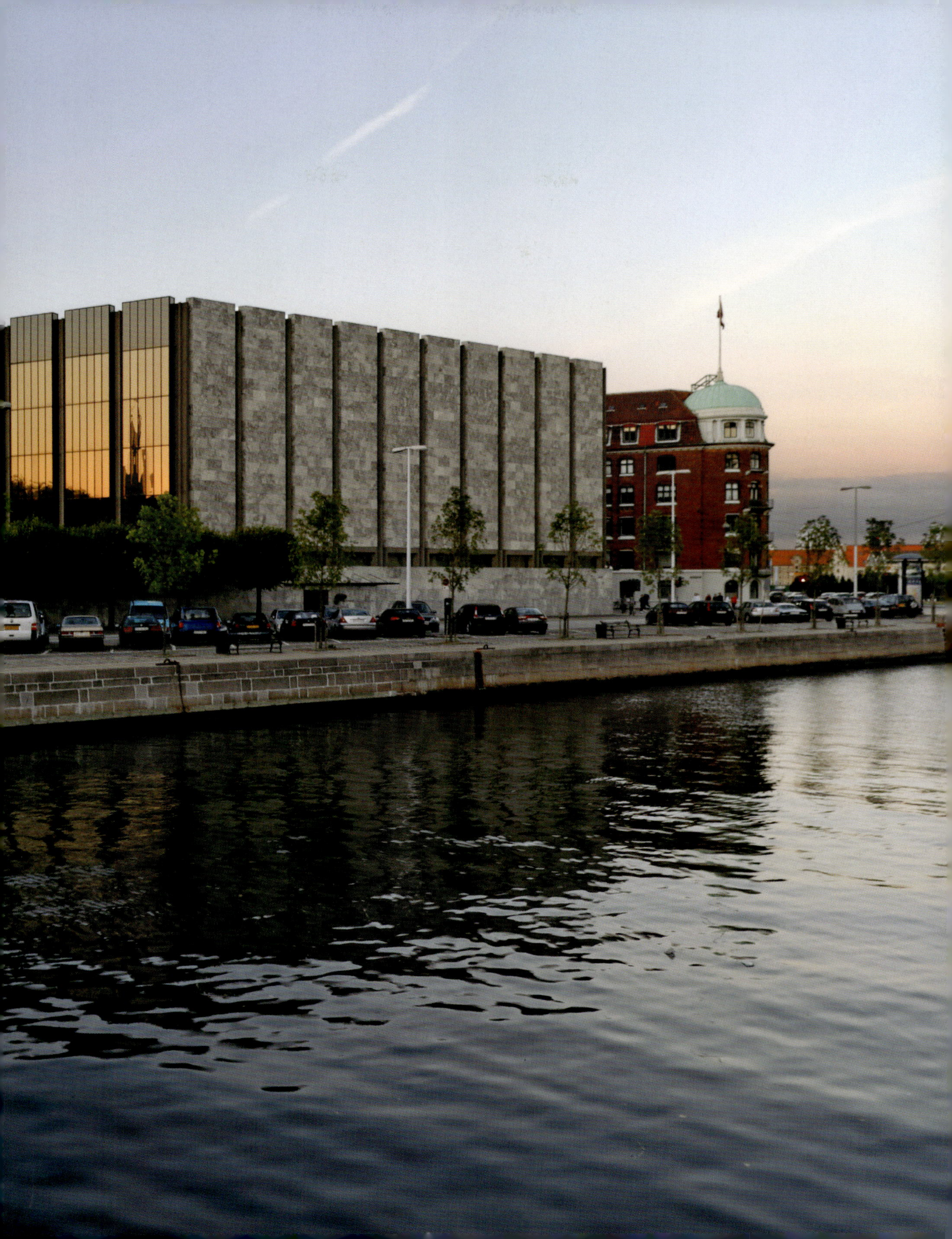

「デンマーク国立銀行」はヤコブセンの代表作であり、これまでのデザインの集大成であり、そして遺作でもある。コペンハーゲンの中心部にある一街区すべてが国立銀行の敷地である。

　全体は、西側半分の低層部と、東側半分の高層部から成る。外観は、ノルウェー産大理石が低層部と高層部の南北面を囲み、周囲の歴史的建築物を鏡のように映し出すガラスのカーテンウォールが東西面を囲んでいる。さらに、銀行という特殊な目的の建物を保護するため、低層部の四方を高い壁で囲んだ。閉鎖的な外観には批判もあったが、内部は意外にも光と植物に満ちた快適な執務空間である。

　南側にある入口の扉をくぐり、湾曲した小さなガラスボックスを通り抜けると、高さ20mのエントランスロビーが現れる。奥に向かって広がる平面形状の逆パースペクティブの先には、天井から軽やかに吊り下げられた階段がある。右手に高くそびえる大理石の内壁にはスリットがあり、時間に応じて床と壁に直線的に光が差し込む。左手の通路を進んだ先の銀行営業室のロビーには、植物が吊られた四角いガラスケースが整然と並んでおり、ガラスケースの天井からは上部中庭からの自然光が降り注ぐ。

"Danmarks Nationalbank" is Jacobsen's representative work, a culmination of his design and also his posthumous work. One whole one block in the center of Copenhagen city is used for the central bank of Denmark.

The building was constructed with a lower part on the western side and a higher part on the eastern side. The southern and northern exteriors were covered with Norwegian marble, whereas the eastern and western exteriors were covered by glass curtain walls that reflect the historical buildings that are opposite like a mirror. Jacobsen built high walls to protect lower part of the building that performed a special task as the bank. Although some criticize the exterior of the building as being contrary to expectations, its interior fulfilled expectations with its lighting, plants and comfortable and spacious offices.

Through the entrance on the south side and the small, curved glass corridor, you reach the entrance lobby that it is 20 meters in height and widens towards its rear. There is suspended staircase at the end of the lobby. The slits in the marble walls on the right side admit natural light to enter, which creates brightly lit lines of light on the floor and wall. The aisle on the left side leads us to the banking hall. Square glass cases in which plants pots are suspended and arranged in orderly fashion. The case's ceiling admits natural light from the courtyard above to illuminate inside.

植栽にこだわったヤコブセンの外構回りのデザイン。
Jacobsen designed the exterior area paying particular attention to plants.

南側の銀行入口。ノルウェー産大理石の壁面が規則的に並ぶ。

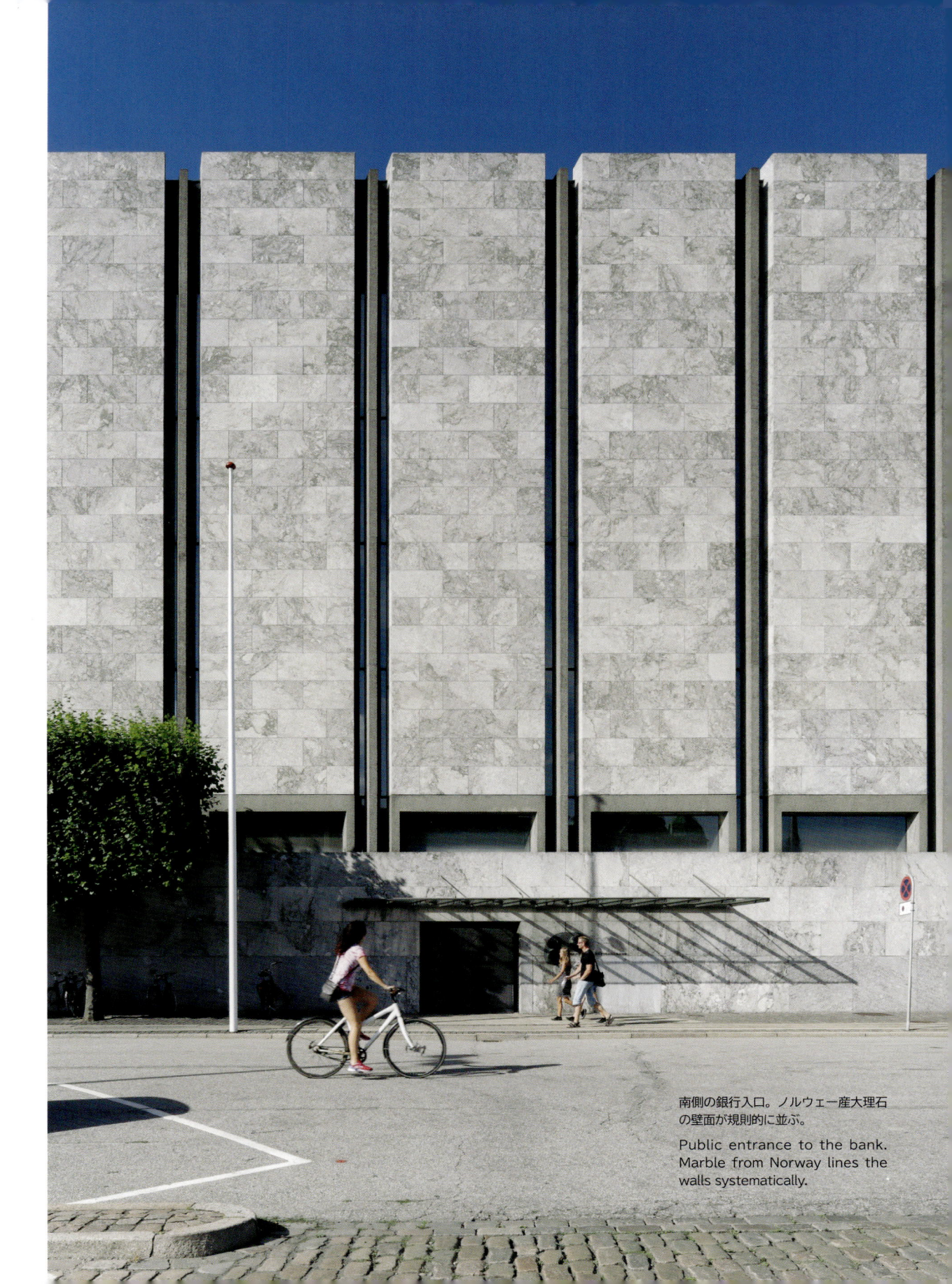

Public entrance to the bank. Marble from Norway lines the walls systematically.

東南のコーナーディテール。大理石とガラスカーテンウォールの 2 種類の外装がファサードに変化を与えている。

Southeast corner details. Having two types of exterior, marble and glass curtain wall, gives this facade character.

軽快なガラス製庇の下の南面にある小さな銀行入口。写真は閉店後、通用口となる建具が地下から上がった状態。開店時はガラス扉に変わる。

Public entrance found under the south glass eaves. Photo taken after closing, and the entrance's fittings moved up from ground. When the bank is open, these will retard underground, revealing the glass door.

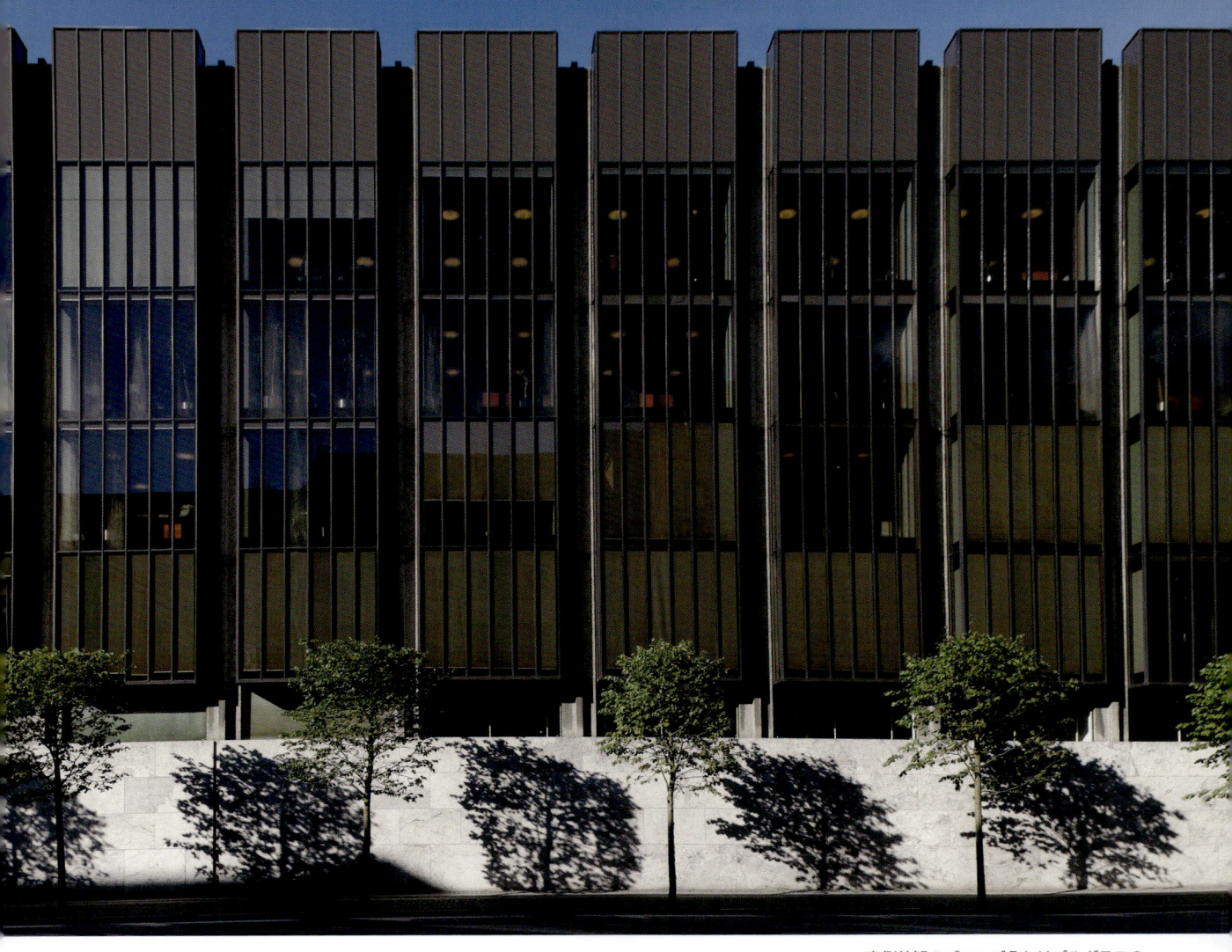

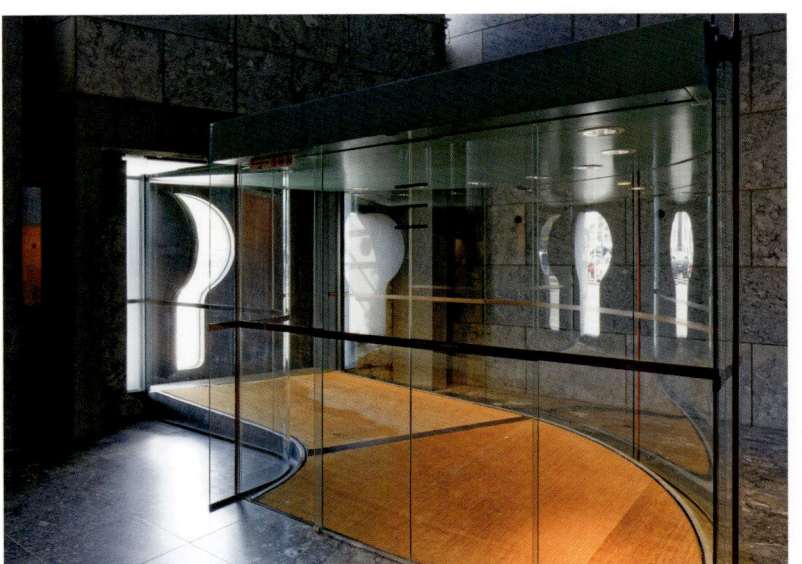

東側外観のブロンズ色トリプルガラスの
カーテンウォール。

Bronze-colored triple glass curtain wall, found on east exterior.

閉店後の入口を風除室側から見る。入口から中に向けて風除室の床が傾斜していて、目線を下げることによりエントランスホールに入る時の視覚効果を最大限に演出している。

View of closed entrance from windbreak room. The floor of the windbreak room declines inwards, lowering visitors' line of sight. This maximizes the visual effect of entering the entrance hall.

The National Bank of Denmark

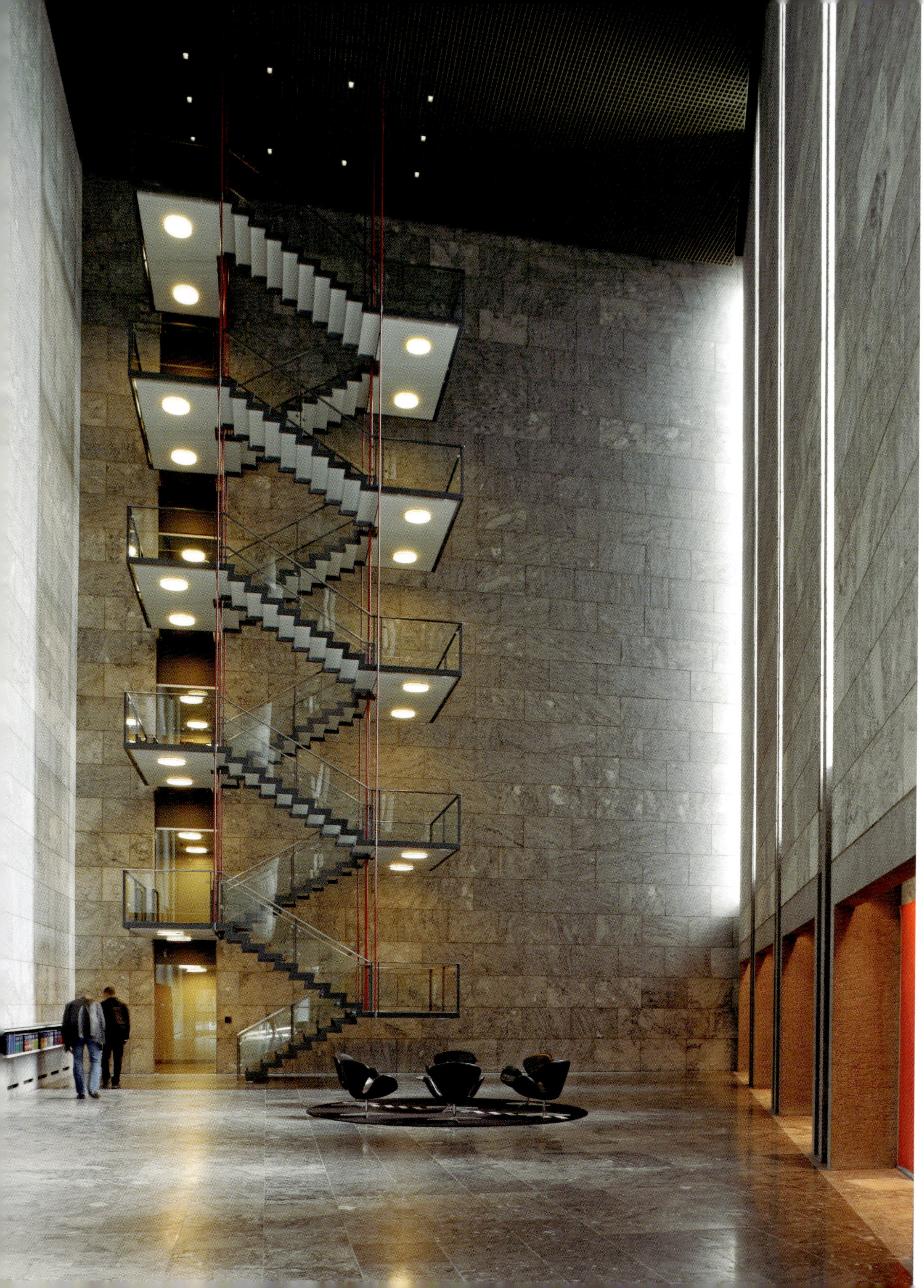

大階段上部からのエントランスホール見下ろし。晴天時には12時前後に南向き外壁の縦長のスリットから光の帯が対向する内壁に棒グラフのように投影される。

View of the entrance hall from atop the staircase. On a sunny day, the vertical slit on the south wall projects a band of light on the opposing wall, around twelve o'clock.

左頁：エントランスホール。天井の低い、下り勾配の風除室を出ると、高さ20mの大空間が現れ、奥にルーバー天井から吊られた大階段が浮遊しているように見える。

Left page: Entrance hall. After passing through a low, declining windbreak room, visitors enter a magnificent space 20 meters tall. The staircase, suspended from the louver ceiling, appears to be floating.

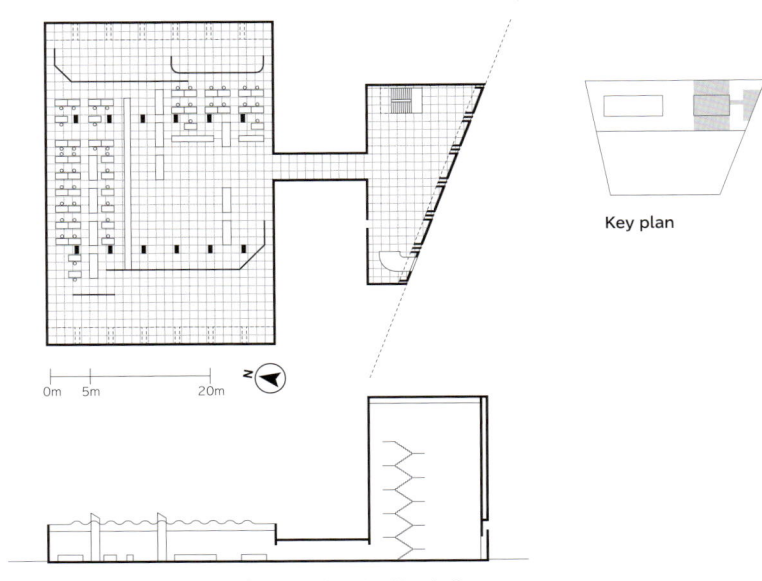

Key plan

Plan and Section of the lobby and the banking hall

The National Bank of Denmark

風除室からエントランスホールを見る。時計回りに回転しながら風除室を抜けると、天井の高いエントランスホールが現れる。

View of windbreak room and entrance hall. A clockwise journey through the windbreak room reveals the tall and spacious entrance hall.

階段側からのエントランスホール。モノトーンでデザインしたカーペットとスワンチェアが大空間を引き締める。

Entrance hall as seen from the stairs side. The black and white carpet, as well as The Swan, bonds the space into one.

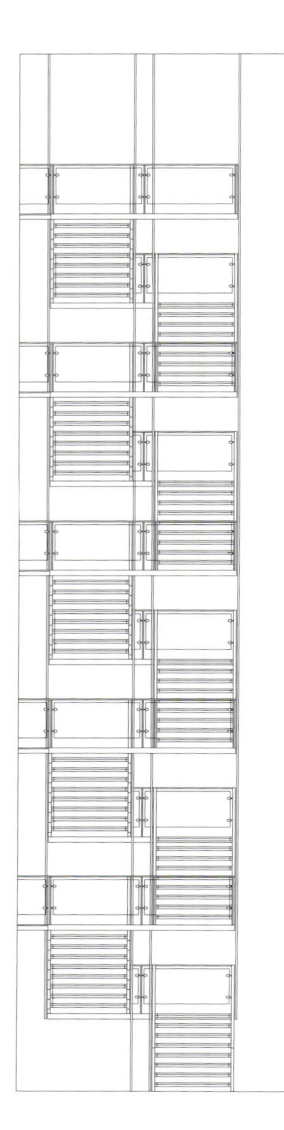

階段踊り場よりエントランスホールを見る。ロドオア市庁舎(p.188)の鉄骨吊階段をさらに洗練させたヤコブセンの直階段の集大成。

Entrance hall as seen from staircase landing. The staircase, an even more refined version of the steel frame suspended staircase than the one at the Rodovre City Hall (p.188), is the culmination of Jacobsen design.

軽快な踊り場が浮遊感を感じさせる。

The light feeling of the landing gives a floating sensation.

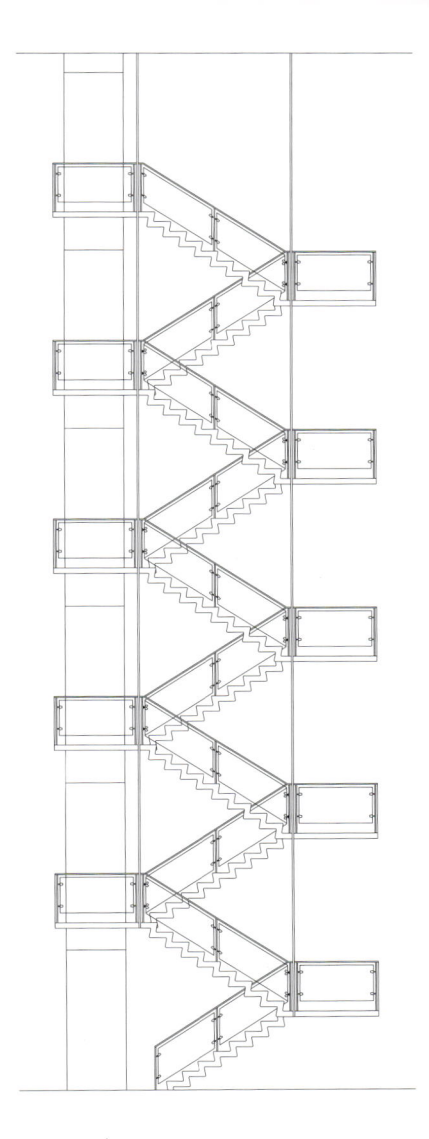

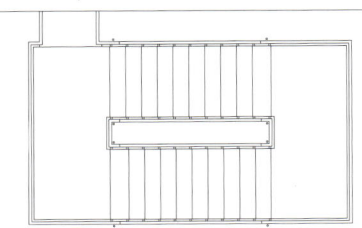

Plan and Elevation

0m 1m 2m 5m

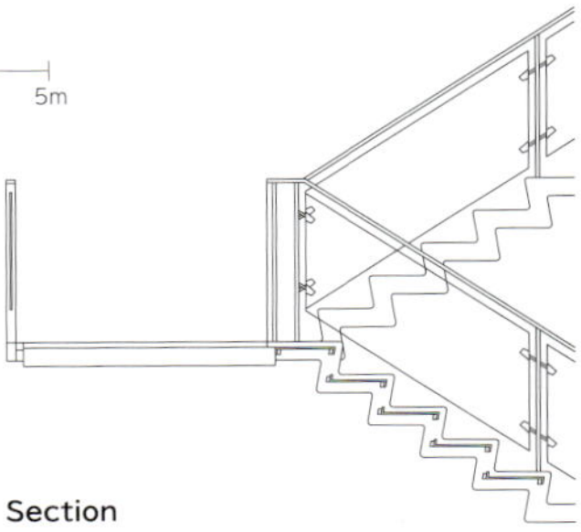

Section

階段ディテール。デザインされたササラ桁の形が美しい。赤く塗られた鋼材が階段を吊っている。
Details on the stairs. The design of the cut stringers is remarkable. Steel painted red suspends the staircase.

階段ササラ桁のディテール。
Details on the cut stringers.

The National Bank of Denmark

営業室から見たエントランスホールへの通路。通路手前の壁面に掛けられた時計は「バンカーズ・クロック」。

Passage to entrance hall, as seen from the banking hall. The clock on the wall is the "Bankers Clock."

営業室にあるトップライトをもつプラントボックス。ヤコブセンが好んだ蘭などの鉢が吊るされている。

Glass cases with a top light, located in the banking hall. Plant pots that Jacobsen loved, such as orchids, are suspended.

営業室全景。トップライトをもつプラントボックスによって空間を仕切りながら、視界をつなげている。天井照明は、もともとはロドオア市庁舎の議場と同じレフランプのアッパーライトが使われていた。

Full view of the banking hall. Glass divides the space without sacrificing visibility. Once, the ceiling housed ref-lamps same as those in the Rodovre City Hall light the ceiling.

2階事務室から低層階の屋上庭園を望む。
View from the second floor office of the rooftop.

抽象的なデザインの屋上庭園。
Abstractly designed rooftop garden.

Key plan

5階の社員食堂から低層部の屋上庭園を見る。
View of the rooftop garden from the fifth floor employee cafeteria.

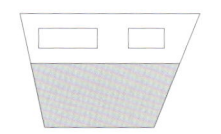

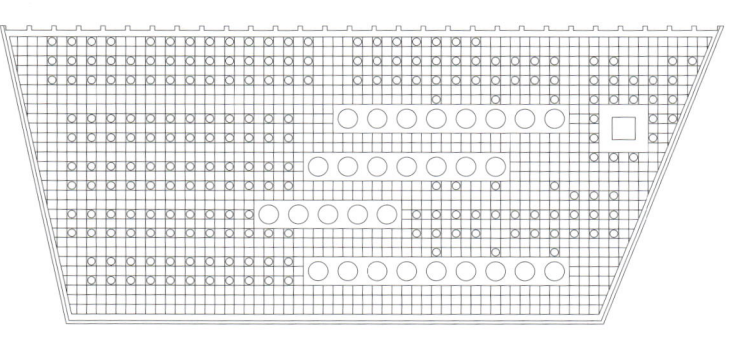

Roof plan of the mintage department

0m 10m 20m 50m

The National Bank of Denmark

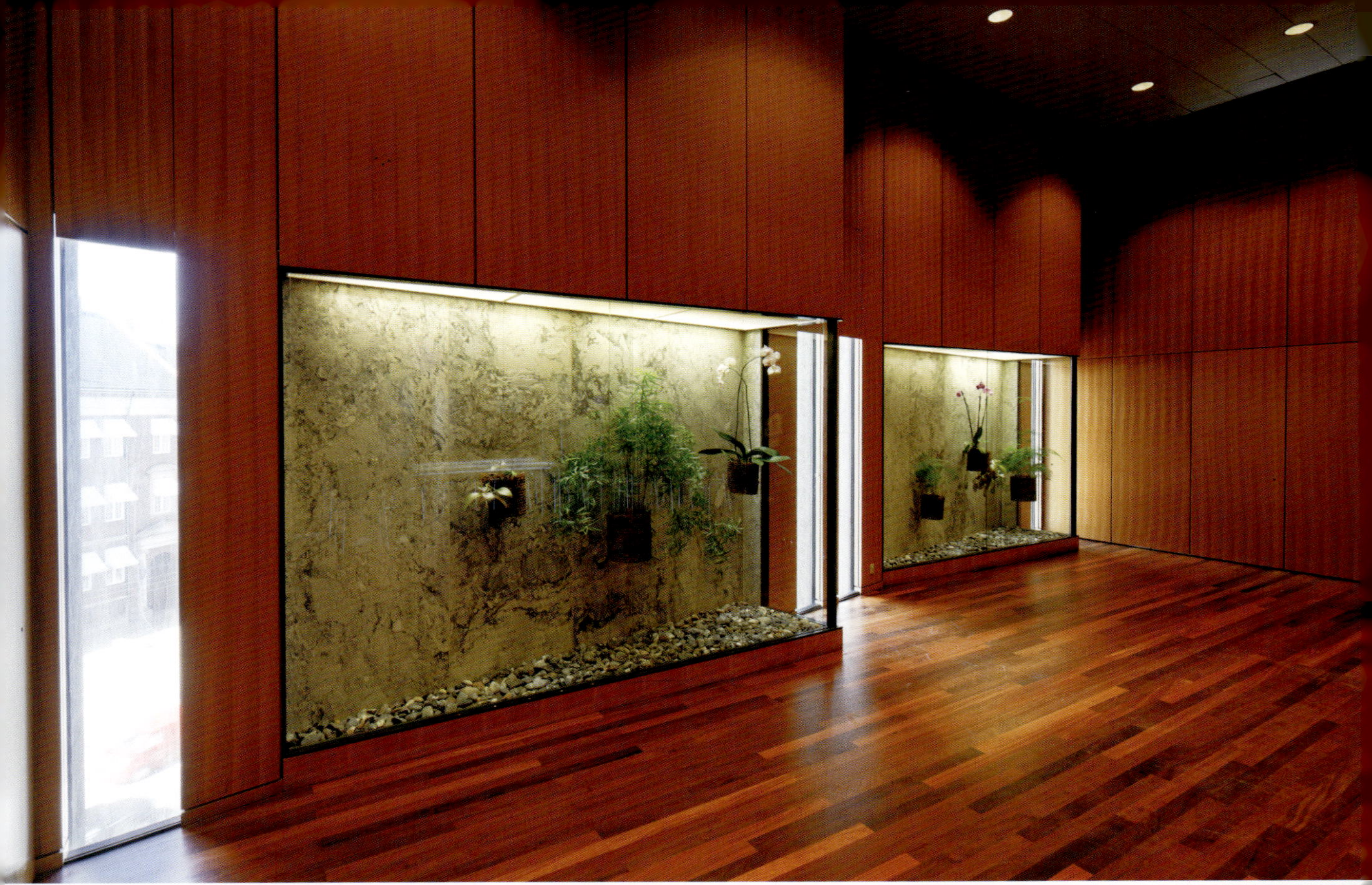
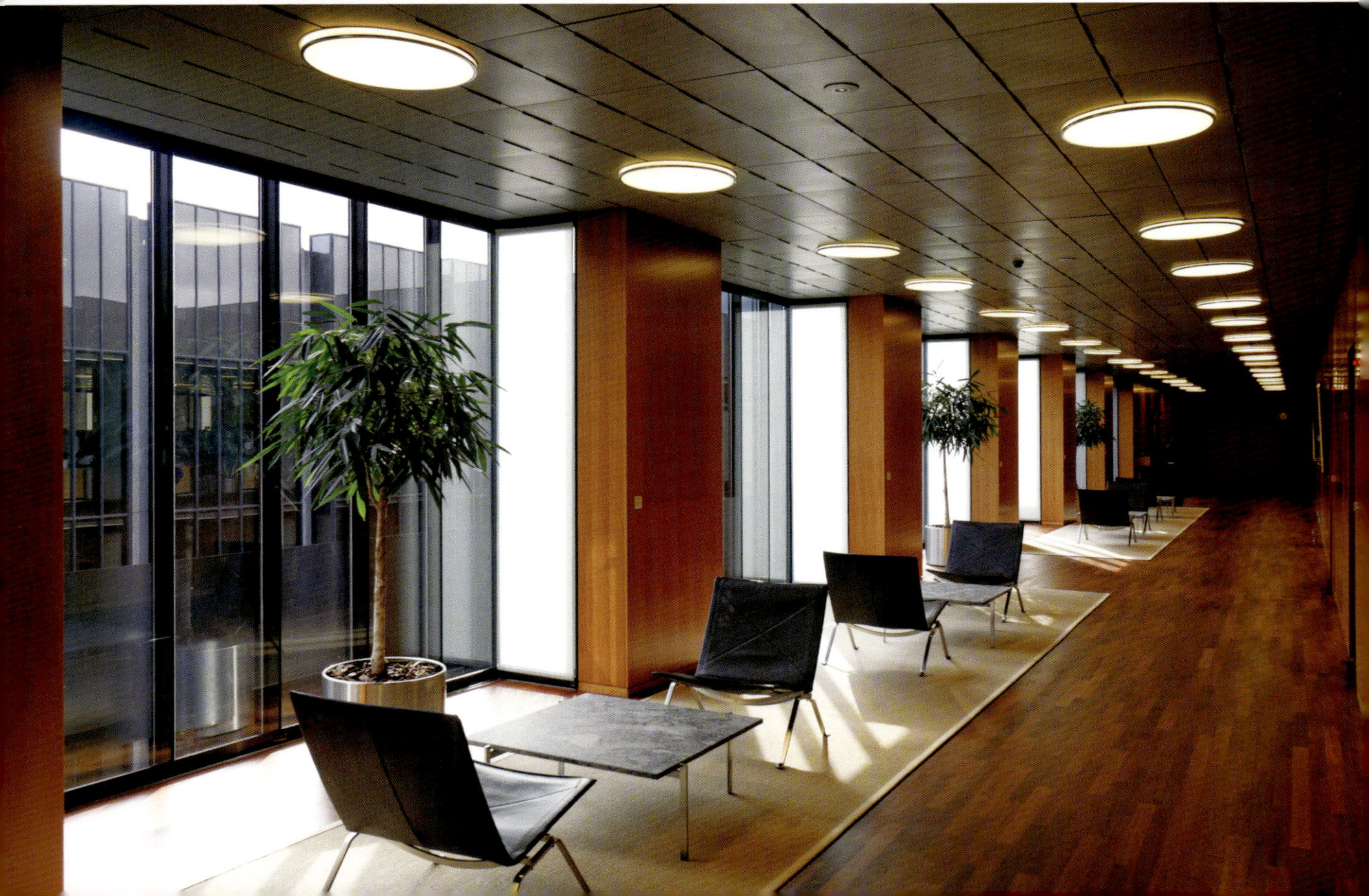

左頁上：5階スモーキングルーム。上部にトップライトのあるプラントケースが雁行して並ぶ。

Left page top: Glass cases with top light are arranged in echelon in fifth floor smoking room.

左頁下：中庭側通路。トリプルガラスのカーテンウォールの内側の空気層には結露防止のニクロム線が仕込まれている。パンチングメタルのシステム天井はスリット部分が吹出口となっている。照明器具は「ムンケゴーランプ」。

Left page bottom: Courtyard-side passageway. Nichrome wire to prevent condensation can be found within the air space of the triple glass curtain wall. The slits in the punching metal ceiling system are wind outlets. Lighting is "Munkegard Lamp."

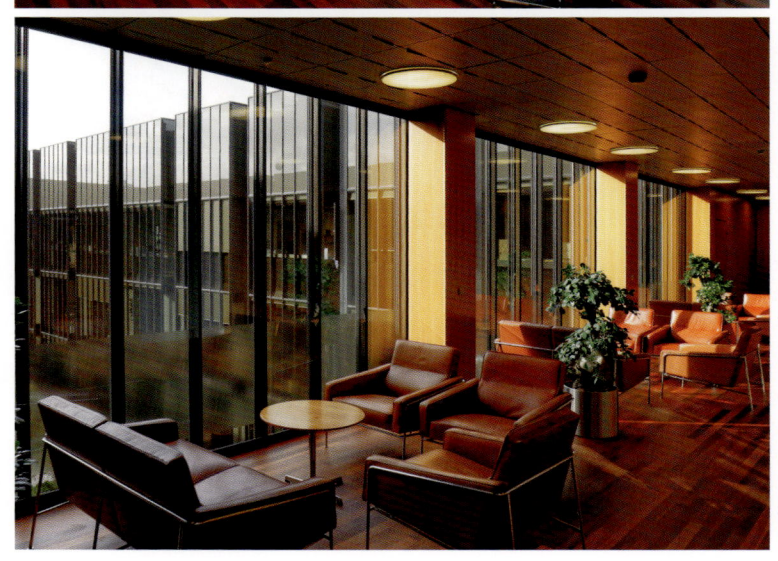

5階の役員会議室（上）。

Top: Fifth floor, executive meeting room.

5階の役員大会議室（中）。

Middle: Fifth floor, large executive meeting room.

5階役員フロアの中庭に面したラウンジ（下）。

Bottom: Lounge facing courtyard, fifth floor, executive area.

The National Bank of Denmark

１期北側高層部の中庭。ヤコブセン独特の造園デザインでまとめられている。

Courtyard in northern higher part of the building. Jacobsen showed his unique gardening design.

ヤコブセンの水彩画による北側の中庭の植栽計画。

A watercolor drawn by Jacobsen shows his planting design for the northern courtyard.

屋上より中庭を見下ろす。正面奥の扉から中庭に出ることができる。

View of courtyard from roof. The door ahead is the entrance to the courtyard.

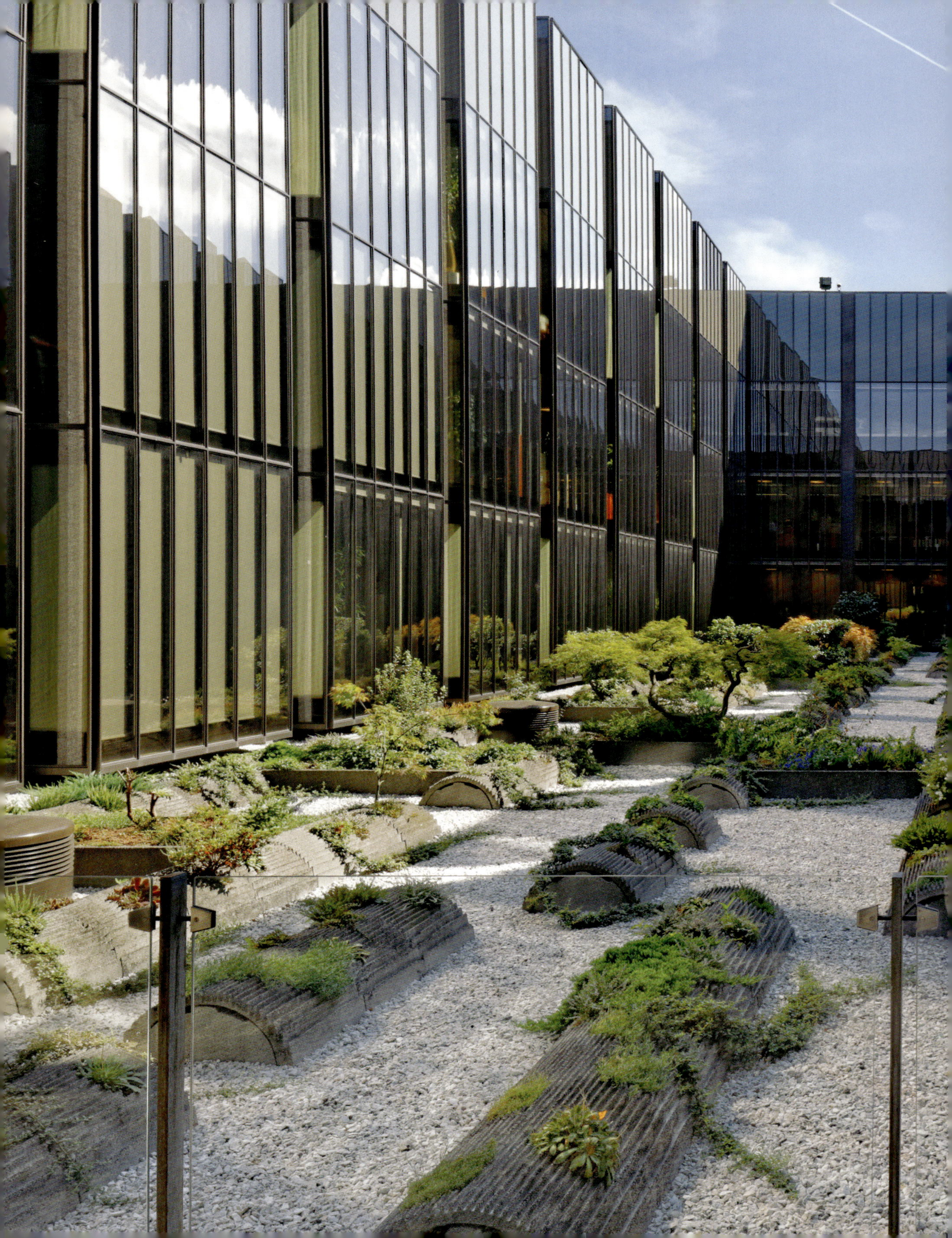

前頁正面奥の扉から中庭に出る。古代の倒壊した円柱をモチーフにしたユニークな植栽。

Entering the courtyard from the door mentioned last page. Unique gardening is themed on collapsed ancient pillars.

THE PRODUCT DESIGN
BY ARNE JACOBSEN

アルネ・ヤコブセンのプロダクトデザイン
鈴木敏彦

アルネ・ヤコブセンは、北欧を代表するプロダクトデザイナーである。彼の名前を知らなくても、「アントチェア」や「セブンチェア」を目にしたことがあるだろう。今や彼の椅子は北欧デザインのアイコンになっているのだ。

　北欧の国々のデザインが「北欧デザイン」と初めて総称されるのは1950年代後半である。きっかけとなったのは1954年から3年半にわたってアメリカ24都市とカナダを巡回した「スカンジナビアのデザイン展」だ。北欧の素材とクラフトマンシップによる上質な日用品は、機械化による安物の大量生産品に嫌気がさしていた北米の生活者に歓迎され、北欧デザインとして浸透した。また、イタリアで3年ごとに開催されたミラノ・トリエンナーレも北欧デザインを強烈に発信する場となった。1957年の第11回トリエンナーレではヤコブセンがグランプリを獲得した。この時の「4130モデル」は以後「グランプリチェア」と名付けられた。

　ヤコブセンはリ・デザインの手法をコーレ・クリントから学んだ。過去の名作にまつわる経験や知恵を捨てず、活用しながら新しいフォルムに昇華していく。デザインのアイデアだけでなく、その時代の最先端の素材と技術を用いたクラフトマンシップが完成度を極める。彼はプロダクトデザインを建築のインテリアエレメントとして開発したが、現在ではその多くがプロダクト製品として人気を博している。生産する企業は、新しい素材、色、加工技術を用いて常に進化した製品を販売する。こうして、ヤコブセンのデザインはオリジナル性を保ちながら現代性をまとうことができ、プロダクトが更新されるヤコブセンの建築は色あせることがない。

　本稿では、ヤコブセンのトータルデザインの一翼であるプロダクトデザインに焦点を当てる。建築の変遷に合わせて5期に区分して紹介する。

Arne Jacobsen is a designer of products that are representative of Scandinavia. You would have seen "The Ant" and "The Seven" without knowing his name. Today, his chairs have become icons of Scandinavian design.

It was in the late 1950s that the design created in Scandinavian countries was first called "Scandinavian design." The beginning was an exhibition of "Scandinavian Design," which was held in 24 cities throughout the United States and Canada over a period of three and a half years starting in 1954. Fine home furnishings made with Scandinavian materials and craftsmanship became popular and known as Scandinavian Design. Consumers in North America welcomed them because they had become tired of cheap and machine-made, mass-produced goods. Also, the Triennale di Milano, which was held every three years in Italy, became a place in which Scandinavian design was heavily promoted and distributed. In 1957, Jacobsen received the grand prize for a chair, "model 4130," which was later called "Grand Prix."

Jacobsen learned the redesign process from Kaare Klint. The important aspects of this are to preserve and employ the wisdom and experience that former designers had cultivated in creating masterpieces and reuse them to create new forms. Not only the idea of design was emphasized, but also craftsmanship with materials and state-of-the-art technology for perfection. Jacobsen designed interior elements for his architecture, although most of them have become popular as product designs. Companies endeavor to develop them with new materials, colors and processing technology. Thus, Jacobsen's designs retain originality and exhibit modernity. Consequently, his architecture has never lost its appeal because his products are always being replaced by new ones.

In this article, I have focused on product designs, which contributed to his total design. To better understand the evolution of Jacobsen's style of architecture, we will examine five phases of his career.

Toshihiko Suzuki

第 I 期 1925–1942
未来の家、ベルビューシアター、ステリング・ビル、オーフス市庁舎、スレロド市庁舎

1925年、23歳のヤコブセンは、カイ・フィスカが設計した「パリ万国博覧会デンマーク館」で椅子をデザインし、銀メダルを受賞する。デンマーク王立芸術アカデミーに入学した翌年の快挙だった。これがヤコブセンのプロダクトデザイナーとしての第一歩である。ヤコブセンはクリントの教えに沿い、正統な肘掛け椅子のスタイルを保ちつつ、これまでの装飾を排除してリ・デザインしている、直線とエッジを強調したシャープさと、背板と座面を籐で編んだ軽やかさが印象的だ。

1929年、ヤコブセンは籐と竹で編んだ「ブラックスラッグ・チェア」を制作し、コペンハーゲンのフォーラム住宅展示会にて実物大モデルの「未来の家」に展示した。同年、ルイスポールセンにフロアランプもデザインして商品化している。ヤコブセンは引き続き竹の椅子に取り組み、1936年に「AJ237 バスケット・チェア」を開発して、「夏の家」のリビングに置いた。

「ベルビューシアター」(p.46) では波打つ形状の座席を、レストランではダイニングチェアをデザインした。いずれもフリッツ・ハンセンがスチーム・ベント・プライウッド(蒸気で曲げた成形合板)で製造したもので、同社はこのダイニングチェアを数年間販売した。

「ステリング・ビル」(p.72) と「セントステファン銀行支店」(1935-1936) ではオーパルガラス製のペンダントランプと真鍮のデスクランプ(1936)をデザインし、ルイスポールセンで製造した。

「オーフス市庁舎」(p.78) では、後に家具デザイナーとして名を馳せるハンス・J・ウェグナー(1914-2007)が家具と什器のデザインを担当した。ウェグナーは1931年に17歳で木工マイスターの資格を取り、コペンハーゲンの工業学校家具技術コースと美術工芸学校家具科で学んだ。そして1940年から1943年までヤコブセンとエリック・ムラーの事務所に勤務して、「オーフス市庁舎」の家具と内装を担当した。「オーフス市庁舎」から感じられる質の高さはウェグナーの助力によるところが大きい。

ヤコブセンは市議会の椅子から、ウォールランプ、ウェディングホールの2連の椅子、玄関ホールのベンチ、灰皿、壁掛け時計まですべてをデザインした。ヤコブセンにはプロダクトデザインのみならず、グラフィックデザインの才能もあった。市庁舎で発表したローマ数字をアレンジした壁掛け時計は「ローマン・クロック」として商品化された。日本でも、「オーフス市庁舎」で用いたアルファベットや数字をヤコブセンのタイポグラフィとして復刻し、マグカップやインテリア雑貨に用いて販売している会社がある。

「オーフス市庁舎」と同時期に設計をすすめ、同年に竣工した「スレロド市庁舎」(p.102) においても、時計、ドアノブ、照明器具そして家具に至るすべてをデザインした。両市庁舎には共通点も多く、共通するプロダクトもある。

Danish Pavilion at Paris Exhibition 1925
Chair with armrest, 1925 / Awarded silver medal

"House of the Future" at Housing Exhibition at the Forum 1929
The Black Slug, 1929 / wicker

Spring Exhibition at Charlottenborg 1937
AJ237 Basket Chair, 1936 / bamboo, wicker, fabric cushions

Phase I   1925–1942
House of the Future, Bellevue Theater, The Stelling Building, Aarhus City Hall, Sollerod City Hall

In 1925 and at 23 years of age, Jacobsen designed a chair for the Danish pavilion, which was developed by Kay Fisker. The chair won a silver medal in the Paris Exhibition. This was a great feat for Jacobsen who had been enrolled in the Royal Danish Academy of Fine Arts for only one year. Jacobsen had taken his first step as a product designer. He followed Klint's design philosophy and created a chair gave an impression of sharpness by its straight lines and edges and of lightness by its rattan seat and back.

In 1929, Jacobsen released "Black Slug Chair" and exhibited it at real size model of "House of the Future" at Housing Exhibition at the Forum in Copenhagen. In the same year, he designed "AJ Floor Lamp," which Louis Poulsen commercialized. Next, Jacobsen developed a bamboo chair, "AJ237 Basket Chair," and placed it into the living room of "Jacobsen's Summer House."

He designed wave-shaped seats for "Bellevue Theater" (p.46), and a dining chair for restaurant. Fritz Hansen manufactured both of them by a steam-vent plywood method and sold them for several years.

For "The Stelling Building" (p.72) and "St Stephen Bank" (1935–1936), Jacobsen designed a pendant lamp using opal glass and a desk lamp using brass (1936), and manufactured them by Louis Poulsen.

For "Aarhus City Hall" (p.78), Hans J. Wegner (1914–2007), who later won fame as a furniture designer, was responsible for the design of the furniture and fixtures. At 17 years of age, Wegner qualified as a Woodworking Meister in 1931. He studied furniture and technology at a technical college, and then enrolled in the furniture course of the Danish School of Arts and Crafts. Subsequently, he worked in the design office of Jacobsen and Erik Møller from 1940 to 1943, where he was in charge of furniture and the interior of "Aarhus City Hall." The fine quality of this building was due to his efforts.

Jacobsen designed everything. This included the chairs for the City Council, wall lamps, benches for two persons in a wedding hall, benches in the entrance hall, ashtrays and wall clocks. He had a talent for both product design and graphic design. The city hall's wall clock, whose face he designed with new typography based on Roman numerals, was commercialized as a "Roman Clock." A company in Japan now has revived the same typography and used it for mag cups and interior goods.

Construction of "Aarhus City Hall" and "Sollerod City Hall" (p.102) proceeded at the same time. Jacobsen designed all aspects of the interior, including clocks, door knobs, lighting fixtures and furniture for both of the buildings. The two city hall projects have similarities and products in common.

Bellevue Theater
Restaurant Chair, 1934 / steam-bent plywood

Bellevue Theater
Theater Seat, 1932-1935 / bent plywood

The product design by Arne Jacobsen

The Stelling Building
The Stelling Pendant Lamp 1937 / glass, metal

The Stelling Building
The Stelling Pendant Lamp 1937 / glass, metal

Aarhus City hall
Light in the city Council Chamber, 1942 / copper, opaque glass shade

Aarhus City hall
Council Desk and Chair, 1937-1942 / wood, leather

Aarhus City hall
Bench and Ashtray, Entrance hall 1937-1942 / varnished wood, copper

304   Arne Jacobsen

Aarhus City hall
Pendant Lamp 1937-1942 / matt glass

Aarhus City hall
Roman Clock, 1942 / glass, aluminum

Aarhus City hall
Wall Lamp, 1937-1942 / opal glass, brass

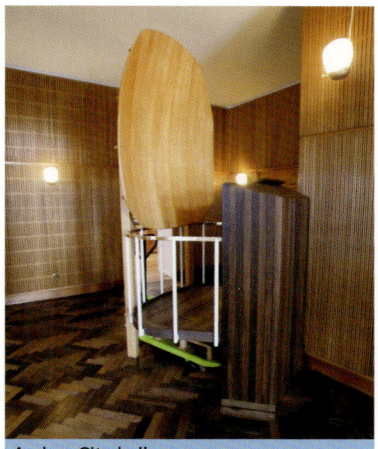

Aarhus City hall
Rostrum, 1937-1942 / varnished bent wood, steel

Aarhus City hall
Aarhus Handrail / brass, steel

Sollerod City Hall
Sollerod Handle, 1939-1942 / wood, copper

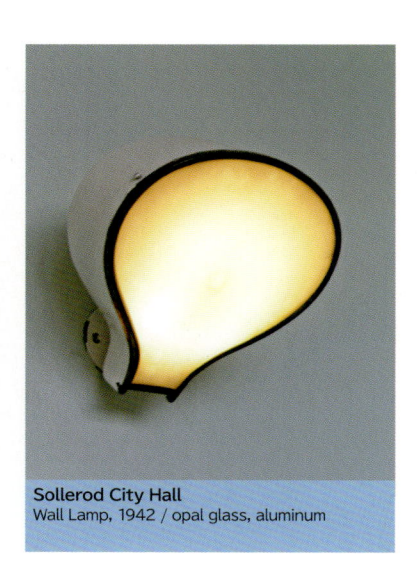

Sollerod City Hall
Sollerod Pendant Pendant Lamp, 1942 / opal glass globe

Sollerod City Hall
Wall Lamp, 1942 / opal glass, aluminum

The product design by Arne Jacobsen   **305**

第 II 期　1943–1946
スウェーデン亡命

スウェーデン亡命時、ヤコブセンはテキスタイルデザインと壁紙の制作に没頭した。ヤコブセンが水彩画を描き、シルクスクリーン技術に熟練していた妻のヨナが布地にプリントした。ヨナは、工芸デザイン学校にてデンマークのテキスタイル・プリントのパイオニアであるマリー・グメ・レチ（1895–1997）に学んだ経歴があった。1944年、スウェーデンのデパート、ノーディスカ・コンパニーにて発表した16パターンのテキスタイルのうち12パターンがスウェーデン・ナショナル・ミュージアムに買い上げられた。デンマークに帰還する前の1945年には、スウェーデン皇太子がヤコブセンのテキスタイルデザイン展を主催し、ヤコブセンは名実共にテキスタイルデザイナーとして名を馳せた。

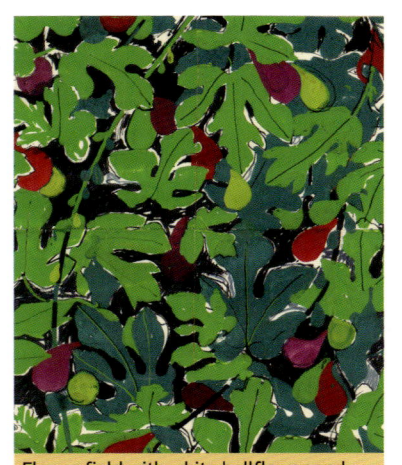

Meadow with horses, 1940s

Flower field with white bellflower and bleeding heart, 1951

Forest floor, 1944

Clover

Phase II   1943–1946
Refuge in Sweden

When he sought refuge in Sweden, Jacobsen buried himself in the creation of textile designs and wall paper. He drew in water colors and Jonna, who was skilled in the silk screen process, printed them. Jonna studied at a crafts and design school under the guidance of Marie Gudme Leth (1895–1997), who was a pioneer in textile design in Denmark. The Nordiska Kompaniet, department store in Sweden released 16 patterns and the Sweden National Museum purchased 12 patterns. A year before they backed to Denmark, the Prince of Sweden hosted in 1945 an exhibition of textile designs for Jacobsen. Thus, Jacobsen won fame as a textile designer both in name and in reality.

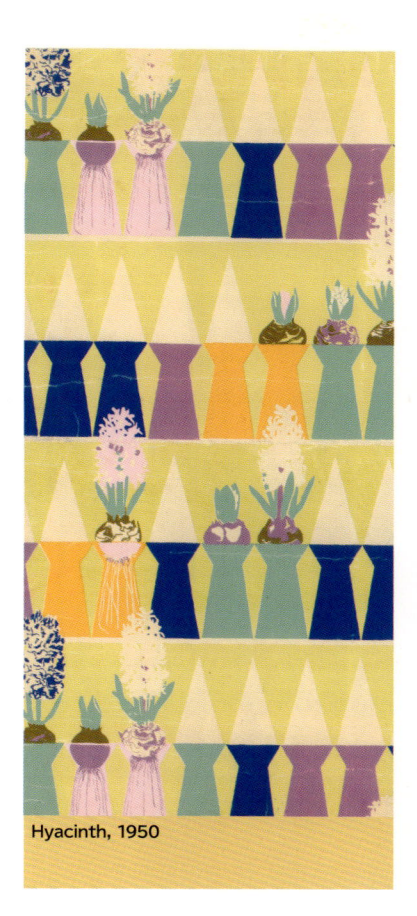

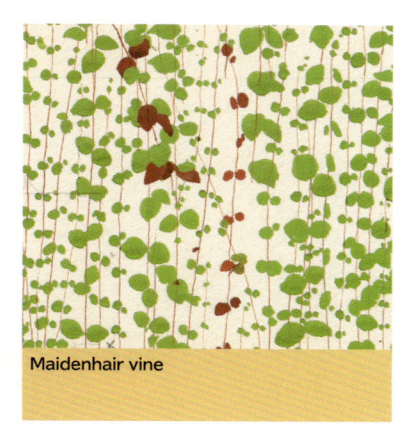

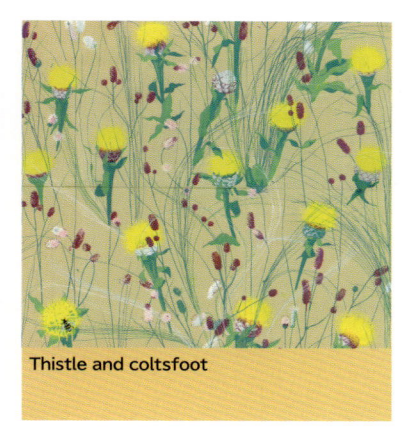

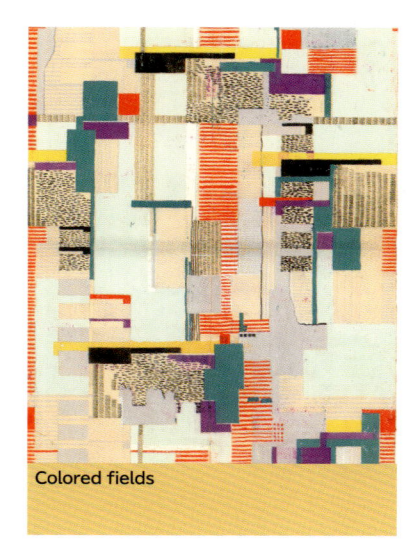

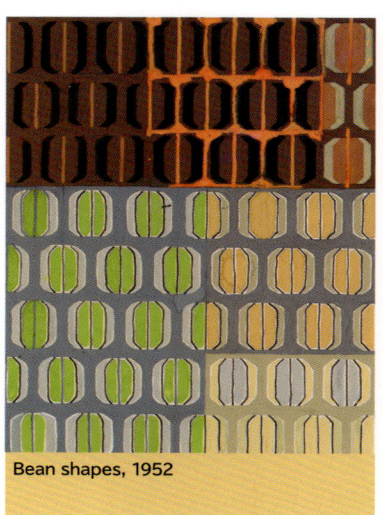

Hyacinth, 1950

Maidenhair vine

Thistle and coltsfoot

Colored fields

Bean shapes, 1952

Cactus

The product design by Arne Jacobsen

第 III 期　1946–1956
ノヴォ治療ラボラトリウム社員食堂、ムンケゴー小学校、ロドオア市庁舎

1952年、ヤコブセンは「ノヴォ治療ラボラトリウム」(p.64) の社員食堂を設計するに当たり、成形合板を用いた新しい椅子を思い付いた。「3100 アントチェア」である。その下地にチャールズ&レイ・イームズが1946年に発表した「プライウッド・チェア」があることを、ヤコブセンは隠してはいない。イームズ夫妻には成形合板の椅子の製法において一日の長があったが、背面と座面を分離して構造材でつないでいた。そこでヤコブセンは背と座を一体化する単純な構造を思い付くが、その制作は簡単ではなかった。どうしても背と座のつなぎ部分にひびや歪みが生じてしまう。その問題箇所を左右から取り除いていくうち、くびれた形状の「アントチェア」が出来上がり、200脚をノヴォの食堂に収めた。

ヤコブセンが好んで3本脚をデザインしたのは、凹凸のある煉瓦の床の上でも安定し、円形のテーブルの周囲に並べやすいからだった。座った人から3本脚は転倒しやすいとクレームがあっても、人間の脚を足せば5本脚になると言ってヤコブセンは譲らなかった。しかし1955年に発表した「3107 セブンチェア」は4本脚で設計した。成形技術と接着剤の進化が、より複雑な形状の成形を可能にし、座り心地に貢献した。

「ムンケゴー小学校」(p.152) では、ヤコブセンは照明、カーテン、透明なアクリルを用いた「ラウドスピーカー」(1955)、小学生用のデスクと2種類の椅子をデザインした。「ムンケゴーランプ」(1955)はルイスポールセン社が発売し、ヤコブセンのインテリアデザインの定番となった。「ロドオア市庁舎」をはじめ、数多くのプロジェクトで使用している。講堂のステージのカーテンの模様は、スウェーデン時代の主流だった花柄から、抽象的な幾何学的なパターンへと変わった。

ヤコブセンとフリッツ・ハンセンは「アントチェア」と「セブンチェア」の生産で体得した成形技術を新作に応用した。「3105 タンチェア」は「セブンチェア」の背面形状を変えたバリエーションのひとつである。「3106 タンチェア」は座面の中心から4本の脚が広がる構造だ。スタッキングには向かないが、1985年に「3102」の製造番号で一時期再販した。

「4130」は1957年の第11回ミラノ・トリエンナーレでグランプリを受賞したため、「グランプリチェア」と呼ばれている。

「ロドオア市庁舎」(p.188) では、議会室に革張りの肘掛け付き「セブンチェア」を収めた。ヤコブセンが「ロドオア市庁舎」のためにデザインした壁掛け時計は、「シティーホールクロック」として商品化された。

Novo Terapeutisk Laboratorium
Chair 3101, The Ant, four-leg chair / bent plywood, steel
Table 3600, 1952 / plywood, steel

Novo Terapeutisk Laboratorium
Chair 3100, The Ant, three-leg chair, 1952 /
bent plywood, steel

Phase III 1946–1956

Canteen for Novo Terapeutisk Laboratorium, Munkegard Elementary School, Rodovre City Hall

In 1952, when Jacobsen design a company canteen for "Novo Terapeutisk Laboratorium"(p.64), he came up with a new chair, "3100 The Ant," in which he used molded plywood. He did not conceal the fact that his inspiration was the "Plywood Chair" that Charles and Ray Eames released in 1946. Although they possessed a bit more experience than him in creating molded plywood chairs, they used a structure to connect the back and the seat. Then, Jacobsen thought of a simpler structure with which to integrate the seat and the back. However, it was not easy to create. Somehow, cracks and distortion occurred in the connecting section of the seat and back. As he removed the defective areas, a chair that had a slender waist emerged. He had created "The Ant." He consequently delivered 200 pcs of "The Ant" to the canteen.

Jacobsen preferred to design a three-legged chair, because it is stable even on a rugged brick floor and such chairs are easy to arrange around a circular table. Although users claimed that the three-legged falls over easily, Jacobsen insisted that a user could count his or her human legs, which gave an additional two legs to the chair, and that with five legs, the chair became stable. However, in 1955 he designed "3107 The Seven" with four-legs. The evolution of adhesive agents and molding technology enabled more difficult shapes to be molded, and contributed more comfortable sheets to be made.

For "Munkegard Elementary School" (p.152), Jacobsen designed lighting fixtures, curtains, transparent and acrylic "Loudspeakers" (1955), two kinds of chairs and desks for students. The "Munkegard Lamp" (1955) that Louis Poulsen released became a regular item of Jacobsen's interior design. He used it in "Rodovre City Hall" and many other projects. He designed abstract and geometric pattern for the curtain of the auditorium's stage, although he only designed floral pattern while he enjoyed refuge in Sweden.

Jacobsen and Fritz Hansen applied the molding technology that they had used in the production of "The Ant" and "The Seven" to a new chair. "3105 The Tongue" with a new chair back was a variation of "The Seven." "3106 The Tongue" had four legs that diverged outward from the center of the seat and therefore was not suitable for stacking. However, it was sold at one time under a product number of "3102." "4130" is called "Grand Prix" because it received the Grand-prix award at the 11th Triennale di Milano in 1957.

For "Rodovre City Hall" (p.188), Jacobsen delivered a leather-covered "The Seven" with an armrest for the Chamber. His wall clock for this building was manufactured as a "City Hall Clock."

Munkegard Elementary School
Desk 1951-1958 / bent plywood, steel
Chiar 3105, The Tongue, 1955 / bent plywood, steel

The product design by Arne Jacobsen

Munkegard Elementary School
Desk, 1951-1958 / bent plywood, steel
Chair 3105, The Tongue, 1955 / bent plywood, steel

Munkegard Elementary School
Munkegard Ceiling Light, 1955 / plexiglass, brass

Munkegard Elementary School
Chair 3103, 1957 / bent plywood, steel

Munkegard Elementary School
Chair 4130, 1957 / bent plywood, plywood

Munkegard Elementary School
Loudspeaker, 1948-1957 / plexiglass

Munkegard Elementary School
Stage curtain / fabric

Munkegard Elementary School
Trapeze curtain, 1956 / fabric

Rodovre City Hall
Ceiling Light, City Council Chamber, upward turned ref-lamps

Rodovre City Hall
Series 7, 1955 / bent plywood, steel

Rodovre City Hall
City Hall Clock, 1956 / glass, aluminum

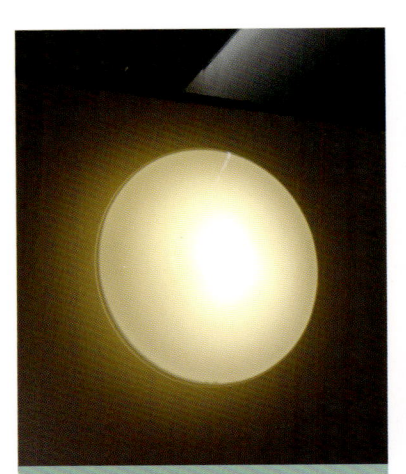

Rodovre City Hall
AJ Eklipta / AJ Discus, 1956 / blown glass

Rodovre City Hall
Chairs attached to the wall, unused state

Rodovre City Hall
Chairs attached to the wall, in-use state

The product design by Arne Jacobsen　311

第 IV 期 1956–1958
SASロイヤルホテル

1956年、SASスカンジナビア航空はコペンハーゲンの中央駅前に北欧の玄関口として最新鋭の旅客ターミナルと近代的なホテルの建設を決めた。「SASロイヤルホテル」(p.212)の設計を依頼されたヤコブセンは、最新のホテルライフを実現するためにトータルデザインを徹底する。ホテルの開業が新聞に取り上げられた際に「電気のスイッチまでもデザインされたホテル」と紹介されたほどだった。ヤコブセンはインテリアを構成するエレメントを開発しては、自分のイニシャルを冠して次々と製品化していった。1956年、カール・F・ピーターソン社から「AJドアハンドル」を発表した。1957年、客室用にシェードが動く「AJランプ」、バーカウンターにプレキシガラスの「バー・ペンダント」、Aミケルセン社からステンレス製の「AJカトラリー」を発表した。1958年、フリッツ・ハンセン社からロビー用に「エッグチェア」と「スワンチェア」、客室用に「ドロップチェア」、レストラン用に「ジラフチェア」を発表した。さらにさまざまな大きさのコーヒーテーブル、グラス、砂糖と塩と胡椒入れといったテーブルウェアを手掛けた。1959年、ルイスポールセン社からレストラン用に「AJロイヤル」、フリッツ・ハンセン社からロビー用に「ポットチェア」を発表した。これは植物の鉢を吊り下げたガラスケース（ウィンターガーデン）の前に並べる椅子であった。この他にも、絨毯やカーテンをデザインし、1960年には、ついに「SASロイヤルホテル」のトータルデザインが完成した。

現在では改装によってほとんどのインテリアが変更されたが、唯一、「アルネ・ヤコブセン・スイート」という606号室にて当時のデザインを見ることができる。606号室の扉を開けるとまず前室がある。天井の照明器具は「AJエクリプタ」である。正面に「AJドアハンドル」を用いた主室の扉が見える。扉を開けると「エッグチェア」、「スワンチェア」、「シリーズ3300」、「スタンダードランプ」が「テーブル3515」を囲んでいる。家具の色はコペンハーゲンの街並みを彩る屋根と同じ緑青色だ。目の粗い半透過のカーテンを閉めれば、テーブルセットと奥のベッドルームが仕切られる。四方の腰壁と化粧台と引出しには木目が魅力的な南洋材のベンゲが用いられている。この腰壁の溝に沿って「SASサイドランプ」を左右に動かすことができる。化粧台の天板を開けると自動的に内部の照明が点く。その前にはオリジナルの「ドロップチェア」がある。部屋の壁の一部はショーケースになっていて、「SASロイヤルホテル」のためにヤコブセンがデザインした鍵やキャンドルホルダーやカトラリーが飾られている。

ヤコブセンがデザインしたカトラリーは斬新なフォルムが特徴である。スタンリー・キューブリック(1928-1999)が監督した「2001年宇宙の旅」(1968)の食事のシーンに使用されたほどである。機能的には宿泊客に不評を買ったため、レストランではすぐに使われなくなった。現在では最上階のレストランである「アルベルトK」で夕食時に使用されている。

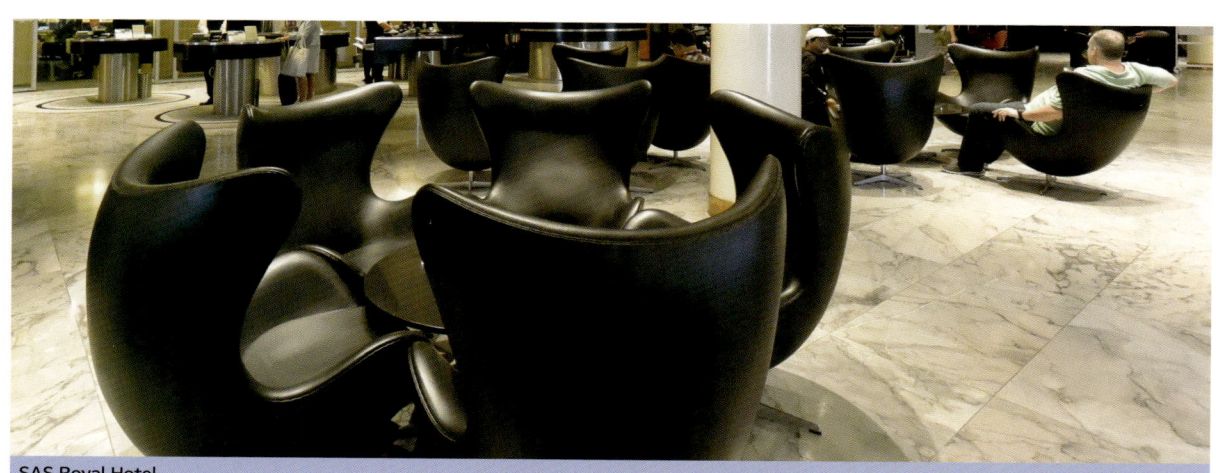

SAS Royal Hotel
The Egg, Hotel lobby, 1959 / polystyrene shell, leather, molded aluminum

Phase IV 1956–1958
SAS Royal Hotel

IIn 1956, Scandinavian Airlines System (SAS) decided to build a state-of-the-art terminal building and a modern hotel, "SAS Royal Hotel" (p.212) in front of the Copenhagen central station as a gateway to Northern Europe. They asked Jacobsen to create the latest in hotel living. Consequently, he created the total design of the hotel. On the opening day of the hotel, the newspaper reported that, "Even the electric switch was also designed." Whenever Jacobsen developed elements for the interior, he included his initials in their names. Examples include the "AJ Door Handle" for Carl F Petersen in 1956, the "AJ Lamp" for guestrooms and the "Bar Ceiling Lamp" using plexiglass for the bar counter for Louis Poulsen, "AJ Cutlery" for A Michelsen in 1957, "The Egg" and "The Swan" for the lobby's lounge, "The Drop" for guestrooms, and "The Giraffe" for the restaurant by Fritz Hansen in 1958. Moreover he designed various sizes of coffee tables: glasses, containers for sugar, salt and pepper, etc. In 1959, Jacobsen released "AJ Royal" by Louis Poulsen for the SAS restaurant, and "The Pot" by Fritz Hansen to place in front of the glass cases (Winter garden) in the lobby. He also designed carpets and curtains and, finally, the total design of the "SAS Royal Hotel" was completed in 1960.

Although most of the interior design of "Arne Jacobsen Suite" has been changed due to refurbishment of the hotel, room 606 retains the interiors of those days. When you open the door of room 606, you enter a front room. "AJ Eklipta" is used as ceiling light fixtures. Before you is the door to the main room with an "AJ Door Handle." "The Egg," "The Swan," and "the series 3300," "Standard Lamp" are located around the "3515." The color of the furniture is the same as the bluish-green of the building roofs in Copenhagen. When you close the loose-textured and semi-transparent curtain, the table set and bed rooms behind are divided. Attractively-grained, tropical wood, is used for the continuous wooden knee wall, four walls and drawers. An "SAS Side Lamp" can be moved along a channel in the knee wall. Opening the table top of the dressing tables turns on bright lamps. The room contains a replica of the original "The Drop." Part of the wall in the room serves as a show case of the key, candle holder and cutlery that Jacobsen designed for "SAS Royal Hotel."

The cutlery Jacobsen that designed has a distinct novel shape. It was used for meals in a movie entitled "2001: A Space Odyssey" (1968), which was directed by Stanley Kubrick (1928–1999). However, hotel guests have complained that it is not user friendly and the restaurant stopped using it. A restaurant on the top floor, "Albert K," employs it today, but only for dinner.

SAS Royal Hotel
The Swan, Hotel lobby, 1959 / polystyrene shell, fabric, molded aluminum

SAS Royal Hotel
Standard Lamp 28710, 1957 / metal support and base

SAS Royal Hotel   The Egg, Room 606, 1959 / polystyrene shell, specially ordered colored fabric, molded aluminum   The Swan, Room 606, 1959 / polystyrene shell, specially ordered colored fabric, molded aluminum   Table 3515, Room 606, 1958 / teak or rosewood, aluminum   Series 3300, Room 606, 1956 / specially ordered colored fabric, chrome steel   The Drop, Room 606, 1958 / polystyrene shell, specially ordered colored fabric, steel

SAS Royal Hotel
Curtain partition, Room 606 / fabric close up

SAS Royal Hotel
Curtain partition, Room 606 / fabric normal view

SAS Royal Hotel
Dressing table and drawers, Room 606, 1958 / wenge, formica, steel

SAS Royal Hotel
SAS Side Lamp, Room 606, 1957

SAS Royal Hotel
AJ Light, Cafe Royal, 1957 / aluminum, steel, wrought steel

SAS Royal Hotel
Tableware, Room 606, 1958 / steel plated with silver
candleholder, ashtray, stemmed goblets, condiment set: salt, pepper and mustard

SAS Royal Hotel
AJ Flatware, Restaurant, 1957 / steel plated with silver

SAS Royal Hotel
AJ Door Handle, 1956 / bronze, white or gold coated, matt or polished finish

SAS Royal Hotel
Room key of SAS Royal Hotel, Room 606 / bronze

The product design by Arne Jacobsen

第Ⅴ期 1959–1971
セント・キャサリンズ・カレッジ、デンマーク国立銀行

オックスフォード大学「セント・キャサリンズ・カレッジ」(p.230) もまた、ヤコブセンがカトラリーから家具に至るまでトータルデザインを手掛けた場所だ。

「セント・キャサリンズ・カレッジ」は全寮制である。夕食時には教授と生徒が食堂に一堂に会する。教授陣は食堂に入る前に黒いガウンをまとう。ハリーポッターの映画に出てくる食堂のシーンはイギリスの私立校における食堂の伝統的なイメージである。ヤコブセンは教授陣の長いテーブル席を際立たせ、特別な場所にするために「ハイバックチェア」をデザインした。1962年に試作し、1965年の家具展でフリッツ・ハンセン社から発表した「オックスフォードチェア」である。背板を低くして肘掛けを付けた会議室用の「ローバックチェア」もある。また、テーブル上には1962年にルイスポールセン社で製造した「セーラーズハット・ランプ」という照明を設置した。

1963年、学生寮の一室を有効に使うため、デスクと椅子、イージーチェア、引き出し式のベッドをデザインした。図書館には肘掛け付きの「セブンチェア」と「スワンチェア」、ラウンジには円形のコーヒーテーブルと「ポットチェア」、講堂には1本脚のセブンチェアを並べた。

1967年、ヤコブセンは義理の息子が副社長を務めるステルトン社からステンレスのテーブルウェア、「シリンダライン」を発表した。コーヒーカップ、ティーカップ、水差し、調味料入れ、プレート、灰皿がすべて円筒で出来ている。ヨナの息子であるペーター・ホルムブラッドはなんとしても義理の父にデザインを依頼したかったので、半年をかけて懇願し、ついに夕食時のナプキンにスケッチを描いてもらった。何度も試作を重ねて完成したこのシリーズは1967年にID賞、1968年に米国インテリアデザイナー協会デザイン賞を受賞した。

「デンマーク国立銀行」(p.278) はヤコブセンの遺作であり、トータルデザインの集大成でもある。これまでのプロダクトデザインを総動員し、さらに新たなプロダクトを開発した。1969年、まったく新しいコンセプトの水栓金物をボーラ社から発表し、同年ID賞を受賞した。1969年、スカンジナビア家具フェアにて「セブンチェア」の完成形である「3108エイトチェア」を発表した。1970年発表の肘掛け付きの「3208 リリーチェア」は、包み込むような形状でシリーズ最高の座り心地を実現したものである。1971年、ヤコブセンは永眠した。当時の担当者であったプロダクトデザイナーのテイト・ヴァイラントが現在もヤコブセンのデザイン監修を引き継いでいる。

例えばフリッツ・ハンセンでは成形の難しさから1980年代に「リリーチェア」の生産を終了したが、2007年に成形技術の向上により再度生産を始めた。この時、現代人の体格に合わせてサイズをオリジナルよりひと回り大きくした。2012年、「セント・キャサリンズ・カレッジ」の創立と「オックスフォードチェア」誕生50周年を記念して、フリッツ・ハンセン社はオリジナルの「オックスフォードチェア」を発売した。背面から座面にかけて布地や皮を張るフロントパディング仕様で改良した。

ヤコブセンの建築がいつまでも色あせないのは、こうしてインテリアを構成するプロダクトが常に進化しているからだ。

St Catherine's College
Outdoor benches / Wood seat attached to the brick wall.

Phase V   1959–1971
St. Catherine's College, Danmarks Nationalbank

"St Catherine's College" (p.230) was another project for which Jacobsen provided the total design from cutlery to furniture. "St Catherine's College" is a boarding school. Its student and academic staff come together in the Hall at dinner. Professors don black gowns before entering the dining room. The dinner scene of the Harry Potter Movies portrays a typical dining room of a private school in England. Jacobsen designed the "Oxford High Back Chair" to highlight the long table for faculty seating and to make it a special place. Jacobsen created a prototype in 1962, and released it at a furniture exhibition for Fritz Hansen in 1965. He also created the "Oxford Low Back Chair" with armrests for the conference room. He designed lighting "Sailor's Hat," which was commercialized by Louis Poulsen, on the tables.

In 1963, Jacobsen designed furniture that would be more suitable for the limited space of a dormitory room. This included a desk and chair, easy chairs, and a drawer type of bed. For the library, he provided a circular coffee table, "The Pot," "The Swan," and "The Seven" with armrests, and "The seven" with one leg for a lecture theater.

In 1967, Jacobsen created stainless tableware, the "Cylinda Line," for Stelton where his son-in-low worked as Vice President. Coffee cups, tea cups, jugs, seasonings containers, plates, and ashtrays are all made in cylindrical forms. Peter Holmblad, a son of Jonna, wanted Jacobsen to design them differently and pestered his stepfather to do so for more than six months. Finally, Jacobsen agreed and sketched a design of a new line of items on his dinner napkin. After conducting many trials, a new series of utensils was completed and received an ID Prize in 1967, as well as the International Design Award of the American Institute of Interior Designers in 1968.

"Danmarks Nationalbank" (p.278) was a posthumous work of Jacobsen and the culmination of his total design. He used in this project every product that he had ever designed. In addition, he developed new products. In 1969, he released a faucet that was based on a totally new concept for Vola and received the ID Prize. He released "3108 The Eight," which was his final design of "The Seven" at the Scandinavia Furniture Fair in the same year. In 1970, he released "3208 The Lily," which was the most comfortable for users of the designs in that series. Jacobsen passed away in 1971. Teit Weyland, a former member of the staff of Jacobson's studio, has taken over the supervision of design as a product designer.

In the 1980s, Fritz Hansen stopped the production of "The Lily". However, it was resumed in 2007 because of improvements in molding technology. At that time, its size was modified to better suit it to the physiques of modern people. In 2012, Fritz Hansen improved the original "Oxford Chair" with upholstery, such as cloth or leather on the seat and the back of the chair. The architecture of Jacobsen never fades because his products enhance the interior and are constantly evolving.

St Catherine's College
The Oxford Chair, Hall, 1962 / plywood, metal high back

St Catherine's College
The Oxford Chair, 1962 / plywood, metal low back

The product design by Arne Jacobsen

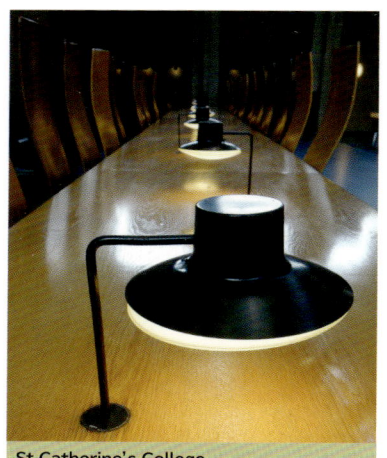

St Catherine's College
Table Lamp, Hall, 1962 / metal, glass

St Catherine's College
Sailor's Hat Lamp, Hall, 1952 / opal glass shade

St Catherine's College
Cylinda line, 1967 / stainless steel, satin finish
salt and pepper sets

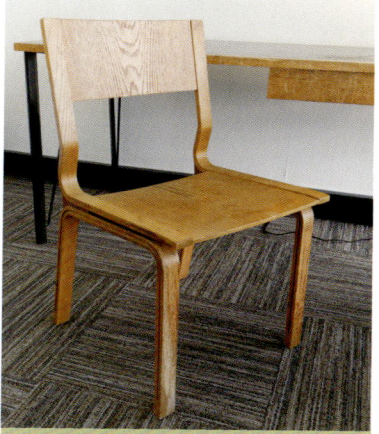

St Catherine's College
Standard chair, study bedroom, 1963 / oak
plywood   Desk, 1963 / plywood, steel

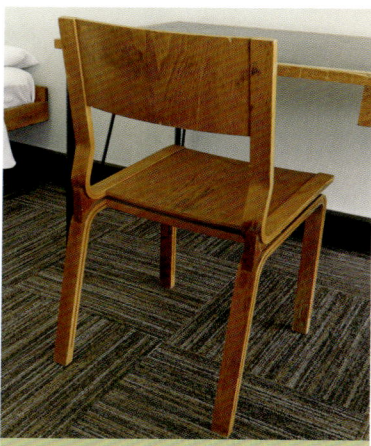

St Catherine's College
Standard chair
The other side.

St Catherine's College
Sofa bed, study bedroom / oak plywood
The couch doubles as a pull-out bed. When pulled out, it becomes a bed.

St Catherine's College
Easy Chair, study bedroom, 1963 / oak
plywood

Danmarks Nationalbank
Glass case, The banking hall / glass, plant pots

Danmarks Nationalbank
Glass case, The employee lounge / glass, plant pots

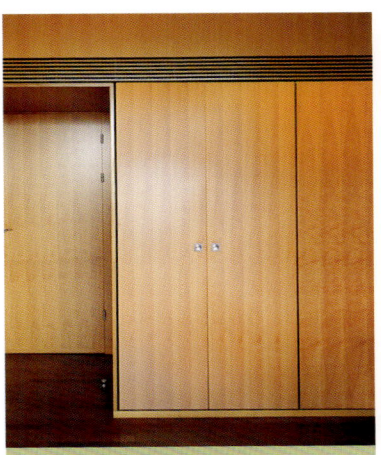

Danmarks Nationalbank
Office's cabinet wall / pear tree veneer, maple
The deep cabinet is closed.

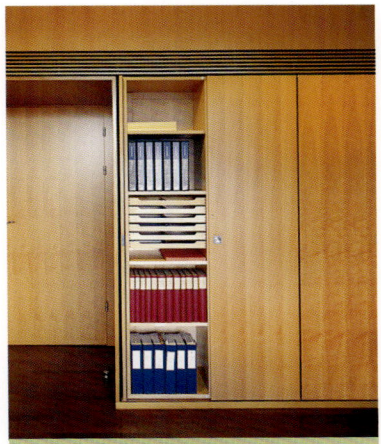

Danmarks Nationalbank
Office's cabinet wall.
The side-hinged doors slides into the panel wall.

Danmarks Nationalbank
Office's cabinet wall.
The deep cabinet is fully open.

Danmarks Nationalbank
Bankers Clock, 1970 / glass, chrome steel

Danmarks Nationalbank
Vola series, 1967-1969 / chrome steel or enameled epoxy resin

Danmarks Nationalbank
The Lily 3208, 1970 / bent plywood, leather, steel

The product design by Arne Jacobsen **319**

掲載作品MAP
A map of the works listed in this book

① ベルビュー海水浴場　The Bellevue Beach （p.34）
② ベラヴィスタ集合住宅　Bellavista Housing Complex （p.38）
③ ベルビューシアター　Bellevue Theater （p.46）
④ テキサコ・ガソリンスタンド　Texaco Service Station （p.60）
⑤ ノヴォ治療ラボラトリウム　Novo Terapeutisk Laboratorium （p.64）
⑥ ステリング・ビル　The Stelling Building （p.72）
⑦ オーフス市庁舎　Aarhus City Hall （p.78）
⑧ スレロド市庁舎　Sollerod City Hall （p.102）
⑨ スモーク・ハウス　Fish Smokehouse （p.116）
⑩ スーホルムⅠ　Soholm I （p.120）
⑪ ホービュー・セントラルスクール　Harby Central School （p.128）
⑫ シモニュー邸　The Simony House （p.140）
⑬ ムンケゴー小学校　Munkegard Elementary School （p.152）
⑭ ニュエア小学校　Nyager Elementary School （p.168）
⑮ ラウンド・ハウス　Round House （p.180）
⑯ ロドオア市庁舎　Rodovre City Hall （p.188）
⑰ ロドオア中央図書館　Rodovre Library （p.200）
⑱ SASロイヤルホテル　SAS Royal Hotel （p.212）
⑲ セント・キャサリンズ・カレッジ　St Catherine's College （p.230）
⑳ デンマーク国立銀行　Danmarks Nationalbank （p.278）

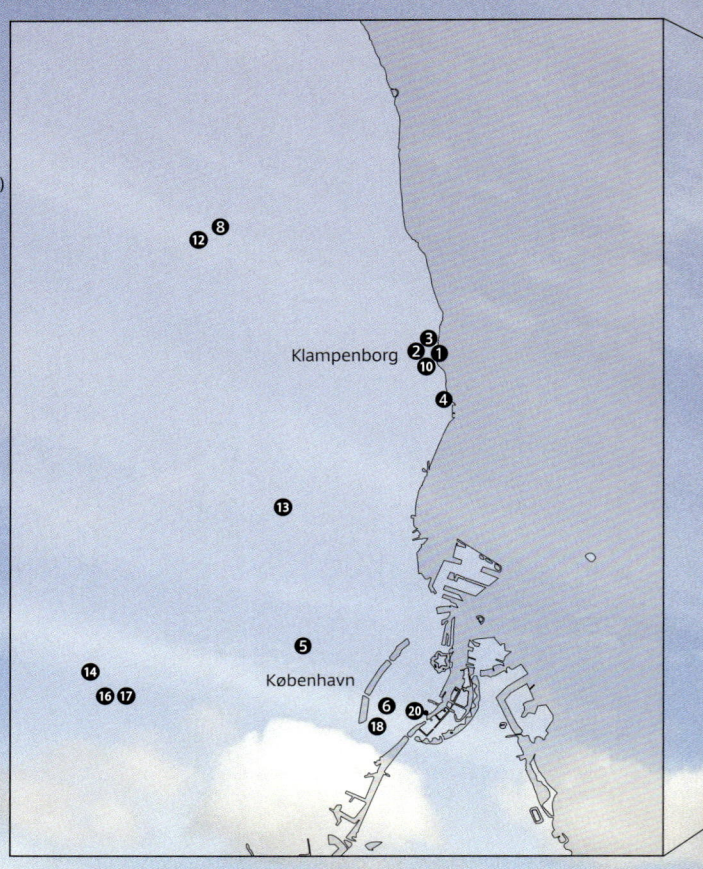

Århus ⑦
Jacobsen's Summer House ⑨ ⑮
⑪
⑲

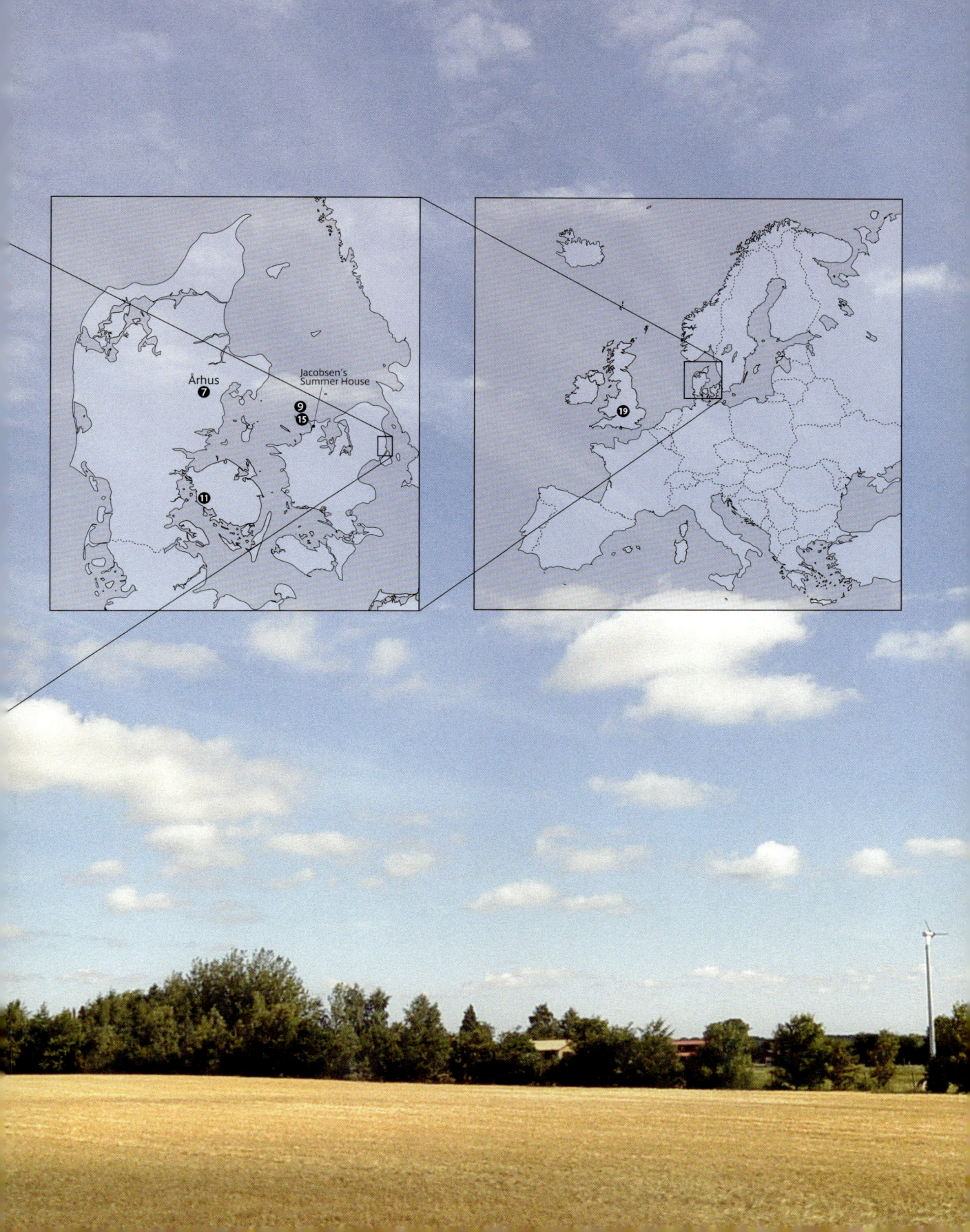

主要参考文献
A COMPLETE LIST OF REFERENCES

書籍　Books

Carsten Thau & Kjeld Vindum, *ARNE JACOBSEN*, The Danish Architectural Press, Copenhagen, 2001 / 2nd edition, 2002

Erik Zahle, *Skandinavisches Kunst Hand Werk*, Droemersche Knaur, Deutschland, 1963：エリック・ザーレ著、森本健次訳『スカンジナビア デザイン』彰国社、1964

Félix Solaguren-Beascoa de Corral, *Arne Jacobsen Approach to his Complete Works 1926-1949*, The Danish Architectural Press, Copenhagen, 2002

Félix Solaguren-Beascoa de Corral, *Arne Jacobsen Approach to his Complete Works 1950-1971*, The Danish Architectural Press, Copenhagen, 2002

Félix Solaguren-Beascoa de Corral, *Arne Jacobsen: Drawings 1958-1965*, The Danish Architectural Press, Copenhagen, 2002

Félix Solaguren-Beascoa de Corral, *Arne Jacobsen: Works and Projects*, Editorial Gustavo Gill, S.A., Barcelona, 1987-89

Kjeld Vindum, *Arne Jacobsen's own summerhouse*, Realdania Byg, Odense C, 2013

Michael Sheridan, *ROOM 606: The SAS House and the Work of Arne Jacobsen*, Phaidon Press Limited, London / NY, 2003

Patricia de Muga & Laura Garcia Hintze & Sandra Dachs, Introduction by Félix Solaguren-Beascoa, *Arne Jacobsen: OBJECTS AND FURNITURE DESIGN*, Ediciones Polígrafa, S.A., Barcelona, 2010

Penny Sparke, *An Introduction to Design and Culture in the Twentieth Century*, Harper & Row, 1986：ペニー・スパーク著、白石和也＋飯岡正麻訳『近代デザイン史──二十世紀のデザインと文化』ダヴィッド社、1993

Poul Erik Tøjner & Kjeld Vindum, *ARNE JACOBSEN Arkitekt & Designer*, Danish Design Centre, Copenhagen, 1995 / 5th printing, 2001

Roger Ainsworth & Clare Howell, *St Catherine's Oxford: A Pen Portrait*, Oxford and Third Millennium Publishing Limited, London, 2012

Stuart Wrede, *The architecture of Erik Gunnar Asplund*, MIT Press, USA, 1980：スチュアート・レーデ著、樋口清＋武藤章訳『アスプルンドの建築──北欧近代建築の黎明』鹿島出版会、1982

伊藤大介『図説　北欧の建築遺産──都市と自然に育まれた文化』河出書房新社、2010

島崎信＋東京・生活デザインミュージアム『美しい椅子──北欧4人の名匠のデザイン』枻出版社、2003

鈴木敏彦＋大塚篤＋小川真樹＋半田雅俊＋村山隆司『北欧の巨匠に学ぶ図法──家具・インテリア・建築のデザイン基礎』彰国社、2012

鈴木敏彦＋杉原有紀『北欧の巨匠に学ぶデザイン──アスプルンド／アールト／ヤコブセン』彰国社、2013

武藤章『アルヴァ・アアルト』鹿島出版会、1968

吉村行雄＋川島洋一『E.G.ASPLUND　アスプルンドの建築1885-1940』TOTO出版、2005

雑誌・カタログ　Magazines & Catalogues

Arne Jacobsen, Dansk Møbelkunst, 2002

2G Libros Books, Arne Jacobsen: Public Buildings, Editorial Gustavo Gili, S.A., Barcelona, 2005

Arne Jacobsen: Absolutely Modern, Louisiana Museum of Modern Art, Denmark, 2002

※アルファベット・50音順
Book titles were arranged by alphabetical order and Japanese syllaby.

クレジット
CREDITS

Photograph / Drawings　写真・図版

Yukio Yoshimura　吉村行雄
All photographs, except those on pages:

Atelier OPA Co.,Ltd.
24, 27, 304 (bottom), 305 (middle, bottom left, bottom center), 311 (bottom center, bottom right), 314, 315 (bottom right), 316-317, 318 (top, bottom)

REPUBLIC OF Fritz Hansen　フリッツ・ハンセン日本支社
8

Arkitektur- och designcentrum
12

The National Bank of Denmark
26, 319 (top, middle)

Danish National Art Library
7, 14-17, 32 (right), 36 (left), 57 (middle, bottom), 63 (bottom right), 77 (middle), 97, 138 (top), 139 (top left), 159, 160 (bottom), 177 (bottom), 195 (bottom), 214 (top, bottom), 221 (top), 306 (top, bottom left, bottom center), 307

The Danish Architectural Press
10-11, 13, 20-23, 25, 36 (right), 56, 98, 296 (bottom), 302, 303 (left), 310 (middle center, bottom left)

Nami Nishino　西野奈美
306 (bottom right)

Shinchosha, *Geijyutu Shincho*, Photo by Seiichi Maeda
© 新潮社『芸術新潮』撮影・前田誠一
310 (bottom right)

Texts　文

Toshihiko Suzuki　鈴木敏彦
All texts, except those on pages:

Yukio Yoshimura　吉村行雄
324-325, 327

Captions　キャプション

Yukio Yoshimura　吉村行雄
All captions, except those on pages:

Toshihiko Suzuki　鈴木敏彦
10-27, 36 (bottom), 56, 57 (middle, bottom), 63 (bottom right), 97, 98 (bottom), 138 (top), 139 (top left), 159, 160 (bottom), 177 (bottom), 195 (bottom), 214, 296 (bottom), 302-319

Architectural Drawings　図面

Atelier OPA Co.,Ltd.
※本書に掲載した図面は、設計時と竣工時の資料を元に作成した。
The drawings appearing in this book were created based on materials from the time of design and the time of completion.

Production Cooperation　制作協力者

■Architectural Drawings　図版制作
Munetaka Ishikawa / Atelier OPA Co., Ltd.　石川宗孝

■English Translation　英訳
Yuki Sugihara / Atelier OPA Co., Ltd.　杉原有紀

■Research Cooperation　取材協力
Jan Thorndal / The National Bank of Denmark
Elisabeth Fogh / Aarhus City Hall
Steen Henriksen / Fish Smoke house, Round house
Jesper Kort Andersen / Rodovre City Hall
Poul Larsen, Boline Andersen Karademir / Radisson Blu Royal Hotel & Radisson Blu Scandinavia Hotel, Copenhagen
Nieller Mandrup / Nyager Elementary School
Jan Overbye / Munkegard Elementary School
James Bennett / St Catherine's College
Alasdair Heath / Downe House
Helle Ryberg, Lars M. Mørch / Novo Nordisk A/S
Ayaho Suzuki, Shinji Yonekura / Fritz Hansen Japan
鈴木理歩、米倉慎二／フリッツ・ハンセン日本支社

■Photography Supply　資料提供
Eric De Groat / Arkitektur- och designcentrum
Mikael Bøgh Rasmussen, Claus M. Smidt / Danish National Art Library
Per Henrik Skou, Martin Keiding / The Danish Architectural Press

■Editorial Cooperation　編集協力
Nampoosha　南風舎
Ayako Onodera　小野寺綾子
Seiichi Maeda / SHINCHOSHA　前田誠一／新潮社
Nami Nishino　西野奈美
Shinji Aratani / Louis Poulsen Japan　荒谷真司／ルイス・ポールセン・ジャパン

あとがき
吉村行雄

　初めてヤコブセンの作品を見たのは、私がヨーロッパ旅行の3度目で北欧を回った時だった。格安航空券を手に入れ、1978年5月の連休を利用して当時一番安いルートだった南回りでデンマークに入り、初めてコペンハーゲンの「デンマーク国立銀行」のエントランスロビーに立った時の感動を今でも思い出すことができる。設計の仕事を始めた頃、書店や図書館などで目にした、ヤコブセンの洋書にあった営業室の天井照明をどうしても見たくて、立ち入り禁止だった営業室に通じる通路の前で、ガードマンにしつこく頼み込んで通路奥の営業室手前まで入れてもらった。やっとの思いで、この年できたばかりの営業室とその天井照明の効果に感激したのを、昨日のことのように思い出す。

　私の北欧関連の本は、2005年の『アスプルンドの建築』（TOTO出版）に続いて、2冊目となる。9年後にやっと2冊目というゆっくりとしたペースである。1冊目のアスプルンドも、撮影を始めてから20年を要しているので、今度はその半分の時間で出版できたともいえる。もともと建築家を志して、大学で建築を専攻し、社会に出てからは設計実務を経験してきたので、私の建築写真の捉え方、取り組み方はほかの写真家の方とは少し違うかもしれない。振り返れば、学生時代に近代建築史の講義が面白く、ぜひこの眼で西欧の名建築を確かめたいという思いが人一倍強かったように思える。当時、図書館に行っても北欧関連の書籍はあまりなく、あったとしてもほとんどが洋書で、掲載されている写真は、竣工当時に撮られたモノクロ写真が多く、同じ写真がどの書籍にも使われていることが気になっていた。例えば植物に造詣が深かったヤコブセンが力を入れた植栽についても、彼は10年、20年後の樹木が成長した時の姿を想定していたはずであり、竣工当初の写真では、彼の目指した造園デザインは理解できないのではないかと思っていた。そこで、近代建築の名作が70年、80年経ってどのように使われているのか、環境はどう変化したのかを現地に行ってこの眼で確かめ、写真に撮りたいといつしか思うようになっていた。実際に撮影に出掛けてみると、ほとんどの建物がオリジナルの姿を尊重しつつ、丁寧に維持・管理され、家具のレイアウトなど、現在の使われ方に応じて適切に変更、改修されていることが分かった。それはすなわち、ヤコブセンの建物やプロダクトをこよなく愛し、利用する人びとの、ヤコブセンへの敬意の表れではないかと思う。

　「デブでケチ」という風評で語られることの多いヤコブセンであったが、彼の生み出す作品は建築であれ家具であれカトラリーであれ、いずれも洗練を極めたモダンデザインである。日本ではともすれば家具デザイナーとして見られることの多いヤコブセンだが、幸いにして学生時代に教えを受けた教授が、ヤコブセンのことを、建築から家具、什器、テキスタイルから、日用品に至るまで、その建築に必要なものすべてをデザインしコーディネートする、真の意味での「トータルデザイナー」として評価していたからこそ、私の関心がヤコブセンの創り出すすべてに注がれたのかもしれない。

　本書は私が長年にわたりヤコブセンの作品を観続け、撮影を続けてきたものの中から、琴線に触れた、興味深い建築を選んだ「写真集」でもある。すでに私の北欧行脚は30回を超えた。あとどれだけ北欧建築の魅力を伝える写真を撮り続けることができるか分からないが、私の眼と足で確かめた名作の、今の姿をこれからも伝えていきたいと思う今日この頃である。

Postscript
Yukio Yoshimura

When I visited the Scandinavian countries on my third trip to Europa, I first viewed Jacobsen's works. In May 1978, I purchased discounted air tickets and flew to Denmark on the southern route, which offered the lowest price at that time. I can still remember how I was moved to stand at the entrance hall of Danmarks Nationalbank. When I began to design architecture, I found Jacobsen's book in bookstores and libraries and noticed the ceiling lights in the banking hall of the bank. However, entry by the public to that hall was prohibited. I really had wanted to see it and so I pleaded persistently with a security guard to let me into the passage. Thus, I did enter before the banking hall, but only with difficulty. It seems like yesterday that I was moved by the just-completed banking hall and the effect of the ceiling lights.

This is my second book about Scandinavia, following *E.G. Asplund 1885-1940,* which was published by TOTO Publishing in 2005. The pace is slow. It is now nine years since I published first book. It took me twenty years to prepare the first book, while taking photographs to include in it. So, I can say that I managed to publish the second book in only half the time that I needed for the first. Originally I aspired to become an architect and majored in architecture in university. After graduating and finding a job, I gained experience in design and construction work. Consequently my interpretation and approach to architectural photographs may differ from those of other photographers. When I look back on my school days, I remember that the History of Modern Architecture lectures were of most interest to me. I wanted to visit and see European architectural masterpieces more than any others. Because there were few books about Scandinavia in the libraries, even if the book was almost a Western book and the photographs in it were monochrome, I was anxious to see same photo was printed in every book. For example, while Jacobsen focused on planting, a photo that was taken upon completion did not convey his ideal landscape design to us. He must have planned his plants on how they would appear 10 and 20 years later. Gradually, I came to aspire to take photographs of the actual site, to confirm how the masterpieces of modern architecture had been considered and how the environment had changed 70 and 80 years later. Finally, I visited the site and found that almost all buildings have been carefully maintained and controlled based on respect for their original appearance. The layout of furniture has been changed and modified in keeping with today's needs. I think that this reflects nothing but respect for Jacobsen from those who love deeply and use his architecture and product design.

It had been rumored once that Jacobsen was "fat and stingy." On the contrary, his creative works, such as architecture, furniture and cutlery, all are in a sophisticated modern design. In Japan, he is often regarded as a furniture designer. However, my professor during my school days considered him to be a real "total designer," who coordinated everything needed in the architecture, buildings, furniture, utensils, textiles and home furnishings. Therefore I might have been interested in all of his creative works.

This book was also a "photo album." While I was observing Jacobsen's works and taking photographs, I selected the most interesting architecture - that touched my heartstrings. I have traveled by foot through Scandinavia more than 30 times. I am not sure how much longer I can continue to do this and take photographs to convey the charm of Scandinavian architecture. However, nowadays I am determined to report on the appearances today of masterpieces that I have confirmed with my eyes and feet.

吉村行雄 (よしむら ゆきお)

建築写真家

1946年大阪生まれ。1971年武蔵野美術大学造形学部建築学科卒業後、竹中工務店入社。設計部、広報部、設計本部を経て2006年退職。現在 吉村行雄写真事務所を主宰。北欧文化協会理事、北欧建築・デザイン協会理事、日本建築写真家協会会員。

1998年ニューヨーク、2001年ストックホルムにて個展を開催。国内では個展、グループ展、講演会を多数開催。2007年武蔵野美術大学「芦原義信賞」受賞。

主な写真集に、『Light / Space / Architecture —— The play of daylight in buildings by Gunnar Asplund & Ragnar Ostberg』(Stockholms Stadsmuseum)、『TAKENAKA-A Book of Buildings』(竹中工務店)、『E.G.ASPLUND——アスプルンドの建築 1885-1940』(TOTO出版)、『建築家 前川國男の仕事』(美術出版社)、私製『建築カレンダー』などがある。

鈴木敏彦 (すずき としひこ)

建築家・デザイナー

1958年東京生まれ。工学院大学建築学科修士課程修了。黒川紀章建築都市設計事務所、フランス新都市開発公社EPAmarne、早稲田大学建築学専攻博士課程を経て、1999-2007年東北芸術工科大学プロダクトデザイン学科助教授、2007-2010年首都大学東京システムデザイン学部准教授、2010-2011年工学院大学工学部建築都市デザイン学科教授。2011年より工学院大学建築学部建築学科教授。

株式会社ATELIER OPA共同主宰。北欧建築・デザイン協会理事。日本インテリア学会理事。

グッドデザイン賞／中小企業庁長官賞、アジアデザイン大賞／グランプリ、レクサスデザインアワード2012、iFデザインアワード2014他受賞多数。

著書に、『世界で一番美しい建築デザインの教科書』(エクスナレッジ)、『北欧の巨匠に学ぶ図法——家具・インテリア・建築のデザイン基礎』(彰国社)、『北欧の巨匠に学ぶデザイン——アスプルンド／アールト／ヤコブセン』(彰国社)、『建築プロダクトデザイン——暮らしを劇的に変えるモノと空間の設計思想』(講談社)などがある。

YUKIO YOSHIMURA
(Architectural photographer)

Born in Osaka in 1946, Yukio graduated from the Department of Architecture at Musashino Art University in 1971. He joined Takenaka Corporation where he worked in the design department, the public relations department and the headquarters of the Design Division. Yukio retired from Takenaka Corporation in 2006. He is President of Yukio Yoshimura Photograph Office, Director of The Scandinavian Architecture and Design Institute of Japan and The Nordic Cultural Society of Japan and a member of Japan Architecture Photography Society.

Yukio held an exhibition of his photographs in New York in1998 and in Stockholm in 2001. He has held many individual exhibitions, group exhibitions and lecture meetings in Japan. He was awarded the "Yoshinobu Ashihara Prize" at Musashino Art University in 2007.

His representative photography books are *Light/Space/Architecture The play of daylight in buildings by Gunnar Asplund & Ragnar Ostberg* published for the exhibition at Stockholm City Museum, *TAKENAKA-A Book of Buildings* published by Takenaka Corporation, *E.G. Asplund, 1885-1940* published by TOTO publishing, *Works of Architect, Kunio Maekawa* published by Bijutsu-shuppansha Co., Ltd. and Architecture Calendar published as a private edition.

TOSHIHIKO SUZUKI
(Architect and Designer)

Born in Tokyo in 1958, Toshihiko completed the master's degree program of the Department of Architecture at Kogakuin University. He joined Kisho Kurokawa Architect & Associates, EPA Marne, France (New town development corporation). Toshihiko graduated from the doctoral program of the Department of Architecture at Waseda University. From 1999 to 2007, he served as, Associate Professor in the Department of Product Design at Tohoku University of Art & Design. From 2007 to 2010, he was Associate Professor in the Faculty of System Design at Tokyo Metropolitan University and also Professor in the Faculty of Engineering in the Department of Architecture of Kogakuin University. In 2011, Toshihiko became Professor of the School of Architecture in the Department of Architecture of Kogakuin University.

He is a Director of Atelier OPA Co., Ltd., Director of The Scandinavian Architecture and Design Institute of Japan and of the Japan Society for Interior Studies. He is a recipient of the Awarded Goode Design Award, the Prize of Smaller Enterprise Agency's Director, the Grand-Prix of Design For Asia Award, the Lexus Design Award 2012, the iF Design Award 2014 and many others awards.

His representative books are *Sekai de ichiban utsukushii kenchiku design no kyoukasho (Most Beautiful Design in the World text book)* published by X-knowledge, *Hokuou no kyoshou ni manabu zubou, kagu interior kenchiku no design no kiso (Learn drawings from Scandinavian masters, Basic design of furniture, interior design and Architecture)* published by Shokokusha, *Hokuou no kyosho ni manabu design, Asplund/Aalto/Jacobsen (learning design from Scandinavian masters)* published by Shokokusha, *Kenchiku product design/Kurashi o gekiteki ni kaeru mono to kukan no sekkei shisou (Architectural product design/Design philosophy of objects and spaces to change life dramatically)* published by Kodansha Ltd.

謝辞
(吉村行雄・鈴木敏彦)

ACKNOWLEDGEMENT
(Yukio Yoshimura and Toshihiko Suzuki)

本書の刊行は、多くの方々のご厚意とご協力に支えられて実現した。ここに一部の方のお名前を挙げて、感謝の意を表したい。

　吉村が北欧に興味をもち、写真をまとめるようにまでなったのは、ひとえに大学時代の恩師・故芦原義信先生と、竹山実先生のご学恩によるところが大きい。心より感謝申し上げる。また、武蔵野美術大学名誉教授の島崎信先生には、ヤコブセンについてのさまざまなことをご教授いただき、感謝に耐えない。

　デンマーク在住の小野寺綾子氏には、ヤコブセン取材の折、たびたびお世話になり、デンマーク語の日本語表記にも丁寧なアドバイスを頂戴した。ご厚意に感謝の気持ちを伝えたい。デンマーク・オーフス建築学校に留学の経験のある建築家の西野奈美氏には、情報収集の面で大変協力をいただいた。ヤコブセンに関する資料までご提供いただき、感謝の気持ちは尽きない。また、新潮社の前田誠一氏には、『芸術新潮』の特集でヤコブセンを撮る機会を与えていただいた。これがきっかけとなって本書の発行につながったことは言うまでもなく、改めてお礼申し上げる。そして私事ながら、長年にわたる私のわがままを温かく見守り、時には海外取材に同行して援助してくれた妻・保子にも感謝の気持ちをささげたい。

　鈴木が、このたび思いがけずヤコブセン論を書く機会に恵まれたのは、吉村行雄氏にご高配を賜ったお陰である。北欧建築・デザイン協会SADIではたびたび、北欧で撮りためた写真を見せて頂いた。一緒にデンマークを訪ね、本を執筆する機会を得たことを非常に嬉しく思う。

　ヤコブセン研究の第一人者のデンマーク王立芸術アカデミーのカルステン・サウ教授には、コペンハーゲンのレストランにてお会いして、疑問点についてすべて解説していただいた。さらに関連資料の使用許可についても強力なご支援を賜り、感謝の言葉が尽きない。また、武蔵野美術大学名誉教授の島崎信先生には、ヤコブセンをめぐる北欧デザインの背景についてご教示いただいた。島崎先生はデンマーク留学当時にオーレ・ヴァンシア教授の研究室に所属していたので、3つ隣りのヤコブセン教授の研究室を垣間見たという。ヤコブセン本人のパーソナリティーについても多くの示唆を得た。深く感謝の意を表するのみである。

　最後に、本書の実現にご尽力いただいた関係者の皆様にお礼申し上げたい。デザイナーの緒方裕子氏には、ヤコブセンの魅力を最大限に引き出す見事なブックデザインをしていただいた。そして杉原有紀氏には、現地での撮影交渉から関係先との調整、英訳に至るまで、多岐にわたりご尽力いただいた。その労をねぎらい厚くお礼申し上げる。本書の発行の意義を評価し、編集の指揮を執っていただいたTOTO出版の遠藤信行編集長と、粘り強く編集作業を続けていただいた田中智子氏に心より感謝申し上げる。

This book was published with the support and kindness of many people. We would like to express our appreciation for their help by mentioning some of their names.

　Yukio Yoshimura is interested in photography and became able to publish a book. I owe this to my beloved professors of my university days, Minoru Takeyama and the late Yoshinobu Ashihara. I wholeheartedly thank them for support and tutelage. I cannot thank Honorary Professor, Makoto Shimazaki enough for teaching me of various matters about Jacobsen. Ms. Ayako Onodera, a resident of Denmark, frequently looked after me when I visited that country to compile Jacobsen's works. Her assistance and advice on the Japanese notation of the Danish language was particularly helpful. Thank you for your kindness. An architect, Ms. Nami Nishino, who once studied at Aarhus School of Architecture cooperated with me to gather information related to Jacobsen. I cannot overstate how grateful I am for the various materials about Jacobsen that she provided. Then, Mr. Seiichi Maeda of Shinchosha Publishing Co., Ltd. provided me with an opportunity to take photographs for "Geijyutsu Shincho" magazine, which featured articles on Jacobsen. Subsequently, it goes without saying that the opportunity connected to publish this book. I would like to express my gratitude to him. Excuse me for being personal, but I really must mention the help of my wife, Yasuko. She has followed me with patience despite my selfishness over many years, providing encouragement and occasionally accompanying me on my trips abroad.

　Toshihiko Suzuki was blessed with an opportunity to write about Jacobsen unexpectedly. I am obliged to Mr. Yoshimura for the time and energy that he gave me. When I met him at The Scandinavian Architecture and Design Institute of Japan, he often would show me photos that he had taken in Scandinavia. I am grateful that we visited Denmark together and had an opportunity to write a book. Professor Carsten Thau of The Royal Danish Academy of Fine Arts, who is an authority on Jacobsen, answered completely all of my questions at a restaurant in Copenhagen. In addition, he was of great assistance in obtaining permission to use related documents. I cannot say thank you enough for your continuous support. An Honorary Professor, Makoto Shimazaki taught me the background of Scandinavia design over Jacobsen. When Professor Shimazaki studied in Denmark, he was attached to Professor Ole Wanscher's office. As a result, he sometimes watched Jacobsen at work in his own office, which was only three doors away. I have received many tips about Jacobsen's personality, as a result of Professor Shimazaki's talks. For this, I am very grateful to Professor Shimazaki.

　To end, we would like to extend our appreciation to the many other persons whose energy and dedication made it possible to publish this book. In particular, this includes Ms. Hiroko Ogata, a designer created a fine book design that captured the charms of Jacobsen at his greatest. In addition, Ms. Yuki Sugihara helped us from the negotiations and the coordination with the locals for photo taking of the buildings to the translation of manuscripts into English. We appreciate your time and effort. We also genuinely appreciate the efforts of TOTO publishing including Mr. Nobuyuki Endo, the chief editor, who valued the significance of publication of this book and conducted the editing and Ms. Satoko Tanaka, who provided an unremitting editorial function with skill and persistence.

Arne Jacobsen
ヤコブセンの建築とデザイン

2014年6月20日　初版第1刷発行
2021年1月20日　初版第3刷発行

写真　　　　　　　　　吉村行雄

文　　　　　　　　　　鈴木敏彦

発行者　　　　　　　　伊藤剛士

発行所　　　　　　　　TOTO出版（TOTO株式会社）
　　　　　　　　　　　〒107-0062 東京都港区南青山1-24-3 TOTO乃木坂ビル2F
　　　　　　　　　　　［営業］TEL：03-3402-7138　FAX：03-3402-7187
　　　　　　　　　　　［編集］TEL：03-3497-1010
　　　　　　　　　　　URL：https://jp.toto.com/publishing

アートディレクション＆デザイン　　緒方裕子

印刷・製本　　　　　　図書印刷株式会社

落丁・乱丁本はお取り替えいたします。本書の全部又は一部に対するコピー・スキャン・デジタル化等の無断複製行為は、著作権法上での例外を除き禁じます。本書を代行業者等の第三者に依頼してスキャンやデジタル化することは、たとえ個人や家庭内での利用であっても著作権法上認められておりません。定価はカバーに表示してあります。

Photographs ©2014　Yukio Yoshimura
Text ©2014　Toshihiko Suzuki

Printed in Japan
ISBN978-4-88706-343-3